Gullible's Travels

Gullible's Travels

The Adventures of a Bad Taste Tourist

CASH PETERS

GUILFORD, CONNECTICUT

MARKETPLACE®, THE SAVVY TRAVELER®, BAD TASTE TOURS®, and MINNESOTA PUBLIC RADIO® are trademarks owned by Minnesota Public Radio. Portions of material in this book were originally featured on Marketplace® or on The Savvy Traveler®.

Marketplace® is the nation's largest daily national business show and is heard on more than 322 public radio stations. You can visit Marketplace® on the Web at www.marketplace.org.

The Savvy Traveler® is public radio's entertaining and informative travel program, produced by Minnesota Public Radio and heard on more than 180 stations nationwide. Visit us on the Web at www.savvytraveler.org.

Text design: M. A. Dubé

Library of Congress Cataloging-in-Publication Data
Peters, Cash.
    Gullible's travels / Cash Peters. — 1st ed.
        p. cm.
    ISBN 0-7627-2714-4
    1. United States — Description and travel. 2. United States — Social life and customs — 1971- 3. Peters, Cash — Journeys — United States. I. Title.

E169.04.P475 2003
973 — dc21   2003043426

Manufactured in the United States of America
First Edition/First Printing

For Mandy

Contents

1

The Begotokomugubu

A very unhelpful brothel-keeper ◆ *I spot an old friend traveling at speed* ◆
lunch in Amsterdam's Blue Fug District ◆ *a drifter's sorry tale* ◆ *the* Sound
of Music *tour, and not for the first time* ◆ *a trip down the Paris sewers,
most definitely for the last time* ◆ *Mandy makes a suggestion* ◆ *facts: the
scourge of good reporting* ◆ *somebody else makes the same
suggestion as Mandy* ◆ *back to the brothel*

IT BEGAN WITH A HAIRSTYLE.

As a rule, I don't care for books that open that way—
cryptically. But on this occasion I have no choice because it's
exactly what happened.

August 1999. An overcast morning. I was standing in a
cramped office in Amsterdam's red light district trying to persuade
a Dutchman called Lars, whose company arranges brothel tours,
to take me on a tour of a brothel. A simple enough transaction on
the face of it, you might think ("You run tours, I want to go on one
of your tours, here's a handful of meaningless colored paper that
you Dutch people call money, let's move."), but for some reason
Lars didn't get it.

I can't remember now exactly what his answer was, but the
gist of it went something like this: No.

"Aw, come on, Lars! *Please??*"

Unfortunately his English wasn't too good, and my grasp of
Dutch is nonexistent. To me everything they say sounds like
"Heeeri, hooori, yerdi-oooori, ooori-ooori." So instead I decided
to try a fresh approach, adopting a technique that's worked well in
the past when dealing with foreigners. I call it Shouting and
Pointing.

"HOOKERS!" Jabbing my finger at a poster over his desk:
"ME. INTERVIEW. HOOKERS!"

1

In the picture, four buxom women in garters and low-cut bodices were draped over a leopard-print couch, leering at us like a bunch of mildly inebriated Rockettes; only . . . well, their bodices were a little too low-cut for Rockettes. And the one on the far left had a big nose and thyroid eyes, so I doubt she'd have passed the auditions. But they served my purpose.

"TAKE ME TO THE HOOKERS!"

"Heeeri," Lars protested, shaking his head. "Erdi-nyora-yeeri, ooori-oooori."

Which I can only assume is Dutch for "stop shouting."

And I was just wondering what else I could do short of slapping him to get my message across when, at that moment, I was distracted by something red and shiny that shot by the window outside.

A hairstyle.

Short, spiky, a little unkempt, and very, very familiar.

"*Mandy?*"

Everyone at some point in his life has a Merchant–Ivory moment, and this was mine. Exotic European location; sinewy Victorian alleyway on the Amsterdam waterfront; quite by chance, or perhaps it's Fate, boy meets girl he had a crush on years before but hasn't seen since. Back in those days, she had her own thriving radio production company and he was a floundering reporter in London. But then, as so often happens, the road forked and their lives took different paths. She moved up to be a top commercials director; he moved to Los Angeles and became a floundering reporter there instead. Years went by. Then, one day, she's on a weekend break in Holland; he's trying unsuccessfully to maneuver his way onto a brothel tour, and their paths cross again. (In the movie I think we'll cast Angelina Jolie as Mandy, and Dame Judi Dench can play me, in what will probably be the most challenging role of her career, since I look nothing like her. In particular, I can't wait to see her grow a brown goatee.)

"MANDY!"

Twenty feet away, a set of worn brakes squealed, little shoes skidded wildly across damp cobbles, and the bicycle convulsed to a halt.

Two seconds to pick me out from the crowd, another two for recognition, then . . .

"CAAAAAAAAAAASH! Oh—my—God!"

THERE'S SOMETHING ABOUT AMSTERDAM that makes it perfect for reunions. It's such a restful, civilized, *fun* place, somewhere you can let it all hang out. Alternatively, you can tuck it back in again and just go for a drink.

Pouting prostitutes in tight skirts that, were they any shorter, might be mistaken for elastic bands, pose in windows like mannequins and tap on the glass at you as you walk by. The bodies of teenage louts, fresh off the ferry from England and already unconscious, lie sprawled in doorways, hugging empty bottles of Jack Daniels. And of course at every turn your nostrils are teased by the tang of "naughty smoke" drifting from coffeehouses. Thanks to soft drug laws that could only have been devised by someone who was high on pot, college students fill their free time not the old-fashioned way with silly studying, but by mellowing out over a big fat joint while marveling at the icy blueness of the sky, or debating the relative merits of Original versus Barbecue Pringles, or musing in total earnest about what a real talent Kenny G is.

In other words, you are free to live, and to do so in ways that please *you*, not the government. Holland trusts its adults to behave like adults. I think that's why it's Mandy's favorite hideaway. She's a grown-up with grown-up responsibilities, and yet at the same time she's haunted by a young girl's yearning to run away from home. Whenever the job becomes overwhelming or relationships turn onerous—and relationships *always* turn onerous—she seeks release in Amsterdam, freewheeling alongside canals on a rented bike, crossing back and forth over dinky stone bridges, and drifting down terraces of four-story gabled homes that resemble dolls' houses in their charm, their cuteness, their design, everything but their size—lost in blissful distraction.

"So what brings you here?" she asked as we nabbed the best table in a restaurant with a panoramic view over one of the main canals.

I didn't answer straight away.

And when I didn't, two dazzling peppermint-green eyes locked into mine. "Oh no! Not the museums thing again. You're not back doing that!"

Embarrassed, I raised my menu so I wouldn't have to look at her.

THE MAIN REASON I'D LEFT BRITAIN in the first place was because of "the museums thing."[1] Somehow—don't ask me how; scientists at some of our top universities are working on this right now—very early on in what I laughingly call my radio career, I'd been categorized by producers as the Best Goofy Tour and Kooky Museum Guy in the Business (or the Begotokomugubu for short). And before you say it, I realize it's hardly something you'd put on your résumé, much less reveal to total strangers in a book, but back then it didn't seem like such a bad place to be, you know? And it sure beat the hell out of the ghastly office job I had before it.

Basically what it boiled down to was this: If some screwball in Scotland decided to build a bungalow entirely out of used hemorrhoid cream tubes, I would be dispatched to Anusol Towers, tape recorder in hand, to interview him.

Similarly if a story came down the wires about a new museum dedicated to the history of clotted cream, or stilt-walking, or if it featured the world's largest collection of cracked pipes, or some other insane and pointless infatuation that nobody but the owner and his family, and sometimes not even his family, were interested

1. There was also the family thing, but let's not talk about that. It's too depressing. All I'll say is that my brother thinks I'm crazy, his wife thinks I'm lazy and crazy, and my Dad doesn't know what to think, although I'm sure that, given half a chance, he'd trade me in on eBay for a son who actually does something valuable for a living and doesn't waste his time trying to be a writer, which as everyone knows is "not work." Nuff said.

in, my phone would ring within minutes and, bingo, I'd be off again. And since:

1. wacko attractions are never in short supply (take it from me, 30 percent of the population of any country is absolutely nuts);

2. news programs love including this kind of screwy, light-hearted stuff at the end of a particularly heavy program (it helps leaven the mix and leaves the audience smiling); and

3. no other journalist on the planet would touch this crap with a bargepole (not even a bargepole on loan from the "Bargepoles Thru the Ages" exhibit at The National Museum of Bargepoles) . . .

. . . I was kept very busy.

In no time at all I became a specialist in odd. Then I cornered the market in strange. Shortly after that, weird and goofball were on my beat too. And, last of all, the much-coveted "lovably eccentric." I was at the top of my game!

Trouble is, in the media, once you succeed at something, even if it's something incredibly pitiful and sad, that's all they ever let you do. Result: a decade and a half on, I was still at it. Going to San Diego, California, to look at a chicken with two asses. Going to Lapland to visit Father Christmas's post office. Going to Salzburg, Austria, for the *Sound of Music* tour. Come to think of it, I'd worked for four different radio stations in Britain over the years and at every single one of them an editor had at some point walked up to me and told me about this crazy attraction in Austria he'd just read about.

"It's a tour . . . of the *Sound . . . of Music . . .* movie locations," he would say, speaking in chunks, in case I got too excited and began to hyperventilate.

To which I'd reply, "Wow, you're kidding me! They really have such a thing?"

"You bet. Want to go?"

And within forty-eight hours there I'd be, on a coach rattling down an Austrian hillside with a bunch of other losers, yodeling "The Lonely Goatherd" at the top of my voice, happy as a clam. Why? Many reasons. Because Salzburg happens to be one of the most captivating cities in all of Europe, if not the world. It's one of the few places that Las Vegas still hasn't built a duplicate of, so there are no shortcuts: you really have to get on a plane and go there. Also because, at heart, I guess I'm just a hapless drifter who loves being on the road at other people's expense. But finally— and this is the main one—because I'm a total sucker for cheesy museums and tours. I am. I can't help it. If it's tacky, lowbrow, kitsch, crappy, a third-rate rip-off of something better, or just a splendid idea incompetently executed, for some reason I'm driven to hand over good money to see it.

Even when I emigrated to Los Angeles, where, with my slate wiped clean and my carte painted blanche, I was free to be bold and strike out in any direction that grabbed my fancy, I quickly lapsed into my old ways. Within weeks, a travel show on American public radio offered to broadcast my work and, like a fool, I accepted. So, after that, I guess it was just a matter of time before one of the producers stopped me in the corridor with an idea.

Oh, but not just any idea: *the* idea to end all ideas.

"You know . . . where we . . . should send you?" he said, speaking in chunks.

"THE *SOUND OF MUSIC* TOUR, *again?*"

"I know. This is the fifth."

"But why?" Picking at a salad, Mandy made a bad job of concealing her disappointment. "Why would you even bother?"

"Because they offered it to me," I shrugged, failing to mention that I'm also an idiot.

The tour, like the movie itself, like my career, is locked in time. It's always the same. Starting in the center of Salzburg, you get to see the original convent used in the film (from very far away), two castles that doubled for the Von Trapp family's home—one for the front of the house (also from far away), the other for the rear ("If you squint through the trees, you can just see the chimney.")—then, to a rousing chorus of "Do-Re-Mi," which leaks from the coach's sound system like gas from a grill, it's on to the gardens of the seventeenth-century Hellbrunn Castle and the glass pavilion where Julie Andrews kissed Christopher Plummer, or someone who looked sus-piciously like him.

"This is the original pavilion from the film," one guide assured us, "except for the roof, the windows, the walls, the benches, and the floor, which have all been replaced."

Ooooh!

But apparently nobody cares that it's a fake. Some of the older fans even try skipping around the benches the way Liesl did in the movie, pretending they're sixteen going on seventeen when really they're seventy going on eighty, and very nearly break their necks.

After this you're herded onto the bus for a short drive into the Salzkammergut, a rather convoluted Austrian way of saying mountains, and the climax of the tour: Mondsee Cathedral, where Maria's wedding scenes were shot. Then, with half the coach singing "Climb Every Mountain" and the other half cry-ing, it's back on the bus again, ready for the return trip to Salzburg, where your best bet is to find a bar and spend the rest of the night getting wasted, trying to forget the horror of it all.

One Australian guy who, every time I looked, seemed to be taking photos—of the houses, the mountains, the pavilion, the group—admitted to me later that he had no film in his camera. He was just too embarrassed. I know how he feels. Nobody wants their friends to learn they've been out doing stuff like this. It's camp, it's ridiculous, and it's humiliating—that's what makes it so irresistible!

AT LUNCH MY MAIN COURSE was vegetable lasagna, swilled down with a bottle of Amstel Light. Mandy had chicken. Beyond the window, young girls with bright sunlit faces cycled by in shorts, somehow managing to chat on their cell phones and avoid plunging into the canal at the same time, while inside, the cafe slowly filled with lunchtime traffic. As it did so, a stifling blue fug descended over the room.

Amsterdamians, I quickly discovered, love weed. Any kind of weed. They smoke on trains, they smoke in bars and restaurants, they smoke between mouthfuls of food. I'm sure the cleverer ones have even found a way to smoke in the shower. I mean, they're not a stupid race, so you'd think they'd have put two and two together by now, health-wise. Or maybe, because they know they're going to die before the rest of us, they've simply decided to live for today and to hell with emphysema. Whatever the reason, the product of their combined efforts is this stifling blue fug that engulfs you wherever you go.

Mandy, who evidently is able to multitask and can eat and choke simultaneously, appeared not to mind. "So where else did you go on this trip?"

"Paris. I went down the sewers."

"Oh yeah? What was that like?"

"Like Amsterdam, only underground, and the canals are filled with shit."

No word of a lie. Many tours I go on are billed as interactive. The Paris Sewer Tour only becomes interactive if you fall in. And you could—*easily*. It's a defecatory wonderland in those tunnels, dark and deep and dangerous. Churning brown rivers of pee and poo flow mere inches from your feet. People have been known to throw live alligators down the sewers, and snakes, and other detritus, which means you have no idea what's ahead of you; you could step on *anything*. Plus, as you might expect, the smell is abominable. It gets in your clothes, your hair, everywhere. I was down there thirty minutes in all, and 90 percent of that time was spent with a handkerchief clutched to my mouth, trying not to vomit or tumble over the guardrails.

"Did you know," I said, although Mandy had clearly lost interest in this subject shortly after my opening sentence, "that houses in Paris are numbered not only on the street but also down in the sewers."

"Really?"

"So when your neighbor takes a dump, you can, if you like, stand underneath his waste pipe and . . . you know . . . watch."

"Is that right?" A forkful of avocado faltered halfway to her lips. She discreetly put it down again and chose a carrot instead. "So where else?"

But there was nowhere else. Apart from those two and the brothel tour, which right now was anything but fixed (and which, thanks to the stubbornly Dutch-speaking Lars, was looking increasingly unlikely), my only other planned stop was at the less-than-impressive Museum of Sex. Oddly, for a city obsessed with the subject, Amsterdam's sex museum is a bit dull. Paris has a much better one. On the other hand, they do have a diorama filled with talking animatronic hookers, which has surely got to be worth ten bucks of anyone's money.

"How's your father doing?" A quick change of topic between mouthfuls.

"The same."

"You mean he's *still* not speaking to you?"

"Nah. It's been so long now that I've forgotten why. Either he's jealous that I'm a travel writer and get to go places for free, and he hates me for it, or, well, he just hates me; it's hard to know."

Leaving Mandy shaking her head with despair, I returned to my meal. But it was no use. My lasagna was starting to taste of tobacco. So I threw down another handful of meaningless colored bills and we made our way out into the street.

"You should put this stuff in a book," she said, inhaling oxygen for the first time in ninety minutes.

"About me and my dad?"

"No—the travel stuff. It's fascinating. Who in this world gets to see all the things you see? Chickens with two asses, Animatronic hookers—it's crazy. People love to read about crazy."

"But it's too weird. Nobody will believe it's true. They'll think I'm making it up."

"Okay—I love to read about crazy. Do it for me."

"Well . . ."

I continued to hesitate, not because I didn't want to spend the next six months of my life working on a book that only one person would want to read, but for an entirely different reason. Mandy wasn't to know this, but there's one major overwhelming obstacle to my writing nonfiction of any sort.

The reason reporters carry notepads on their travels is so that they can scribble down important information on the fly. That way they can be certain their stories are accurate. Indeed, in some quarters, I hear, this accuracy thing is all the rage. People even win prizes for it. Well, fine, but it's not for me, I'm afraid. I don't deal in facts. Rather, personal impressions are my currency. Conjecture and supposition are the knotted straps that stop my curiosity-bonnet from blowing off in a high wind. In fact, it's this, I believe, that gives me a certain edge, singling me out from the rest of the journalistic profession. Oh sure, my reporter's notebook is full of scribblings like everyone else's, but look closer and you'll find that 90 percent of them are phone numbers I've jotted down off infomercials, or interesting kitchen ideas, or street directions to the nearest Starbucks—*never* facts. Jeez. I mean, would you invite Stevie Wonder to wallpaper your living room? Of course not. Well, then don't be looking to me to give you information, that's all I'm saying.

Which is why writing a nonfiction book would be kind of tough.

"Nah," I said, offering a different excuse entirely. "I'm done with this crap. Seriously. This is my last year. I'm moving on."

"Fine—so move on." Two unblinking green lasers trained themselves on my face and remained there for the longest time. "But write the book before you do, okay? Tell your story. I really want to hear it."

Mandy went to retrieve her bike, a thunderous old clanking machine that one can only assume was thrown together from fallen Luftwaffe planes at the end of World War II. That, or there's a diesel locomotive somewhere in Holland with half its engine missing. Dragging it upright, she dug a scrap of paper out of the basket. After a quick look to make sure there was nothing important on the other side, she scribbled down her e-mail address and stuffed it in my pocket.

"God, I miss you so much," she said.

Then, pausing only to envelop me in a monster bear-hug, the kind of hug that can, if you're not careful, crack a rib, and amid a flurry of kisses, firm promises to stay in touch, and another hug for good measure, she swung a leg over the crossbar of her downed Messerschmitt, and, teary-eyed, teetered off over the nearest canal.

It was a touching moment. I continued waving at the back of her head right up to the point when it vanished, swallowed up by the crowd. Until the day comes when they're able to measure friendship on the Richter scale, no one will ever really know how fond I am of that little redheaded ball of energy. My flame-haired old flame, as I call her. In a different time, a different place, two different people might have made a go of what we had. Just not then. Not there. And not us.

Feeling strangely empty all of a sudden and aware that something significant had just happened, though I wasn't sure what or why, I grabbed the backpack with my mini-disc recorder and microphone in it and strode off in the direction of Lars's office in the red light district, ready to give him hell.[2]

AND THERE YOU have it.

How thrilling it would be to wind up this brief episode by telling you that the seed Mandy sowed that day in Amsterdam eventually sprouted literary roots and branches and, over time, blossomed into the glorious flowering book-plant you hold in your hands right now. It'd round off the story so neatly, wouldn't it?

Unfortunately that's not how things went.

Rather, about nine months later I was back home in Los Angeles, packing my bags for yet another of these dumb trips, the book idea having slipped my mind completely, when out of the

---

2. The mere fact that the brothel tour is never mentioned again in the whole of this book should be enough to tell you how this turned out.

blue who should call but an editor on the East Coast. She loved my radio stuff, she said, and wanted to know if I'd ever considered writing a book about my travels.

"No," I told her straight. "And anyway, you're too late. Another six months of this and I'm quitting."

"To do what?"

"Not sure. I'm waiting for inspiration to strike."

"Well, while you're waiting, how would you like to write about your final six months as a travel reporter?"

"Not really."

"Are you sure?"

"Absolutely positive. I'm not interested at all. But thanks anyway."

And that, my friends, is how this book came about.[3]

---

3. I should perhaps add that, rather than take "But thanks anyway" for an answer, she subsequently went on to offer me money to write the book, a cunning and quite reprehensible maneuver, frankly, and one that, I'm sorry to say, changed my mind in an instant from "No, I have a problem with facts" to "When do you want it done?"

2

Your Feet, and How to Locate Them

*Life on a budget ◆ the Unnecessary Door ◆ winter: what's **that***
about? ◆ Dr. Scholl and the documented history of the
corn pad ◆ my plans for traveling by zeppelin ◆ who should have
their asses kicked in Chicago ◆ the most despised vegetable in
the world ◆ my first-ever pea-flavored dessert

I T'S NO SECRET, I THINK, THAT PUBLIC RADIO SHOWS
are run on a shoestring. And not just any old shoestring
either; in many cases the cheapest shoestring money, or a lack
of it, can buy. The budgets are miniscule, the pay often
derisory, and the work environment unsettlingly low-key for what
is after all supposed to be a branch of showbiz.

A noble enterprise (indubitably!), a national treasure (without
a doubt!), an admirable end-product (I should say so!), a source of
wisdom and spiritual enlightenment to generations (oh stop it,
now you're just being silly!) — public broadcasting is three of these
things. But it's also very . . . well, cheap. That's why, when
strangers ask me what I do for a living and I'm forced to admit that
I'm a travel reporter for public radio, and they go "Oooh, a travel
reporter! How *glamorous,*" it's all I can do not to lash out at them.

"I bet you fly everywhere first class . . ."

What?

". . . and get to stay in the best hotels . . ."

Are you insane?

". . . and all your expenses are pai . . . OW! What was *that*
for?"

For suggesting I have an easy time on assignment.

Take the hotels. These tend to be what's tactfully known as
mid-range; in other words your room is neither comfortable

enough to be a home away from home nor so basic that you feel like you're in the isolation cell at a detention center. Facilities are . . . actually, I'm in a good mood today, so let's be generous and call them laughable. Most times here's what you get:

1. A bed. "Well . . . duh!" you might be thinking. But believe me, if they thought it'd save a couple of bucks, they'd hang you on a hook in the closet.

2. A table and two chairs by the window. I generally use these to drape my dirty underwear and socks on (something you might want to bear in mind if you check in after me). Alternatively, you could sit on one of the chairs and stare out of the window, though experience has taught me not to bother. Nine out of ten times your room will overlook a brick wall, a generator, the hotel parking structure, or a freeway off-ramp. Indeed, on one occasion I was so surprised to find that my window had none of these but rather an uninterrupted view across the slurry tanks of a neighboring pig farm that I got an instant adrenaline rush and had to lie down.

3. The tiniest of bathrooms. This will contain:

a. A bathtub (cracked). Usually only a half or even a third normal size. Not quite big enough for a human being to bathe in, but ideal if you win a tortoise in a raffle and need somewhere to store it.

b. A shower (cracked). Operated by a single lever. The lever flicks on okay, but just try turning it off! Doesn't matter which way you twist it—left, right, up, down— the water gets hotter and hotter and hotter and hotter and hotter and hotter and hotter, until you leap out, screaming, with ugly red welts all over your face and shoulders (I can't count the number of times I've turned up to breakfast looking like I've just been jogging around the inside of a nuclear reactor. If I had my way, I'd never again shower in a mid-range hotel without taking a plumber in there with me—and to hell with the tabloids).

c. A sink (cracked). The merest touch of the faucet releases a torrent of water, as powerful as any fire hose, that squirts all over your shirt and leaves "I've peed my pants" splashes down the front of your trousers.

d. A toilet (cracked). The seat won't be fastened down properly and will shift mysteriously each time you use it. Also, note the way the first sheet of toilet paper is folded into a V-shape—a needless flourish designed to fool poorer patrons into thinking they've checked in to a classy joint, hahahahahaha.

e. One of those strange novelty carnival mirrors that magnifies your blackheads to the size of Oreos and picks out every last blood vessel in your eyes. *Yeuw.* The mirror comes as standard, along with a basket of toiletries placed there for the specific purpose of being stolen (and, if you're cheap enough to steal them, you'll find they also make wonderful Christmas tree decorations), plus a hair dryer with only two settings: *warm* for your hair and *emergency* for the wet patches on your trousers.

f. Dark brown stains on the ceiling. Kind of a tradition, this. And yes, they're exactly what you think they are. The toilet seat upstairs isn't fastened down properly either.

4. An Unnecessary Door: There's always one more door than you need in these rooms, which is pretty odd in the first place. But then they compound the mystery by keeping it permanently locked. Even if you put a drinking glass to the wood and listen, you can never hear a thing going on. Many theories have been put forward as to what lies behind that door, the most plausible one being that it conceals a long, thin staircase leading down to some strange in-between world, a fantastic land where all the people get along with one another, where rivers and streams are unpolluted, toupees are undetectable, chocolate cake is promoted as a dietary aid, the court system is more interested in dispensing justice than making money for lawyers, corduroy never goes out of style, and Nicolas Cage is considered a good actor. But, frankly, it all sounds so darned improbable that I refuse to believe a word.

Anyway, I digress.

My point is, wherever I go in America working for public radio, though the locations may change, the standard of the hotels never does. I was reminded of this all over again one dismal January night when I hauled my bags through the door of yet another of these infernal two-star penitentiaries and checked in. (Bed: yes. Tiniest of bathrooms: yes. Table and two chairs: yes. Window overlooking brick wall: yes. Unnecessary door: yes.)

For some reason that night, I was in a New York state of mind.

Sadly, in Chicago that counts for very little.

The temperature outside was 28 degrees F and falling, with a wind so brutal that it penetrated the closed window, causing the glass to crackle menacingly and the net curtains to convulse and billow into the room.

Unfortunately, because I live in Southern California, where it's perpetually warm, I don't own any warm clothes. It sounds ridiculous, but I don't. Not even the basics. For that reason, as I emerged from my hotel around nine that first evening in only a T-shirt and jeans and the thinnest of summer jackets and set off, leaning at a 45-degree angle against a tempestuous gale that hacked at my face like a thousand scimitars, in the direction of the nearest coffeeshop, I honestly thought I might die. Or at the very least be scooped off my feet and flung into Wisconsin.

Huddled over a hot chocolate, I stammered to the waitress "B-b-b-bad weather, huh?"—only to watch her reel away laughing.

Apparently this was nothing. The *really* bad weather had yet to arrive.

Chicago is prone to blizzards so intense that they can turn

domestic pets into Popsicles and cause small children to vanish altogether. One minute they're at your side, chattering and giggling; the next, you and a bunch of firefighters are digging them out with sticks. Why is that? Well, I'm no meteorologist, but five bucks says it's something to do with seasonal weather patterns. Though it can't help that the city nestles—no, *cowers*—on the shores of Lake Michigan, which is really an ocean, but everyone's too modest to say so. There's Chicago, then the lake, then nothing at all; the world just sort of ends. So of course when winter arrives, it meets with no obstacles. The wind has free reign, the rain may pour how and where it pleases, and come February, monster snowstorms rampage up and down these broad avenues like panicked cattle, driving Chicagalinos[4] indoors for months and months on end until, eventually, spring arrives, the ice melts, and they can venture out into the streets again to retrieve any children they may have misplaced in December.

On this evidence alone I think a good argument could be made for sticking Chicago on the back of a truck and moving it to Florida, don't you?

This year, though, for once, things were different. A high pressure system heading for Quebec had accidentally reversed into America and gotten its rear wheels bogged down in Illinois (The I-Bet-You-Wish-You-Hadn't-Come-Here State), inflicting bitter cold on northernmost areas, but thankfully no snow, which came as a merciful relief, especially to me. At least I wouldn't be spending the next three days trudging miserably through five-foot drifts in Gap deck shoes.

I WAS IN TOWN TO COVER NOT A GOOFY TOUR or kooky museum for once, but something we felt was closely allied to them: the International Housewares Show, an annual expo showcasing the very latest in home appliances and accessories.

---

4. I'm pretty sure this is the collective name for them. Only pride prevents me from looking it up.

As usual, in an effort to bag the cheapest flight available—
which for some reason is often the most inconvenient flight available, involving long delays, multiple connections, and a seat at
the very back of the tail section (traditionally, I believe, the first
part of the plane to drop off in a crash)—I'd been sent here two
days early. And since the housewares show wasn't due to open
until Tuesday lunchtime, I was left with plenty of time to kill.

Of course other people, let loose in America's third-largest city
for the weekend, would head straight for the sights. They'd check
out the art galleries, take in a play or two, go shopping, and stroll
gamely around the streets and parks, exploring the more interesting byways of this culturally rich society.

Good for them.

Me, I don't want that. I'm looking for danger. I want challenge and adventure and, wherever possible, heaps and heaps of
bizarre nonsense.

So imagine my delight when, while bumming around the
downtown area looking for a Starbucks, I happened upon the
William M. Scholl College of Podiatric Medicine. I'd read about
this place in books and was immediately curious. Not only that,
but as I stumbled through the doors, blue-cheeked and shivering,
I found that this just happened to be the opening day of "Feet
First," a landmark exhibition charting the life and achievements
of Dr. William Scholl. You know, the shoe guy.

THE DR. SCHOLL STORY IS FASCINATING. A bit like the Glenn
Miller story, only with a lot more emphasis on bunions.[5] If you
don't know anything about him—and let's face it, why would
you?—allow me to bring you up to speed.

He was born on a dairy farm in Indiana. Please don't ask me
when; I have no clue. But the history books tell us he moved to
Chicago around the turn of the century, so I think we can safely

---

5. And without the dying-in-a-plane-crash bit at the end. Come to think of it, I'm not
even sure Dr. Scholl had a big band. Or if he did, the museum doesn't mention it.

assume it was before then. New in town and eager to work, he took his first job at Ruppert's Shoe Store on Madison Street and, from what we can gather, was instantly appalled by the state of customers' feet.

Appalled, and yet . . . strangely intrigued.

Don't forget, even as late as 1900 American footwear design was still in its infancy. Shoes were rigid and uncomfortable, like small canoes for your feet. To make matters worse, people back then weren't very bright. Or at least they weren't bright enough to figure out that you needed two different-shaped shoes, one for the right foot and one for the left. Instead, a single shape was made to fit both. (I mean, if it'd been me, I'd have said something. Or bought moccasins. But historical people were notoriously feeble and dim. You could lay any old crap on them and they'd take it.)

Anyway, due to all of this, calluses were rife and ingrown toe-nails a curse. It might still be that way today had it not been for this spunky Indiana farm-boy. Convinced that there had to be a better way, Billy Scholl applied his mind to the problem and very soon hit on the invention that was to be the foundation of his worldwide business empire: the spring-loaded arch support.

Doesn't sound like much, I know, but it changed everything.

One day a regular customer happened by the store and, for fun, young Billy slipped one of these miracle devices into his shoe.

"Oh, dude!" cried the guy—who I imagine must have been from Beverly Hills or Orange County—"It's frickin' awesome. Man, this gadget of yours is, like, a total 'FOOT-EAZER'!"

And with that a global revolution was born! Armed with this catchy name—The Gadget[6]—Scholl, teaming up with his brother Frank and using money borrowed from his father, set up a company called Scholl Manufacturing, and in the years that followed proved to be not only a shrewd entrepreneur with a real flair for innovation and marketing, but also a generous employer, an enthusiastic mentor, and an all-round super guy.

---

6. Changed later that same afternoon to The Foot-Eazer.

I think he was also gay.
"No, he wasn't."
Oh.

I'D TURNED UP AT A VERY AWKWARD TIME. It was late in the
day and Dave, the Museum of Feet's curator, was busy making
final preparations for the "Feet First" first-night party. So the last
thing he needed was a radio reporter hovering around, asking him
a million questions.

Well, he was in luck! Because, although I was most certainly
a radio reporter, I didn't have any questions to ask him at all. In
common with 99.5 percent of the world's population, I'm not
even the teensiest bit interested in podiatry, fallen arches, or Dr.
William Scholl.[7] As far as I was concerned, the sooner this was
over the better. So, with a view to taking in the highlights only, we
set off at a sprint, with Dave trailing two paces behind, and me trying to think of things to ask him.

"So what's this?"
"And what's that over there?"
"And what does this do if I push it?"
"I'm pushing it, Dave, but nothing's happening. Why?"
"What d'you mean, the electricity's off?"
"*Oooh*—the world's largest shoe!"

Given the unsavory nature of the subject, the museum manages to be both absorbing (to a degree) and informative (up to a
point). There are large plaster models of feet, photos of diseased
toes, a computer that graphically simulates bunion operations, a
cabinet filled with "shoes through the ages" (which succeeded in
proving beyond any shadow of a doubt in my mind that stilettos
are the Devil's work), and finally, just when you've reached the
point where you think it can't get any more interesting, you find
yourself standing in front of a glass case dedicated entirely to the
history of the corn pad.

In addition, if you ask nicely, the staff will tell you how to

___
7. And this number is growing, I believe.

locate your own feet (I don't think I'm giving too much away when I say the technique involves pointing at the ground) and, once you've found them, what to do next.

It took me thirty minutes to tour both galleries, although I imagine anyone with Attention Deficit would be in and out of there in under ninety seconds. The final exhibit I came to—but only because I'd gone around the wrong way—was the first thing visitors see as they enter the exhibition: a blow-up photo of Billy Scholl. And you know what? I was shocked.

Shocked, and yet . . . strangely intrigued.

You'd expect anyone who's *this* consumed by foot diseases to be a goofy-looking doofus who prances around town wearing a cape and goggles, or something weird like that. But Scholl was no doofus. He was a prime cut of manhood—a bit like Zorro on his day off, and kinda foxy in a Tom Selleck sort of way. *Woof!* So quite naturally you're thinking, "Hm, foxy, eh? I bet he was a womanizer." Well, that's what I thought too, but apparently not. Foot diseases were his big thing and they dominated his world almost to the exclusion of all else.

"Dr. Scholl lived very frugally at the Athletic Club," Dave told me. "A bachelor all of his life . . ."

"Oh, so he was . . ."

"No, he was *not* gay."

Before I could probe further, the subject was quickly changed by throwing in a Trivial Pursuit question: "Name one person who was on the first commercial jet flight between New York and Paris."

"Ethel Merman."

"No. Dr. Scholl."

"Oh, of course, it's so obvious now! Hahahaha."

In addition: "Scholl was also one of the first people to ride across the Atlantic on a zeppelin. That was his outlet. He liked adventures. Outside of that, his company was his world."

"And he had no time for women?"

I don't know why this bugged me so, it just did.

"He had time for women," Dave insisted, steering me toward a device that plays song parodies about podiatry (I swear to God), "but they didn't necessarily appreciate the schedule that he kept. One woman he was engaged to broke off the engagement when he failed to show up for dinner three dates in a row, because he had meetings and problems at the factory."

"*John Brown's baby has a corn upon his toe . . .*" sang the machine.

"And you swear to me he wasn't gay?"

"Not a chance. The guy just liked his work."

Hm.

"*Hey, sister, Scholl sister, Scholl sister, Scholl sister . . .*"

Moving on . . .

This isn't a large museum, and yet they manage to offer a veritable cornpadcopia of distractions for those who share Scholl's fascination with feet. However, since I'm not one of them, why was I wasting a single unnecessary second here?

One thing I did come away with, however, was an enduring awareness of the incredible pounding each of us gives our heels and toes every day, and we don't even realize it. The feet I use, for instance, are the original pair I was born with, so they've seen a lot of action over the years, traveling thousands of miles.

"In your lifetime," Dave told me as I was leaving, "you will walk around the earth four times." A pretty wild prediction, coming from a man I barely know. Although, thinking back on some of the producers I've worked for, that is *exactly* what would happen. They'd have had me walking across whole continents, and even oceans, if they thought it'd save them a few bucks on their travel budget.

I WARMED TO CHICAGO VERY QUICKLY. Not the city so much, although it's pleasant enough, with a racy kind of vibe, but the local people, who are *so nice*. They smile warmly at you when you meet them. They say "Hi, how's it going?" for no particular reason other than that you're standing right there and they have to say *something*. And if you're lost and you ask them for directions, they won't send you entirely the wrong way just to be devilish, the way English people do. That's why Midwesterners are the best. In fact,

I don't know what they could have done to make my stay more pleasant or more comfortable.

Oh, hang on—yes I do! There is one group of people in this city that in my opinion deserves to have its communal ass kicked, and if possible with the world's largest shoe. Pass legislation, start a vigilante group, hire ninjas—I don't care how you do it, just see to it that regular ass-kickings are administered to everyone on the following list:

1. waiters.

AT THE LOW- TO MID-PRICE RESTAURANT END especially— which, let's face it, is the only one I'm familiar with—I found the level of service to be abysmal. That evening, after leaving the Museum of Feet, I staggered vainly around downtown against an excoriating gale, entering one establishment after another, and four altogether, desperate for something to eat.

In the first restaurant I was left standing by the "Please wait to be seated" sign for so long that I lost all sensation in my toes. After twenty minutes of being totally ignored by everyone from the hostess on down—"What is it? Am I invisible?" I snapped at her as she walked right past—and when *still* nobody had stepped up to greet me, I turned and, grumbling loudly, retreated into the street. And I bet the bastards ignored that too.

In the second, I sat down at a table, by this time totally ravenous, only to find that every item on the menu had artichokes in it: salads, soups, entrees, and, if I'd bothered to look, probably the desserts as well. Now, that may be fine for some, but I don't happen to like artichokes. They remind me of cactus. However, my stomach was growling badly and I was desperate, so I asked the waitress very politely if the chef might possibly prepare me a Chicken Breast in Artichoke Sauce as per the menu, but leave off the artichoke sauce, only to have her glare at me as if I was on day-release from a Tourette's clinic.

"Leave off the artichoke sauce? That's the best bit."

"But I hate artichokes."

"That's ridiculous. You don't know what you're missing."

"Look, can I have a Chicken Breast in Artichoke Sauce without the artichoke sauce or not?"

"I don't know. You'd have to speak to the manager."

"Okay. And where is he?"

"It's his night off. He'll be in tomorrow."

"Anyone else?"

"I'll go fetch the deputy manager."

But I couldn't bear to wait for his verdict; I already knew what it was going to be. So the moment she disappeared through a nearby doorway, I grabbed a leftover dry roll from the basket on a nearby table and walked out, vowing as I went that I would never ever visit The Artichoke Palace again. And I mean it, too.

At least I had a roll, though, which gave me something to chew on while I traipsed the streets for several more minutes searching for something better. After trying a couple of other restaurants along the way, neither of which really appealed, I finally settled on a place I've been to many times: TGI Friday's, where I know the food is adequate, the service consistently upbeat, despite the fact that the waiters are made to wear striped red-and-white outfits that make them look like they've just been squeezed out of a tube, and the welcome is chipper bordering on hysterical.

"Hey heeeey, welcome to T.G.I. Fridaaaaaaay's. How are yooooou?"

"Up to the point where you said 'how are yooooou?' in that silly voice, I was doing fine," I thought.

Stumbling windblown into the warm, I laid immediate claim to a table and ordered, without being given a menu, a pea soup as my appetizer and salad as a main course, together with my recreational drug of choice, a strawberry margarita. The margarita would help fill in time 'til the soup arrived.

"You got it," my overjolly waiter chirruped, scurrying away.

But that was where it got weird, because the soup didn't arrive first, my salad did. And when I pointed out to him that he'd brought them in the wrong order, his response was so way out there that ludicrous doesn't adequately describe it.

The soup, he said, would—in a fascinating twist on convention—be coming later. "Er . . . why?"

Whereupon he launched into a bizarre improvised cock-and-bull story about how salads are easier to prepare because they're cold, whereas hot soup, well, that takes *forever*, so he'd be bringing it after the main course, like a pea-flavored dessert. "Is that okay?"

"No. It's *not* okay," I groaned. "In what city this side of Hell is pea soup considered a pudding?"

But already I'd been written off as a difficult customer, I could tell. With that, he sidled away to confound someone else with his brainless logic, only returning one more time to my table, much later on when I was halfway through my pea-flavored dessert, to ask the ITQ, the Inevitable Tip Question: "And how are we doing over here?"

Grrrrrrrr.

I didn't reply. I just glowered at him darkly. Also, when the time came to pay, I tipped him a penny for putting his hat on the right way round and stormed out, mentally relegating my previously beloved TGI Friday's to a personal blacklist, just below The Artichoke Palace, as somewhere I never intend to visit again.

That's it. I've said my piece about waiters. The rest is up to you, Chicago.

Let the ass-kickings begin.

3

The Hamster Wheel

*What we can learn from men in dull gray suits ◆ I put the fun in
funeral parlor ◆ transport problems ◆ glittering times at the International
Housewares Show ◆ a new use for Sarah Brightman ◆ nosying shamelessly
around other people's homes ◆ setting fire to my past ◆ I have a spiritual
epiphany ◆ then I go taunting product demonstrators ◆ a bad experience
with Jimmy Neutron, Boy Genius*

C
HICAGO IS A CONVENTION CITY.
To a traveler, that means only two things:
**1. Half the people you run across as you walk
around town will have mysterious plastic name tags
dangling from a string around their neck**.

At first I was puzzled. I thought maybe they were just total
imbeciles who kept forgetting who they were. But not so. Turns
out it was a whole bunch of executives and salespeople who'd
flown in for the International Housewares Show and whose parents had given them names so preposterous—"Hoss J. Pinkerton
IV, Chairman, Pinkerton's Good to Go" or "Goliath X.
Trimbleweather, CEO, Trimbleweather Hose & Pipe"—that they
couldn't wait to stick them on a tag and show them off to people.

Personally, I've always rebelled against being tagged, mainly
because Cash is a preposterous name too and I loathe it when
people squint at my tag and chuckle, "But it's okay if I give you a
check, right? Hohohohohoho!" Actually, I'm thinking of awarding a prize to the 100,000th person to say that to me. It should
happen any day now.

Also, revealing one's identity too soon can undermine one's
mystique. Not that I have much mystique, but I'm reluctant to
squander what little I do have on a bunch of strangers who, when

they find out who I am, are only going to laugh at me anyway. Hohohoho.

2. Each evening, once the show's over for the day, the bars in mid-range hotels all over town will be full of bored-looking salesmen and executives (sometimes they're women, but mostly men), in dull, homogenized gray business suits, sitting alone.

I see these guys everywhere I go. Invariably they look suicidal. At a loose end, they spend the entire time after dinner hunched in a chair, sipping a rum and Coke as they rhythmically scan the pages of the latest John Grisham without taking in a word.

Sip and scan. Sip and scan. That's all they do.

Oh yes, and glance at their cell phone. They do that a *lot.*

Sometimes they'll even pick it up and stare at the screen for no reason, or press buttons at random, or idly scroll down one menu after another.

"Hey. You!" Sometimes I fantasize. I imagine standing close to one of these guys, but hidden, perhaps behind a pillar. "Yes you, in the dull, homogenized gray suit noodling on your phone."

"Who said that?"

"Put down that fast-paced novel by one of America's premier thriller writers and reflect for a second. Do you honestly believe you were put on this earth to wear that stupid suit and struggle in a boring job and drown in car payments and credit card debt and wear a plastic tag around your neck with your name on it?"

"Look, what the hell is going on? Come out from behind that pillar."

"You deserve better than this, my friend. You have a destiny. Rise to it. Do it now. Climb off the Hamster Wheel. *Find a way* before it's too late!"[8]

"Okay, that's it, I'm calling the cops!"

And off he goes. It's the same every time. They won't listen.

They know they screwed up somewhere along the line—but where? I mean, by all accepted standards, these guys have it all: the house, the car, two kids, money in the bank, good job, annual

---

8. I also do a great Marley's Ghost, if you're interested.

bonus and benefits, three vacations a year—every element of a perfect mundane existence is right there at their fingertips; yet inside they're boiling mad. And incidentally, this is going on right now all around the world, not just America. "How is it that every day feels like a slow nosedive into Hell?" people are asking themselves. "How come I bought into all of this? Got stuck in a rut, too old to switch tracks, too tired to cheat on my wife, just one more loser, as gray and homogenized as this suit I'm wearing, holed up in a mid-range hotel room with a bath too small to lie in, a toilet seat that shifts around when I sit on it, and an uninterrupted view of a brick wall? What went wrong?"

What went wrong?

Not many questions fascinate me, but this one does, if only because I too am an object of pity. From where those guys are sitting, they probably think I'm one of them: another anonymous drone propping up the bar in a strange hotel, scanning a John Grisham, sipping at a strawberry margarita (and before you say anything, I know it doesn't look good, okay? But I hate rum and Coke), waiting for my cell phone to ring.

Which it doesn't.

Therefore are we saying I screwed up too? At my life's end, when I find myself *still* reporting for public radio and standing in the bathroom of yet another mid-range hotel with a gun to my head—and this is not as far-fetched as you may think—will I look back on the sixty or seventy years I spent on this planet and say to myself, "You're telling me *that was it?* That was all there was?"

Apparently so.

THE NEXT MORNING DAWNED BRIGHT and even chillier than the day before. After breakfast, Jim, my producer, called from the studio in L.A. with a bright idea.

Never a good thing, this. Producers with bright ideas are like children with flamethrowers. You know there's going to be damage, you're just not sure how much. But that's what happens: I'm bumbling along nicely on my own, not harming anyone, then quite unexpectedly the studio will call with an assignment. "Go here." "Do this." "There's someone we'd like you to meet." "I've had a bright idea." In that respect, my life is not unlike an episode of *Mission Impossible,* only with all the interesting and exciting parts taken out.

"*Since you have time on your hands,*" he said, "*we thought you might like to go to Palatine.*"

"Why?"

"*It's close by, and they have an unusual miniature golf course.*"

"Oh yeah? What's unusual about it?"

"*It's in the basement of a funeral parlor.*"

"Oooh!"

And there you have it. That's my problem right there. In this business, you have to know when to say no to things, and I never could.

"NO, I have no interest in miniature golf courses, however unusual"; "NO, I don't want to fly to Texas to meet a man who collects toilet seats"; and "NO, I definitely, *definitely* do not want to see a chicken with two asses, thank you very much."[9] That's how it should be—a firm, decisive refusal every time. Instead, I'm weak. At the first glimmer of anything even remotely trashy, I buckle like warm vinyl. "A miniature golf course, you say? In the basement of a funeral parlor? Oooh!"

And before I can stop it, the nightmare has begun all over again.

PALATINE IS ON THE TASSELED FRINGES of what's called the Chicago Metropolitan Bedspread, although you'd never know it; the two don't seem even remotely connected. Over that way you have the big city, the bustling, breakneck hub of all things good and popular; over here, only forty or so miles away but it may as well be on the Moon, is Palatine, a flat, lifeless pocket of suburbia that feels like a model village whose creator died shortly before completing it.

---

9. I found the chicken with two asses at Kathy's Freak Farm in San Diego. Admittedly, it was dead and in a glass case. Even so, that hideous creature, with two dozen eggs sitting beneath it (six per ass), still comes to me in dreams.

I arrived at Ahlgrim Acres Funeral Home and Miniature Golf Course on a Monday, which, as I quickly discovered, was Delivery Day.

At the rear of the building, three workmen labored against a biting wind, wrestling caskets off the back of a truck. This being the Midwest, we immediately exchanged smiles, shook hands for no reason, and talked about nothing at all for several minutes. And as we did, my eyes wandered through the open doors of the funeral home, where, at that moment, the same biting wind that was slowly peeling the skin off my face was also ruffling a tuft of ginger hair belonging to a fourth guy. He was so quiet that I hadn't noticed him before. Not that he was shy or anything, or hiding, just dead.

"Oh my God—a corpse!"

Before I could run away, or freak out, or even crap my pants— all of which were in the cards—a tall, jovial, gray-haired man came striding around the corner toward me, grinning broadly.

This, I found out, was Roger Ahlgrim, and he grins a lot. Some might say too much, given that he runs a funeral parlor. What makes the guy *really* special, though, is his fondness for miniature golf. So passionate is he about it that, in 1964, he decided to build himself a special nine-hole course downstairs at the family funeral home. That way he could get in a game whenever he had a spare moment.

"It was only for our family and my kids' friends. I had no intention of its becoming public really. Then word got out. Our daughter would have sleepovers in the lounge, which is right next door to the miniature golf course . . ."

"With dead bodies upstairs?"

"Yes. Their parents didn't mind. They understood. So everyone had a good time."

Hm.

The setting, when you reach the basement and Roger has turned the lights on, is not unlike a cross between TGI Friday's and a slightly ragged end-of-the-pier amusement arcade. Signs and bric-a-brac litter the walls and there are pinball machines and computer games to keep non-golfers busy. The course itself offers nine holes and lots of obstacles: a lighthouse, a windmill, and so on. But Roger, being somewhat cheeky and evidently no respecter of good taste in these things, couldn't resist tweaking things here and there to make the concept a little more "in keep-ing." This he did by giving it a death theme. So there's a skull that lights up, a haunted mansion, a casket with a fake dead body in it, and even a cemetery with tiny tombstones—"The names of our employees are on those."—each item put together with so much affection and such a morbid sense of fun that it's almost guaranteed to bring a smile to the lips of the recently bereaved.[10]

"So do you want a game?" he asked finally, holding out a club.

"Er . . . well, I don't know. I've never played before."

"Oh, it's great fun," he laughed. "Come on. I'll show you."

First, let me just say something. One of the rules of broadcast journalism is that the journalist must be seen to participate in the event he's covering. It happens all the time, especially on local TV news shows, where starchy reporters with bad hairstyles try to shatter any impression the audience might have that they're over the hill and have no sense of humor, by taking their jacket off (but leaving their tie on!) and "mixing it up" on the streets—rapping in Ebonics, break dancing, or flying Chinese kites, things they would never do in a million years if they weren't being paid for it. In news circles this kind of report is considered hilarious. Editors love it. But really, all it does is confirm something the viewers sus-pected all along: that the journalist in question is a humorless no-

---

10. Funeral people are peculiar types, by the way. If you're ever in Houston, Texas, and you're in need of a good laugh, you might want to take yourself to the National Funeral Museum. The guy who gave me a tour was one of the most chipper people I've ever met in my life, in or out of a funeral museum. For at least an hour he let me fool around in hearses and play with a bunch of novelty caskets shaped like onions and chickens, although he seemed to draw the line at my idea that we climb inside a coffin together and wait 'til the security guard came around, then leap out at him shouting "BOO!" —so I guess even chipper folk have their limits. The best bit of the tour *by far*, though, was when he sat and played an old funereal pump organ while I stood alongside him singing a medley from *Grease*. Outstanding! I highly recommend it.

hoper who'll stoop to virtually anything to get approval. That's why I refuse to do stuff like that. Always have. It's a lesson I learned very early on in my career—*never participate in anything*[11] —and it's stood me in good stead ever since.

On this occasion, however, I relented. Finding myself with a whole day to fill and (this being Palatine, Illinois) nothing whatso-ever to fill it with, for once I abandoned my principles and over the next half-hour trundled about the room behind Roger, merrily knocking my ball (and sometimes his too) along narrow chutes, up slopes, under windmills, down tubes, through haunted mansions, and over, between, and across a variety of steps, funnels, and wavy hillocks. (Incidentally, memo to miniature golf-course designers: without all these obstacles the game would progress a lot faster. I mean, c'mon, guys, what *were* you thinking?)

By the time we'd done, I was quite exhausted. And yet, despite having an unfortunate handicap—I can't hit a ball straight to save my life—I somehow prevailed, managing to finish the course a mere 349 over par, which, as any seasoned pro will tell you, is pretty respectable.

Once we were done and I'd squeezed every last drop of enter-tainment value out of hitting balls with sticks, Roger turned off the lights and we slipped back upstairs again, passing en route the chapel of rest. And that—oh dear God—*that* was when I caught sight of my second dead body of the day. Imagine: forty-six years entirely cadaver-free, then kaboom!—two stiffs in the same morning.

The guy lay in a plain casket, wearing the glasses he died in and a formal suit he probably kept just for church, job interviews, and funerals (his own included). The flesh on his face was tight about the cheeks, and had been given a light dusting of makeup. (Imagine Joan Rivers with her mouth sewn shut, it was a bit like that.) In fact, on a cursory glance, he looked for all the world as

---

11. I have since extended this beyond my professional assignments into everyday life, and it works like a dream.

though he'd just returned from a trip to Wal-Mart to buy embalming fluid and decided to take a wee nap to get his breath back. Amazing. I only hope I look that good when I'm that age, and that dead.

And you know what? For a moment there I was even envious.

After all, here was someone who knew how the story ended. No more second-guessing for him. Unlike the rest of us, still busily scribbling the chapters, he'd checked out. Gone. The clock had stopped running and the pressure was off. Now he was able to lie back, put his feet up, and tally the pluses and minuses of his eighty-so years.

Did he win or lose, I wondered? Did he hitch his wagon to a star, or chain it to a fire hydrant and wonder why it wasn't going anywhere?

Sadly, I'd caught him at a bad moment. He was dozing eternally and not up to answering questions.

Furthermore, I still have no clue who the old codger was (now, *here* would be a good place for a plastic name tag!). And since this was a while ago anyway, whether he came through finally and won the game of life or ended up 349 over par is academic. In either case, he's already compost.

Lucky bastard.

Which brings me, though perhaps not as smoothly as I would have liked, to the International Housewares Show.

TRADE SHOWS ARE BIG BUSINESS. Big, huge, enormous. And the International Housewares Show is the glittering granddaddy of them all.

Every product, every device, every gadget humanly imaginable is on display here. If there's an exciting new design of bucket on the market, or a wooden spoon that "breaks all the rules," or a toaster that not only browns your bread but also impresses a facsimile of Sarah Brightman's face on every slice, then in all probability you'll catch it here first. Some companies even bring a handful of next year's products with them, gadgets so spiffy, so new, so *now*, that quite honestly they make anything you saw at the show this year look positively half-assed.

Not long ago the housewares expo dug its heels in and became an annual fixture at McCormick Place, Chicago's three-halled concrete and glass colossus conference center. This was located less than a mile from my hotel.

Normally I'd have walked it. I don't mind walking. Walking's like real exercise, only without the swollen joints and the showering afterwards. According to the map, the well-tended grassy common across the street would have taken me all the way there, making for an ideal summer morning stroll. If this had been summer. Which it wasn't. That day, Chicago was freezing in the kind of deep midwinter they write Christmas carols about, and of course I, being dressed for a Hawaiian luau, was not about to go walking anywhere. No, some alternative would have to be found.

As far as I could figure out, the choices were as follows:

- **I could rent a car.** Not an option. I'm hopeless with machines. I have problems operating even the simplest of devices: soap dispensers, door chimes, you name it. By the same token, my skills as a motorist tend to be very point-and-click: I switch the vehicle on, aim it in the direction I want to go, press a few buttons that look as if they might contribute to that "moving off into traffic" thing, grip the steering wheel 'til my knuckles turn white, and from then on pray to God that nothing gets in my way. A friend once observed that I drive a car the same way Luke Skywalker flies fighter planes: I close my eyes and rely on The Force, reaching my destination eventually, but by another's hand. For that reason and no other, I drive only if I have to.[12]

---

12. And yes, I'm fully aware that if ever I'm up in court on a traffic offense, this paragraph will be read out very slowly and with great glee by the prosecution while I'm shouting, "My God, what is wrong with you people? Can't you take a joke?" from the witness box.

- **I could take public transport.** Are you *insane?*

- **Somebody could drive me.** Six times out of ten, this is what will happen. An assistant from the Chamber of Commerce or the Convention and Visitors Bureau will stop by and take me where I want to go. Not that they want to; they have a thousand things they'd rather do than chauffeur me around. But you know what? I'm persistent. In the same way that "a smile is just a frown turned upside down," I regard "no" as a mispronounced "yes," so usually it's easier for them to grab their car keys and take me than to stand there listening to me whine on about how unhelpful they're being and threatening to picket the building.

- **I could catch a free shuttle.** Ah, *now* you're talking! My credo has always been, "If it's free or it's a cow, milk it." Free shuttles are a positive boon to anyone either too lazy to walk or too cheap to take a cab, and, as luck would have it, I fit snugly into both camps. The housewares show, I found, had arranged free coaches to take exhibitors and ticketed attendees from their hotels to McCormick Place, and though I was neither an exhibitor nor a ticketed attendee, I *was* staying in a hotel, and hey, one out of three wasn't bad, I thought, so I jumped aboard anyway.

AS I SHUFFLED THROUGH THE DOORS to McCormick Place behind a long line of people, I was handed a press pack by a small, rather plain woman who'd been given the job of meet and greet.

"I'm a big fan of your show," she gushed. "I listen to you all the time."

"Oh yeah? That's nice."

"Your reports are so great. You're my favorite."

"Thanks."

It's always nice to be recognized. Sadly, it doesn't happen very often. And when it does and I hear listeners singing my praises,

I'm absolutely convinced they don't mean it at all and what they're really thinking is: "Forty-six years old and still doing five-minute travel reports for public radio. *Such* a waste."[13]

"You always bring a smile to my face."

"That's very sweet of you," I replied, and bowed to receive one of those awful plastic name tags around my neck.

CHAS PETER, it said.

"Enjoy the show, Chas. Keep up the good work."

"I will. And thanks again."

Sometimes I come close to sobbing.

WALKING ONTO THE FLOOR OF THE SHOW that day was an epiphanous experience for me. Like finding that Heaven does exist after all; it's not just some mythical carrot dangled by the Church before a few sinner-donkeys to tempt them onto a more righteous path; it's real. More than that, Paradise is decked out in burnished chrome and glittering fairy-lights and is stacked to the rafters with thousands upon thousands of sleek, enticing, next-generation consumer durables for you to ogle, caress, and coo over.

Straight away, a blonde bikinied model caught my eye.

"Hi," she said brightly, handing me a leaflet.

"Hello," I replied, and she giggled. (Women *love* my sense of humor.)

So we got to chitchatting, and she began telling me how she'd been ordered by the manufacturer not only to lounge in this foaming whirlpool bath for the best part of a week, but to do so with glamorous insouciance, as if she was actually enjoying it. That was the hard part. The day had barely started, but she'd already been lounging for so long that her fingers had wrinkled like curtain fabric and her carefully toned thighs were turning to putty before her eyes.

---

13. This is a peculiarly British trait, by the way. We can never accept compliments. Say something nice and we're convinced you're lying; be horrible to us, and we get upset and storm off. You can't win. Frankly, if I had any advice for you at all, it would be to ignore us altogether. Stick with people you understand.

"How long do you have to sit there for?"

"'Til five o'clock," she said.

"Oh yeah? Not long to go, then."

I looked at my watch. It said 11:15.

Moving on. Out of the corner o . . .

"I get lots of breaks, though!"

I'm sure you do. Anyway, out of the corner of my eye, I'd just spotted Model No. 2, another blonde. She was busy on her knees, trying to deflate a king-size stowaway air bed. Once she'd done that and it was lying flat on the floor, she set about inflating it again with a pump. And once she'd done that she set about deflating it again. Up and down it went. Inflate, deflate, inflate, deflate, inflate, deflate, inflate, deflate . . . ten times in one hour.

"Aren't you exhausted?" I asked.

"No. I love it. It's a great air bed. Would you like to lie on it?"

"No thanks. I . . . er . . ."

I had no good reason really. I just don't like making an exhibition of myself at . . . well, exhibitions. Fortunately, there was no shortage of other volunteers. So, stopping only to crack a joke at the expense of Model No. 1 who was slowly shriveling to nothing in her whirlpool, I waved goodbye to Model No. 2 and left her to it.

Inflate, deflate, inflate, deflate, deflate, inf . . .

Hang on—you missed one.

Deflate, inflate, deflate, inflate . . .

That's better.

SOMETIMES ON THE WEEKENDS when I'm home in L.A., my partner and I circle the neighborhood looking for "Open House" signs. We have no intention of buying anything, we just love nosing around other people's personal belongings—What have they got? What does it do? How expensive was it?—ogling their choice of bathroom fixtures, laughing at their gym equipment or their meditation room or their collection of porn videos and Scientology books. It's the best hobby *ever*.

And it doesn't matter how many houses we visit, I never cease to be blown away by how much junk people collect. Little junk, big junk—trinkets, knickknacks, souvenirs, toys, mementos, a thousand objects bursting from drawers, heaped on shelves, cascading out of closets; more junk than they could ever use or know what to do with. And that's just the junk you can see. Open any cupboard door—and I *always* open cupboard doors—and still more junk tumbles out, pushed forward by the junk behind it. Some items may have been received as gifts; the rest one can only assume were bought deliberately, then, when interest in them dissipated, about twenty minutes later, hurriedly crammed under stairs, behind sofas, up chimneys, anyplace there's room, and forgotten about. Junk, junk, junk.

I, by contrast, am not the acquisitive type. I don't seek to own or control or possess, and never have.

Before I moved to America in the late 1990s, I decided I had to make a clean break of things, and the only way to do that and ensure there'd be no turning back, was to start burning my bridges in England. Or if not actual bridges, then everything else I could lay my hands on.

So, secretly, one moonless May night, I gathered up almost every item I owned—that's to say, whatever I wouldn't be bringing with me to the States—packed it into four cardboard boxes and drove it to a remote field in Yorkshire.

I remember I'd prepared a small ceremony, nothing grand or terribly profound, just a few words I'd lifted from a New Age book and scrawled on a piece of paper to mark the occasion: about the significance of creating a crossroads in one's life, releasing the old and inviting in the new. Clichéd hippy nonsense really, but it was quite sincere at the time.

Once that was done I took a match and set fire to the pile.

Now, we're not talking big items here, before you write in. No Louis XIV armoires or Steinway grand pianos were incinerated that night,[14] just clothes, books (including the New Age book), and a few personal items: photos, some family stuff, mementos from school, college, and my travels, together with the boxes I'd brought them in.

It was harder to do than I'd imagined. Some of these "treasures" I'd been holding onto for thirty years and, barring incident, I'd have held onto them for another thirty, I'm sure. But all the while I kept telling myself, "It's just junk. You'll be freer without it. Besides, you can't go so far and *not* do the rest, can you?" So I continued feeding the flames with memories, and stared entranced as my past blistered and sparked, flickered and turned black, and finally dissolved into smoldering ashes before me. Four boxes, I'd been thinking as I drove here — that's a lot of stuff. It could take an hour at least. But in the end everything I'd brought vanished in under fifteen minutes.

Last of all, I threw in the piece of paper upon which I'd written my ceremonial words, and when that was no more, kicked over the embers and left.

A week later I was in America. As May handed the baton to June, year-wise, I stepped off a plane in Los Angeles with only two bags to my name, feeling light and liberated and optimistic. It was a remarkable moment. Though what's even more remarkable is that four years later, if I'd had to leave again, I could still have crammed everything I owned into those same two bags.

Alas, all that changed the day I attended the International Housewares Show.

---

14. I had so few possessions at the time that it quite startled people. "This is everything you own?" friends would say, eyeing ten objects arranged on a table. But I'd never bought an apartment or house, only rented; and since the places I stayed in always came furnished, I never had to buy anything to put in them. Besides, as a freelancer in public radio I could never afford possessions anyway. (Oddly, it didn't seem quite as sad back then as it does when I'm describing it to you now.) Possessions are an encumbrance. They represent restriction, tie you down. Speaking as a Buddhist — oh yes! — my view is: "Life needs elasticity." You have to be free to change, to move on as the opportunity arises (this isn't strictly a Buddhist principle, it's more a foolproof way to avoid your creditors; but it still holds true) and you can't be flexible if you're weighed down with junk, can you?

What I saw at McCormick Place in Chicago sowed seeds in my soul—dark, devilish seeds of discontent and avarice so strong that not even the sturdiest of spiritual shovels could have rooted them out.

On every side, all I could see was acre upon rolling acre of electricals and mechanicals: pristine state-of-the-art devices, each one promising slavishly to cater to my needs. Needs I never really had, and still don't, but who cares? A part of me was already willing, even as I was looking on and purring over them, to develop needs *specifically* for these devices to cater to. Fawning over burnished steel toasters, dancing around juicers and vacuum cleaners, letting my fingertips drizzle across the rippled surface of sandwich makers and then ovenware and soft furnishings and non-stick utensils, I came this close—*this* close, mind—to breaking at least three of the Ten Commandments, in particular the ones about not worshiping false idols, not coveting your neighbor's ass, and not buying a Rowenta steam iron until you've tried the full range of quality European models (I forget which commandment that is; the fourth or fifth, I think).

Household objects I've lived without for decades I suddenly found I wanted.

A waffle maker, for instance.

I don't even *like* waffles. Except perhaps as packing material. But after only the briefest of demonstrations, during which two black metal jaws stamped out an entire plateful of waffles seemingly without human intervention . . . ("Would you like a taste? They're waffle-icious," declared a woman in a white coat whom I was obviously meant to mistake for a scientist.) . . . I knew I could no longer function as a complete person unless I owned one.

Same goes for the True-Air plug-in air purifier, a fan that sucks unpleasant smells out of your kitchen. I've never heard of it, never wanted it, and have no use for it. But the instant my eyes happened upon True-Air's subtle curves and creamy white casing, I couldn't resist.

"Say you're having a fish fry," said the overexcited saleswoman, wiping my drool off the handle with a rag, "and you invite friends over . . ."

"Actually, I don't cook."

"You don't?"

"Can't."

She began laughing, but uncertainly, in case I wasn't joking, which I wasn't. "Well, it's a wonderful product anyway."

"Does it remove the smell of Lean Cuisines?"

"It does." She laughed again, this time in a "you're frightening me, please leave" kind of way. And when that didn't work, and sensing that I was the type of guy who'd stick around making dumb comments until she gave me a free one, she grabbed a True-Air from the pile, shoved it in my hands, and sent me on my way.

I'll never use it, of course. There are no cooking smells in my kitchen, simply because there is no cooking in my kitchen. Ever. Still, just owning a True-Air was enough. It felt good and looked good, and filled me with a strange, unfamiliar kind of inner satisfaction, as well as an overwhelming desire to let something burn or boil over the moment I got home.

Chop-chop-chop-chop-chop-chop-chop-chop-chop-chop-chop-chop. . .

Elsewhere, the sound of a hyperactive Japanese chef dicing onions rattled around the rafters like tommy-gun fire.

Pausing for a moment: "Aaa row!" he said, his voice amplified thirty times by the Japanese speaker system. "Wittaker. Foblijen. Wiv coom en peer. Vor de—onions!"

Chop-chop-chop-chop-chop-chop-chop-chop-chop-chop-chop-chop-chop-chop-chop-chop-chop-chop-chop-chop-chop-chop-chop-chop-chop-chop-chop-chop-chop-chop . . .

Not far from him, an out-of-work actor dressed in a chef's apron to make him look less like an out-of-work actor was heckling the crowd, proclaiming the benefits of baking cookies in a microwave oven. Actually, the benefits are few, it turns out. They're rubbery, way too hot, and taste like puppy chow. And I think the out-of-work actor must have known it too, because when I offered him one, he wouldn't take it.

. . . chop-chop-chop-chop-chop-chop-chop-chop-chop-chop-chop-chop . . .

My heart goes out to product demonstrators, it really does. The hell these people put themselves through to promote machines that in many cases they, along with most of the rest of the world, but *especially* they, could care less about.

"Look, everyone, at how wonderfully clean the carpet is now. The bloodstains have almost completely vanished . . ."

"And if I give this a quick twist—there! You see how easy it is to put a door back on? That, my friends, is the miracle of Hinge-B-Screwed."

And where there weren't demonstrators, there were guys in suits, dull and homogenized and gray. Hundreds upon hundreds of them. More than I've ever seen in my entire life; more than I knew existed. On phones. In meetings. Shaking hands. Talking with quite spectacular passion about toaster ovens and brooms and china tea-sets and lawnmowers and valves, objects you and I have trained ourselves to be quite blasé about. So many plastic name tags, so many wagons chained to fire hydrants. What a mess.

"Hey. You!"

"Aw jeez, not *again*. I thought I made it clear last night, stay away from me."

"You must have had such potential when you were young. Now here you are, middle-aged, married, stuck on the Hamster Wheel."

"I happen to enjoy my job, alright?"

"But you're selling iron lungs for a living. How can you enjoy that?"

"They're not iron lungs, they're barbecues."

"Well, anyway, you're throwing your life away . . ."

"How d'you know? How come you know so much about me?"

"I know, because I did exactly the same as you. I had an ordinary job for eight years. I conformed, and I wasn't happy. I felt unfulfilled, the way you do."

"But you're *still* not happy or fulfilled. Look at you: forty-six and still doing five-minute travel reports for public radio."

Ouch!

Anyway, there are millions more just like him, is my point. You see them everywhere, each one just bumbling through, doing the best he can, praying for a break from the interminable rotation of that Hamster Wheel. It's so sad.

   . . . *chop-chop-chop-chop-chop-chop-chop-chop-chop-chop-chop-chop* . . .

Oh yeah, and this guy will have arthritis in his elbow by the time he's fifty!

IT HAD BEEN A VERY LONG DAY. I must have walked ten miles of red carpet at least, experimenting with one amazing gadget after another; interviewing people; badgering men in gray suits 'til they ran away. Come 5 P.M. I was quite pooped. (You want to know how bad it got? Even a display of patterned ironing-board covers failed to excite me—*that's* how bad!) Maybe I'd return another time and see the rest, but for now I needed a margarita, some hot food, and fresh air, in that order. And I was just staggering toward the nearest exit, past a tired but smiling Goliath X. Trimbleweather—evidently this had been a banner year for hose & pipe—when, just then, right out of left field, along came my worst nightmare.

Jimmy Neutron, Boy Genius!

Aaagh!

Actually, it's not him in particular that I dislike, more "men in foam costumes with big plastic heads" in general. My history with them is not good. Indeed, it's so bad that I'm beginning to think I may be foamaphobic.

During one particularly horrible incident at a Fruit and Vegetable Expo years ago I remember getting into a fight with a guy dressed as an avocado. I'd asked if I could interview him, but his PR woman wouldn't let me. ("I'm sorry. Avocados don't talk," she said in all earnestness. Well, duh!) However, not one to be deterred by a refusal, I went ahead anyway, shoving my microphone up the inside of his costume.

"Stop that!"

Too late. Already I'd unbalanced him. He was perched on the hood of a convertible at the time and when I lunged forward he rolled right off the other side, taking the PR woman with him. It was dreadfully humiliating for all concerned, and there have been many occasions since then when I've wished I could set the record straight by apologizing to the both of them, and perhaps giving them a free True-Air each. Whoever you are, if you're out there and you're reading this, I'm very, very, *very* sorry.

People in foam costumes are a recurring hazard at trade shows and conventions. You see them all the time, dressed as giant fruit, dinosaurs, Teletubbies, birds, butterflies. They're always relentlessly perky. They're paid to be. And they *always* have the same sinister fixed grin on their face, stretched wide and beaming. This, to my mind, is what makes them so goddamned irritating.

Beneath the foam exterior, earning an honest buck and trying not to feel too humiliated doing it, is some poor actor whose agent has persuaded him to be the object of derision for a day by putting on big white cartoonish gloves and an oversized molded head to prance around in, waving at people. It's dark and insufferably hot inside there. The actors can't hear or be heard. Not clearly anyway. So they're under strict orders never to say anything to anyone. Doesn't matter how you torture them—stomp on their face, kick them, wrestle them to the ground, punch them, insult them, do your very worst—they won't utter so much as a squeak. And of course the fixed plastic smile will keep right on smiling.

When Jimmy Neutron, Boy Genius intercepted me, he did so at the worst possible moment. Except for a rubbery microwaved cookie—and half of that I'd coughed back up into my hand and thrown away—I'd not eaten a thing since breakfast and I was close to dropping. But of course he wasn't to know that; he was just a man in a dumb costume promoting a movie.

Being a genius, he spotted my microphone from far away and thought, "Oh great! A PR opportunity." Next thing I knew, he came bounding over with his handler. (There's always a handler. His job is to lead the actor around obstacles, to field questions — and mostly it's the same question: "Does he speak?" "No." — and wherever possible to stop small children biting his legs.)

"Pleeeeeeease stop that," I groaned as Jimmy Neutron began tickling me.

But he couldn't hear, or see my smile-turned-upside-down.

Tickle-ickle-ickle. Chunky gloved fingers groped my abdomen.

"Look, I'm not in the mood, okay?"

And anyway, I'm in radio. What use to me is someone who doesn't speak?

Tickle-ickle-ickle-ickle.

"Hey, pal, for the last time, will you please . . ."

Ickle-ickle.

But he wouldn't be told. Just kept on pummeling my stomach until I reached a point where I couldn't take a single second more. One minute I was calm, then I snapped. No, I didn't just snap, I *exploded* with rage.

Luckily for him I'm British. When a Brit explodes with rage, you really can't tell. As a race, we're masters of wry understatement. Low-key is written into our DNA, which can be both a strength and a weakness. Instead of erupting into tirades of screamed threats and abuse, the way Italians do or the Spanish, we bottle it up. So even though, on the inside, I was seething with fury, what came out of my mouth was a restrained and, given the circumstances, perfectly reasonable: "If you don't stop doing that right now, sunshine, I'm going to punch you in your big fat plastic head."

I guess after this I was expecting a fight to break out. Certainly the foundations had been laid. But the handler, whose sole function so far had been to stand around giggling helplessly, finally sobered up. Deciding that this wasn't helping ticket sales, he grabbed the actor's hand and pulled poor Jimmy Neutron, Boy Genius across the hall to safety.

Hurrah! Sweet victory.

Sadly, however, as with so many victories in life, it was to be fleeting.

The might of the foam army is great, and, as I would later discover, although one battle may have been won and significant gains made, the war between human beings and human beings wearing enlarged plastic heads was not over yet. Not by a long shot.

4

Fun Times in the House of Hate

*A night in Boston ◆ a brief history of the American Revolution
(focusing mainly on tea) ◆ why the people at my B&B hated me ◆
Lizzie Borden: what a scheming bitch! ◆ preparing to visit the
Museum of Dirt ◆ the Ice Maiden cometh, and goeth ◆ mea culpa
◆ the return of Alan Ladd (briefly) ◆ a buccaneer's pledge*

I 'D BEEN WARNED ABOUT BOSTON, NOT ONCE, BUT A
hundred times, since coming to America.

"Don't go," friends would tell me.

"But why not? I heard it's a great place."

"Oh sure, it's a great place alright, if you like exquisite architecture, historic monuments, stretches of open parkland, clean
air, variable seasons, and wonderful restaurants."

"Which I do."

"Ah. Yes. That's what *everyone* says. Until they go there."

"Why? What happens when you go there?"

"Er . . ." And voices would trail away to nothing, as if there was
some ominous little secret they all shared which none of them
wanted to be the first to tell.

Time and again I heard the same thing. "Boston? Oh yes, a
fine city. Shame about . . ."

"About what?"

"Er . . ."

Well, this made no sense. You can't live life that way, through
the prism of other folks' preconceptions. You have to experience
every aspect firsthand and then make up your own mind.
Simplistic, I know. Oprah-ish almost. But that's how I look at it.
So, turning a deaf ear to their remonstrations, I bought myself a
cheap airline ticket and se . . .

"Don't say we didn't warn you."

. . . oh be quiet . . . and set off on a nine-day expedition to Boston, ready for anything that might come my way.

HOTEL ROOMS IN BOSTON ARE NOT CHEAP. It would help if they were, but they're not. As I quickly discovered when I tried to book one, the most paltry accommodation available in the convenient downtown area was beyond our show's budget. *Way* beyond.

So once again it fell to me to start cutting corners, forsaking the just-about-bearable mid-range stratum this time in favor of something lower and infinitely more humbling: a bed-and-breakfast. And even then, to my horror, it took hours of Web surfing and many phone calls before I found a place we could afford, settling in the end on "The O'Hare Family Guest House. Comfortable rooms. Mouthwatering breakfasts. South Boston."

"Hm. South, eh?" I thought. That sounded kind of far.

South Boston, it turns out, is a predominantly Irish community, dating back to the nineteenth century when thousands of European settlers arrived at Logan Airport (at least one assumes they flew; the boat would have taken days), equipped with nothing more than the clothes on their back, a ragged copy of *Frommer's* in their pocket, and the name of a modestly priced B&B written on the palm of their hand, eager to begin a new life. Something tells me Boston was probably on the ocean back then, because a considerable shipbuilding industry appears to have thrived here. Or perhaps the ships were built inland and carried to the sea. At any rate, much of the dockyards' workforce, including boilermakers, welders, stevedores, riveters, and ship-carriers, were Irish immigrants and they lived, many of them, in South Boston.

Naturally, the neighborhood's gone to seed. These days, it's a rundown working class enclave of terraced houses, smoky pubs, and rough corner cafes where the employees have tattoos and teeth missing, and they laugh uproariously at you if you ask for a salad.

According to guides I'd been reading, Boston as a whole is abundant in weird and dopey museums, enough to keep me highly amused for the whole week, and so, before leaving L.A., I'd put in a series of courtesy calls to various curators to let them know I was coming. I'd also called the B&B owners to tell them to expect me 9 P.M. Sunday.

"*Oh good. That's great,*" Donna O'Hare's lilting brogue tinkled down the line.

(I have *such* a soft spot for Blarney Folk, really I do. I think my great-grandparents were Irish. That, or they once holidayed in Cork, I forget which. Either way, there's an undeniable fondness that goes back generations.)

"*We'll see you Sunday, then. Bye.*"

Hm. And so, excited at the prospect of being administered a medicinal dose of Old Country hospitality, I'd scratched "find a B&B" off my to-do list and hung up.

Little did I know that the O'Hares, in common with most other Bostonites,[15] have no truck whatsoever with Old Country hospitality, or anything even remotely approaching it. Not only that, but, to my horror, I found that the reasons for this, and there are many, lay in the year 1773.

IN 1773 THE BRITISH PARLIAMENT PASSED a wicked piece of legislation called the Tea Act, imposing a tax on all tea imported into the Colonies.

The locals were in uproar. "Ye infernal bounders! Forsooth, 'tis intolerable what ye do"; or however they spoke back then.

But King George III was a tough old bird and refused to budge, which only made the colonials madder still. However, rather than do the obvious, i.e., boycott imported tea and switch to coffee, or even freshly squeezed juice, which is better for you anyway, they instead launched a full-scale civil uprising out of

---

15. Again, I'm guessing here. It might pay you to double-check the collective noun before you start using it in conversation.

Boston, intent on driving out the greedy British. Of course, I can't vouch for the truth of any of this, although I'm afraid we Brits do have rather a history of trying to take over other people's countries and then being driven out again with our asses on fire, so it's probably about right.

In the years that followed, much blood was spilled. And much tea. Until the Colonies broke away from Britain entirely to form their own country. They decided to call it America, and after a bit of a slow start it went on to become quite a hit among the international community, especially the British, who have since moved back here by the thousands. Very soon we'll own the place again, you'll see; *then* you'll be sorry.

Anyway, the point is, and this is what so surprised me: three hundred years down the road, they've *still not gotten over it*. King George III moved on and went off to pick, and lose, a fight with someone else (India, I think). But not the Bostonites, oh no. Incredible as it may seem, they continue to bear a deep-seated grudge against Brits, one they won't admit to, but which they ram home at every conceivable opportunity. In fact, had I been aware of such rampant hostility, I would almost certainly have looked elsewhere for a place to stay—Pittsburgh perhaps—or at the very least not been quite so surprised when, at the appointed hour of 9 P.M. a week later, after dragging my bags for forty minutes in a driving rain up hills, under bridges, around parks, and crisscrossing a grid of streets until I hit Emerson Street North, I arrived on the doorstep of Donna and Gerry O'Hare's B&B only to find that, as part of their extensive preparations for my arrival, they'd locked the door and gone out.

WHEN THE COUPLE FINALLY DID MAKE an appearance, forty minutes late, with a curt hello but no explanation or apology, I was welcomed into their home the way a family of mice might welcome in a ginger tom. Turned out they weren't husband and wife, as I first thought, but an Irish brother and sister team who'd fallen into the bed-and-breakfasting biz by default, after everything else they'd tried in life had failed. At that point, I gather, it was either open their house to guests or run off and join a circus.

"This is where you'll be," Donna—trim, chalky face, Nancy Drew haircut—said, steering me down some steps to my room.

On the phone she'd called it "the servants' quarters," stirring up images of a below-stairs Edwardian nook lit by hurricane lamps and filled with soft armchairs, lumbering old-style brass bed-frames, and chintz. But it was nothing of the sort. This was like somewhere you'd hide Anne Frank, a claustrophobic grotto with mysterious slime stains on the walls, curling carpets, and only the top half of a window (the bottom half disappeared into the cellar). I've never seen such squalor in all my life!

Call me spoiled, but I'm used to comfort. I am. I'm used to places where the TV doesn't just turn on and off, it also picks up different channels as well; where the ceiling is higher than my forehead, where the light switch can be operated by means other than jamming a screwdriver into the casing, and where the drawer space is an actual *space*, and not crammed with knickknacks, bro-ken toys, and underpants left behind by previous guests.

Flopping down on the bed, I found that someone had placed a handwritten note on the nightstand. "Breakfast will be served at 8:00 A.M. prompt," it said. *"don't be late.* Thank you."

There was a second note behind the door: *"No smoking* in rooms. If you do, we will ask you to leave." Squeezed underneath in smaller writing was a supplementary clause: "And *no secret puffs* at your window! Thank you."

Oh yeah? And what window would that be, I wonder?

THAT FIRST NIGHT I SLEPT SURPRISINGLY WELL, waking only thirteen times. This I put down to my fear of being late for breakfast. And it worked, because on the dot of 7:59 A.M., washed and dressed and anxious to get started on the first day of my trip, I slipped downstairs to the dining room, only to find yet another message waiting for me:

"Good morning. Breakfast is a fixed menu. *No special requests.* Thank you."

When I asked him what this meant, Gerry—short, pudgy, with a rasping voice reminiscent of peanuts grating in a blender—told me of an elderly American lady who'd once stayed at the house. "One morning she's at the table, right where you're sitting now, and she asks for black coffee and dry toast. Bold as you please."

So?

"*Black coffee and dry toast!*" His eyes popped with incredulity. "Well, I told her, 'Madam' I said, 'in this country we put *cream* in our coffee and *butter* on our toast, and *that* is how it will be served to you. Thank you.' I mean, the *nerve* of these people. And that's when we put that little sign up."

Oh—dear—God!!

Now, back home, just to fill you in, I'm strictly an organic oatmeal and banana guy in the mornings, with maybe a little English breakfast tea (the untaxed kind) to swill it down with—something simple and unfussy; and I'd planned on asking the O'Hares for the same. But to hell with that now. Being British, and therefore hopeless at confrontations, I submitted to their fixed menu without so much as a whimper, forcing down a fruit yogurt, a short stack of pancakes drenched in maple syrup, two strips of bacon, two eggs that were supposed to be scrambled but looked as if they'd just been slightly toyed with then put aside for ten minutes until they were cold and rubbery, like something a dog might play with, and a cup of fresh-brewed coffee. Ugh!

Finally, before Gerry could return to ask "How was breakfast?"—because I hate lying—I leapt from the table, grabbed my stuff, and ran for the street.

THE FIRST MUSEUM ON THIS TRIP was something called The Lizzie Borden House, a popular New England tourist attraction that had recently been voted the world's No. 1 Scariest Place by what I guess is the world's No. 1 authority on the subject, The Travel Channel.

When I called the owners from Los Angeles the previous week, they said they'd opened the place as a bed-and-breakfast not long ago and if I wanted to stay overnight I could, adding that, if I did, they'd let me sleep in the actual room where sixty-nine-year-old businessman Andrew Borden was brutally murdered all those years ago.

Oooooooooooh!

Yet, oddly, the idea of spending eight hours in a space once occupied by a butchered corpse held only minimal appeal. Besides, I was already settled in my own B&B, and since this would only mean exchanging one set of fairly horrific circumstances for another, I returned a polite no, opting for something altogether less nerve-jangling: a guided tour.

I DON'T KNOW IF YOU'RE FAMILIAR with the Lizzie Borden story. If not, here's the short version.

THE LIZZIE BORDEN STORY

Lizzie Borden killed her parents with an axe.

Probably.

The End

That's all there is to it. Frankly, I'm surprised whole books have been written and entire TV movies starring Elizabeth Montgomery made about the subject, because when you get down to basics, it's really a cut-and-died case.

The murders happened at 92 Second Street, in the little country town of Fall River, Massachusetts. On the night of August 4, 1892, rich young social butterfly Lizzie Borden waited 'til after dark, then crept into her parents' room and promptly and methodically struck them about the head (she enjoyed night-clubbing apparently). Back then, kids didn't have TV or video games, so I guess slaughtering your mom and dad was a bit like the Playstation of its day. Anyway, once dead, Andrew and Abby Borden were scattered liberally about the house—him on the downstairs sofa, her on the floor of the guest bedroom—where they remained until Bridget, their Irish maid, found them the next day. My guess is that, on entering the room, she probably clutched her cheeks and screamed like a banshee. Victorian maids were always clutching their cheeks and screaming like banshees. It was kind of a tradition.

Of course, when poor people get murdered, which they do a lot, nobody much cares, but the Bordens had stacks of cash and so their cold-blooded execution was THE big international news story of the period, *period.*

Straight away, Lizzie became the chief suspect, on account of the fact that she did it, and she was arrested and tried for double homicide. Yay! Yet even though the girl's alibi was as shaky as hell ("I was raised by lobsters and have been living for the past thirty-two years in a small cave under the sea" being, I think, the main thrust), and despite the fact that at the inquest and preliminary hearings, she changed her story about twenty times, and ignoring clear prosecution evidence that, twelve hours after the crime, she bundled up the dress she'd been wearing and burned it in the kitchen stove, the jury returned a verdict of not guilty. (Really, does anyone still believe that this archaic system works? You'd be better installing a giant roulette wheel in every courtroom and spinning your way to justice.)

"It was the O. J. Simpson trial of the previous century," the house's current owner told me. "The case was never solved; and just as O. J. was acquitted but was generally thought of as being guilty, although Lizzie was acquitted, many people thought she was not innocent."

As I said, a lot of books have been written about the murders. Some of them were hatchet jobs, but the better ones, with such provocative titles as *The Girl in the House of Hate* and *Lizzie Borden: Did She, or Didn't She?*,[16] as well as a bunch of mementos and other Borden-related souvenirs are available from the Fall River Historical Society.

But you don't care, do you?

I thought as much.

---

16. My own book, *Yes, She Did. Now Quit Asking,* will be in bookstores next spring.

FALL RIVER IS ABOUT AN HOUR'S BUS RIDE outside Boston. As luck would have it, 92 Second Street was directly opposite the coach station, which meant that, having left lots of time for getting there and becoming hopelessly lost (which is what normally happens), I actually found myself knocking on the door about thirty minutes early (which *never* happens!).

The three-story Victorian Greek-revival-style mansion is a little uninviting, from the outside at least. Not dirty or neglected, just . . . well, cold. Intimidating. Indeed, if you didn't know, you might think it was built for an episode of *The Twilight Zone*, then abandoned once the production wrapped.

As it turned out, all the surplus minutes I'd accumulated by arriving early were wasted as I spent half an hour hammering on the front door, only to find that the entrance was not where I thought it was. You get in by passing through the print-shop building farther along the street.

Once inside, you can't help but be struck by the eerie authenticity of it all: the chintzy Victorian decor, the furnishings, the atmosphere. Everything is exactly as it was on the night of August 4, 1892. Of course the bodies have been cleared away and someone's vacuumed around, otherwise it's identical. Using actual crime scene photos, the owners dutifully re-created the sitting room, the parlor, the dining room, and the rest, matching wallpaper and carpets, replicating the antique chairs and tables, the doors, the fittings. It's all *toooo* spooky.

Photos of the Borden family adorn the walls upstairs, including Lizzie, who was surprisingly pretty, in that starched, frigid, glum-faced, untouchable way that sent Victorian men wild, and her sister Emma, who, as a child, looked like a small gorilla and, to be honest, didn't improve much with age. They even have on display—and this will be pointed out to you with awe and reverence as you walk by—a period-style costume worn by Elizabeth Montgomery in the made-for-TV movie about the murders, which I never saw, though I doubt it was as good as *Bewitched*.

This, to me, though, is what makes the Borden House experience so much scarier than sleeping in your average house of hate—the fact that it's all so well thought out, so exquisitely pre-served. That's why I could never stay overnight; I'd be terrified. Not of ghosts or spooky goings-on, or God forbid of being mur-dered, but of breaking something—knocking over an antique lamp while doing the macarena, or running with scissors and acci-dentally tearing a hole in the Elizabeth Montgomery dress. They don't realize it, but I did them a huge favor by turning down their offer. Oh yes.

Others, however, are not so timid. They do sleep there. Many more, playing the amateur sleuth, trek through the house hoping to find clues that might have been overlooked by detectives a century ago, and again by decorators when they completely renovated the place. Others, realizing what a futile exercise that is, prefer instead to drape themselves over the couch where Andrew Borden's body was found and pretend they've been bludgeoned.

Anyhow, it's all very absorbing. Although, as you leave—and I left remarkably quickly—the major question on your mind is: Whodunnit?

They've had a number of clairvoyants come in and try to solve the murder using their psychic powers, though you won't be sur-prised to learn that each one of them came to an entirely differ-ent conclusion.

"It's possible Lizzie did it," Michelle, the manager, summed up the findings. "It's also possible her uncle, John Morse, com-mitted the crime."

Ah.

"Or Bridget the servant, who was working here at the time."

Hmm, I see.

"One of the books even suggested that Mr. Borden had an ille-gitimate son who committed the crimes."

Oh, well, why didn't you say so? It was clearly him, then.

"Another theory is that one of Lizzie's boyfriends, who Mr. Borden didn't think was good enough for his daughter, did it."

Or him.

"Personally, I think it was a conspiracy between Lizzie's older sister Emma and their uncle, John Morse."

Oh, yes, yes, yes. So basically, everybody did it. Though, if you ask me, I say they're all wrong. I believe it was far more straight-forward: During the course of the evening a particularly robust game of Twister got out of hand and Andrew and Abby Borden slaughtered themselves. That's it. Lizzie Borden was innocent, the trial was a sham, and this is my final say on the matter. (I should give talks on this, I really should.)

THAT SAME AFTERNOON I DECIDED to drop in on the local tourism people. Whenever I visit a major town, it's my custom to stop by the offices of the Visitors Bureau or the Chamber of Commerce or whatever else they have, to say hello. I don't stay long, just an hour or two, while I pick up leaflets, use their phones, their computers, their bathroom, their vending machines, their fax, their photocopier, their paper, their pens, and whatever else is lying around—generally drawing on their abundant resources in any way necessary to help make my poorly funded excursions run more smoothly. (If it's free or it's a cow, milk it—remember?) And in almost every case the staffers, appre-ciating the value of a spot of radio publicity, are eager to help. After all, that's what they're paid for, right? To help.

Well, not in Boston apparently.

"I'd like to visit something called the Museum of Dirt," I told the gray-faced mannequin who stepped out to greet me. We shook hands. It was like pulling the lever on a slot machine. "D'you know where it is?"

"I'm sorry, I don't," she said, already unhappy with the way this was going.

"But you have an address for it, right?"

"No, we don't."

"Well, maybe you could go look."

"I don't need to look."

"If you don't know it, then you need to look."

"I don't need to look because I already looked."

"No you didn't."

"*Yes I did.*"

"How could you have looked, you haven't moved from this room!"

I swear to God, if bickering was an Olympic sport, I'd take home the gold.

"I looked some time ago. And we don't have it."

"Well, perhaps you should look again. It might be there now."

"I . . ."

At this point, the Ice Maiden faltered.

A thought had crossed her mind: "The sooner I help him, the sooner I'll be rid of him," which, strangely enough, is what most people think when they meet me.

And for a moment or two there I watched her teeter on the brink of giving in. But then something else took over. Something sinister and quite maddening. I'm not sure what you'd call this erratic mood change, though I believe the technical term for it is sheer snooty, arrogant, unyielding, bull-headed obstinacy, and as far as I can tell it's peculiar to people who live in and around Boston.

"No. I'm sorry," she snapped. "I can't help you," and walked out.

Damn the woman.

Then I remembered: In my notebook I had the number of the museum's PR girl. I forget her name, but let's call her Lisa, which is a pretty safe bet since 75 percent of PR people worldwide seem to be called Lisa. Even the men. So I grabbed the nearest phone and dialed.

"I'd like a tour of the Museum of Dirt please."

"*I'm sorry, Mr. Peters-s-s, but that's not gonna be possible.*"

"Why ever not?"

"*They're moving-g-g, and the museum's all in boxes-s-s.*"

It didn't help that she had this weird voice pattern that extended every fourth word or so by an unnecessary two syllables. Incidentally, I should add that it was because of this woman that I was here in the first place. She'd e-mailed me in L.A., bursting with enthusiasm, encouraging me to come. When I reminded her of this, though, she brushed it aside without a second thought.

"All I can say is-s-s, 'mea culpa-a-a.'"

"What the hell are you talking about, mea culpa? I travel three thousand miles to be here and you tell me it's canceled?"

"Sorry–y–y. The museum's closed. I can't help you-oo-oo."

"Goddamnit!"

Slamming down the phone I turned to find the Ice Maiden standing behind me, a smirk of smug satisfaction tweaking her anchovy lips.

"So you won't tell me where it is?"

"I don't *know* where it is," she insisted. "Now, if you don't mind, I'm very busy." ("It's 3:15. In five minutes' time, I have to go outside and glare disapprovingly at a coach-full of tourists.")

"Fine!" Springing to my feet with the verve of a strapping young buccaneer destined for the high seas, I snapped shut my notebook and swore by the seven golden fleeces of Sinbad to track down this Museum of Dirt that nobody would let me see. It might take me a few days, but I would find it, oh yes, and when I did I would fix up an appointment with the curator *personally*, and insist that he give me a guided tour. And Lisa—well, Lisa could go screw herself-f-f.

"To hell with you all!" I cried, bounding across the office toward the open window. Then I thought better of it. "I don't need your help." I turned by the door and threw her a defiant wave, like Alan Ladd from the rigging. "Madam, I bid you good day."

But it was wasted effort. Madam had already walked out.

Boston people do that a lot.

RETURNING TO THE B&B THAT NIGHT, I wasn't in the best of spirits. It had been a depressing day all round; Boston was starting to bring me down, and I was desperate to shut myself away in the hundred-dollar-a-night mold-stained clutter-pit I called my room and go to sleep. However, my mood improved considerably, I have to admit, the moment I entered the house and discovered that, while I was out, my bags had been removed from Anne Frank's Hiding Place and put in a bright, plush, beautifully decorated room on the second floor. Oh boy! This one had windows and a working TV and a comfortable bed, and *everything*. And of course more little notes:

"Sunlight *ruins* carpets. Pull shades down when leaving room. Thank you."

And by the telephone: "Please keep calls *short* (5 minutes). Thank you."

And not forgetting the one on the mantelpiece: "No wet towels on furniture. Thank you."

The O'Hares had taken pity on me, moving me to somewhere bigger and brighter and, more to the point perhaps, actually worth the money I was paying. No longer would I be made to feel like the insane relative nobody talks about, tucked away below stairs. Without knowing it, I had passed some rudimentary initiation test—the tourist equivalent of hazing—devised by the O'Hares to weed out troublemakers, the reward for which was being treated like a respectable human being for the rest of my stay.

Hurray!

And to celebrate, I spent a very enjoyable evening dipping towels in the sink and draping them over the furniture.

5

The Old Woman with an Armchair Glued to Her Ass

Mr. Moussef asks for a fork ◆ *MOBA* ◆ *Lucy in the Field with Flowers*
◆ *Joseph, Mary, and teddy-bear Jesus* ◆ *the Six Hallmarks of
Bad Art* ◆ *tracking down the Museum of Dirt* ◆ *a touch of unpleasant-
ness in a Boston library* ◆ *close encounters with the Bostonites: grrrr*
◆ *a visit to the* Cheers *pub* ◆ *the Moussefs disappear* ◆ *a sticky
breakfast confrontation*

I WAS ALARMED TO LEARN THE NEXT DAY THAT A couple of new guests had checked in to the B&B—a Mr. Moussef and his wife. Alarmed because this was not long after 9/11, a fear-filled time when almost everyone in America, anticipating further terrorist atrocities, had the jitters about anything and anyone Middle Eastern. It was a wholly regrettable situation that generated much inter-racial anguish for a while, and also, I'm sorry to say, caused a dark pall of suspicion to hang over breakfast that particular morning as the Moussefs— who turned out to be, not members of an as-yet-unapprehended Al Qaeda cell, but an extremely pleasant French-speaking couple down from Canada for a sightseeing tour—sat in silence across the table from me, trying to figure out why they'd only been given one fork between them.

"Don't ask me," I mimed when they looked my way.

Just then, Gerry crept in with a plate of brownies, fresh from the packet, and set them down on the table.[17] Without a word, he made to leave again. As far as he was concerned, speaking to guests

---

17. I assumed at the time that chocolate fudge brownies were a local delicacy and everyone in Boston eats them for breakfast. I, on the other hand, would rather stick needles in my eyes.

only invited replies, and replies might lead to conversation, and from conversation it was but a few short, very dangerous steps to actually being pleasant to them, a prospect that filled him with dread. But he hadn't gotten halfway to the door when Mr. Moussef chimed up in broken English: "Could I 'ave another fork, pliss?"

Uh-oh!

Unfamiliar with the rules — "No *special requests*. Thank you." — a guest had unwittingly spoken out of turn. We all watched anxiously as Gerry, his neck glowing a deep crimson, slowed to a stop. "Sure," he said through gritted teeth.

"And more coffee," Mr. Moussef added. "Pliss."

Man, this guy had balls!

Frozen in his tracks, as if he'd just been caught shoplifting, then preserved cryogenically, Gerry allowed his head to sink to his chest. After a few seconds and with a protracted sigh, he raised it again and in that ghoulish grating voice of his, said, "Another fork! More coffee!"

"Pliss."

"You know, it's amazing. You've only been with us twelve hours and already you're ordering me about."

"Pardon?"

Mr. Moussef had clearly not read the signs. *Why oh why hadn't he read the signs?*

"Oh — nothing," Gerry seethed, then he stormed off down the hall to the kitchen, leaving the poor Moussefs to exchange glances of utter incomprehension, before turning to me again.

"Hey, don't involve me in this. You sort out your own fork problems."

Sound callous? Well, maybe. But I had my reasons. Two years ago someone bought me the *Fawlty Towers* compilation boxed set for Christmas, so given this type of bitter hotelier-patron dispute I know precisely what comes next: Someone gets hit in the head with a spoon.

Besides, I had a train to catch and a crap museum to see. Busy, busy, busy.

So, fleeing the brushfire of Gerry's wrath, I grabbed the rest of my pancake and a ripe banana from the bowl and darted out of the door.

MY CRAP MUSEUM DU JOUR promised to be one of the best ever, although it was quite a long way away—in Dedham, Massachusetts.

Actually, Dedham sounds like it might be a nice place, doesn't it?

Located southwest of Boston on the Charles River, this is one of the oldest colonial settlements in the Massachusetts Bay region, so not unreasonably I was expecting something quaint, perhaps even a little English-country-villageish maybe. And certainly there *are* country villages in England just like it, but they're nowhere you'd want to visit. Dedham, defying all expectations, turns out to be quite nondescript. In fact, it takes nondescript and raises it to new heights. Maybe I was in the wrong part of town. Maybe there were countless dreamy treats tucked out of sight up neighboring side streets—a windmill, a lighthouse, a haunted mansion—waiting to be explored and reveled in. But it was a very big maybe.

However, what I *did* find more than made up for what I didn't.

Dedham, you see, has a community theater. Normally I wouldn't mention this, since I'm no fan of the provincial arts. Given a choice between sitting through an amateur production of *Joseph and the Amazing Technicolor Dreamcoat* and dipping my face in a pan of hot fat, I'd opt for permanent disfigurement every time. But this one is different. Inside the community theater at Dedham there is something so delightful and extraordinary, so utterly, thoroughly, amazingly amazing that it leaves me with no alternative but to say "Oh—my—God!" and wish upon you the joy of someday traveling to Massachusetts and experiencing this wonder of wonders for yourself.

I'm talking, of course, about the Museum of Bad Art.

"WE ARE THE *OFFICIAL* MUSEUM OF BAD ART," the PR woman told me, as if a measure of exclusivity would somehow enhance the experience. Her name was Elaine, but I'm going to call her Lisa.

"Who declared you official?" I asked.

"We did!" she said.

Fair enough.

The walls of the museum are covered with artwork. But not just any artwork: some of *the* most abysmal artwork ever produced, 240 items altogether, many of them thrift-store dreck or the low-end renderings of painters and sculptors with not a breath of talent between them.

• To your left, a painting of three dead gorillas lying alongside a two-headed man. ("This arrived anonymously in the mail," Lisa said, "which is not unusual at all for us.")

• Behind you, a strange two-dimensional object. ("It's either a ski slope with a face, or possibly a dog in a veil.")

• To your right, a thoughtful clown with two noses, hugging a monkey. ("We call this one 'Pals.'")

• Over there, an acrylic landscape so nightmarishly rich in symbolism that I defy any rational human being to explain what the hell's going on. A four-year-old child would get spanked for doing something this bad. Strictly speaking, it's not the painting they should be hanging, it's the artist.

"A lot of them know they're not good," Lisa admitted, wincing as she caught sight of a Chinese guy wearing glow-in-the-dark trousers and carrying two giant Christmas tree decorations. "What they are is sincere, and that's important to us. If it's not sincere, we don't think it's art."

The very first painting in the collection, the one that started it all off, was "Lucy in the Field with Flowers," and that takes pride of place here, on the wall next to the stairwell leading down to the gents' urinals. When you see it, you'll laugh so hard that your lungs may burst. What it is is a portrait of an old woman in a blue dress.

"Maybe she's sitting and maybe she's standing, but there is certainly a red chair attached to her behind. And those are B-52s in the sky." Which, by the way, is a glaring primrose yellow. Blue, I guess, would clash with her dress. "We also think there's a forest fire over there."

"Oh, is *that* what that is?"

To this day, "Lucy" remains unbeaten in its sheer bloody awfulness. By any standard of aesthetic appreciation it's a travesty, and, like so many of the exhibits here, would make a super gift for a blind person. Oddly, though, it almost didn't survive at all. Scott Wilson, the Esteemed Curator of the museum, found it lying on the curbside in 1992 after someone with taste had thrown it away. Admittedly, Scott's first impulse was probably to throw it away also—stick his foot through the canvas and sell the frame.

But then . . .

I dunno, there's just something about that old woman with an armchair glued to her ass, sit-standing in a burning meadow during a B-52 fly-past that uniquely catches the eye *and* turns the stomach at the same time. So instead of doing what he should have done to "Lucy"—pour flaming kerosene over her and stand guard 'til every last migraine-inducing brush stroke had been incinerated—Scott actually took her home, bless him. And that night a monumental new world movement was born, a movement the French, with their customary flair for hitting on exactly the right word,[18] refer to as *le bad art*. (Don't waste time looking it up. Roughly translated into English, it means "bad art.")

Since then hundreds of similar paintings have flooded in. Only about one in ten makes the grade—and that's a pretty low grade, remember—but the very best of the very worst, the true abominations, now hang in four special galleries at the museum, preserved for all eternity. Or longer.

---

18. Or *le mot juste* as the French would say. There! They did it again!

Their titles alone give you some clue to the horror that dwells here: "Madonna and Child III," "In the Cat's Mouth," "Suicide," "Circus of Despair," and "Peter the Kitty."

"What's this?"

I'd come to a halt before a picture of what seemed to be a startled-looking girl with more hair than is strictly called for, involved in fisticuffs with a chicken.

"Hmmm." Lisa drew close, squinting at details. Then she took four paces back and contemplated the whole for several moments, before concluding with some gravity that, as far as she could tell, and without referring to the curator's files upstairs, it was indeed a startled-looking hairy girl fighting a chicken.

We stood there giggling helplessly.

It's this, to my mind, that makes the Museum of Bad Art so refreshing. Try going to the Getty and laughing at their collection: they'll show you the door. But not MOBA. Laugh at *their* collection, and they'll simply show you a picture of a badly drawn door—they have several—and lead you on to the next gallery.

BEFORE WE GO ON, I HAVE TO CONFESS—as incredible as it might sound, but it's really just a lucky coincidence—that here is one subject of which I have firsthand experience.

Years ago, when I was in England, I used to live with a bad artist.

His name was Neville: thirty-four, divorced twice, financially independent, bad hair. Neville treasured a single, unswerving dream, he told me. He'd all his life wished to become a master painter, which is an entirely admirable ambition, I think, and probably would have been quite attainable too, had it not been for one small detail that at the time it seemed almost churlish to mention: he had absolutely no talent. And I mean not a scrap. Zero. In Neville's world, perspective was as mysterious a concept as nuclear fission. "I didn't quite bring that together, did I?" he would say about a triangular horse or a road that started small in the foreground then grew steadily wider as it rolled toward some distant horizon. Almost every subject seemed to elude capture by his skill-less hand: landscapes, animals, birds (his geese looked like he'd been eating cottage cheese and tripped), people, fresh fruit—you name it, he couldn't do it.

"Neville, why is that pineapple blue?"

"It's not a pineapple, it's an orange."

"Ah." *(Pause for thought)* "Neville, why . . . ?"

"Oh shut up, I'm trying to concentrate."

Last time we ran into each other, it was at an exhibition he mounted in Camden Town, London. The theme was The Nativity. Every day for months, two professional models—one man, one woman—had come to his studio and sat on barstools to pose as Joseph and the Virgin Mary, gamely draping themselves in bedsheets and wrapping tea towels around their heads to get into character. Since no real baby was available—Neville's second wife having been given custody, and the female model being seventeen and unable to conceive at such short notice—a teddy bear was made to double for Jesus and squares of paper towel for swaddling clothes. Meanwhile, the artist hovered Matisse-like over them, slapping gouache frenziedly on canvas, recording every last curve, line, and fold.

Weeks later, on a delightfully balmy evening, a few friends and I, in a show of moral support, but also because we enjoyed laughing, stopped by the exhibition to catch the result of all his hard work.

"Welcome, welcome," Neville cried, thrusting a glass of cheap champagne in my hand. He was wearing a beret. "All great artists wear berets," he said. And bad artists too, evidently. "Wander around at your leisure. The paintings marked with little red spots are sold."

For a full twenty-five minutes I paced the floor, checking out the displays, and saw only one red dot on a painting, put there, I'm sure, by Neville himself to get the ball rolling.

As I said, this was several years ago, so the exact title of the show escapes me, although "Things I Have Smudged" would not have been inappropriate. Of the twenty or thirty paintings spread around two rooms, in 90 percent of them Mary and Joseph were little more than indistinct blobs. (In the other 10 percent they didn't appear at all.) No eyes, no mouths, hands with superfluous fingers, two-dimensional feet pointing straight down (a bit of a trademark for Neville), and picked out so vaguely from an over-busy background that you wondered why he needed models; he could have done them from memory and still gotten them just as wrong.

Added to which the baby Jesus, cradled in Mary's arms, had been given a black nose and rounded ears on top of his head! I swear *I am not making this up.*

Heaven only knows what medication the artist was on, or what happened to his paintings after the exhibition—although two words spring to mind: "enormous" and "bonfire"—but I was convinced at the time that, even if I lived to be 108, I'd never see anything as godawful as that exhibition ever again.

Just shows how wrong you can be!

TO BE FAIR TO THE ARTISTS WHOSE WORK is featured in the Museum of Bad Art, their paintings are at least challenging. They invite the viewer to step up and interact with them, though admittedly it's hard to interact when you're recoiling with your hand over your mouth.

What's shocking is how much dross Scott Wilson and his friends have managed to accumulate. The exhibits fill several white-walled galleries in the basement of the community theater, and then—just as you're saying to yourself, "Well, that wasn't too bad"—an entire storeroom next to the gents' urinals.

"It's temperature controlled," Lisa assured me as we walked in, "to prevent mildew."

A huge mistake, this. In the majority of cases the onset of mildew would only be an improvement.

Anyway, we spent the next few minutes sifting through dozens of odd items: a bad owl standing on a bad twig, a bad curvaceous woman with bad hairy armpits, and so on—and as we did so, I began to realize that there are six hallmarks that set bad artists apart from their more able contemporaries. Therefore, in case this book should ever become culturally significant and a revered reference work for art scholars—don't laugh; it *might!*—here they are:

- **Bad artists can't draw hands.** So they'll usually be tucked behind a book or a vase, or allowed to run off the edge of the canvas, giving the impression that the subject's arms stop at the wrists. Or mittens will be worn. Or the subject's sleeves will be too long. Similarly, if the artist can't draw feet either, then shoes are helpful in avoiding most screwups. Failing that, the subject will be standing in long grass, or paddling in shallow water, or, in a pinch, crouching.

- **Landscapes are bloody impossible.** The great masters like Rembrandt and Turner were such craftsmen that they could probably paint a landscape with their eyes shut, whereas when bad artists paint a landscape it only *looks* like they did it with their eyes shut. In bad landscapes, trees and bushes march in formation. Rivers will disappear mysteriously behind a house, a hill, or a boulder and not come out the other side. The sky will be anything but blue—a light tan maybe. Or green. Flowers will be of a species as yet undiscovered. Farm animals and birds will be located very far away so as to render identification difficult. Oh, and grass will be on fire.

- **Perspective creates more problems than it solves.** So bad artists adopt or abandon it as it suits them. Thus, objects in the foreground will be smaller than objects in the background, people will be the same size as buildings, and a rabbit will tower over the hutch it's meant to be living in. Streets, intended to recede into the distance, will remain the same width the whole way, like chimneys, or until the artist grows tired of them, at which point they will veer off to the left and disappear behind the frame.

• **You thought perspective was tricky: You should try painting noses!** In his efforts to get a nose to look right, the bad artist will make many attempts, applying more and more paint until there are so many layers on the canvas that the subject really does have a full-size three-dimensional nose.

• **A lot of bad art is "mixed media."** Another way of saying "the artist glued stuff on," either to hide some glaring error or simply because he believed—wrongly, as it happens—that it would enhance the aesthetics of the work. Truth is, most times, nothing would enhance the aesthetics of the work, other than perhaps thirty seconds with an acetylene torch. In the mixed-media field, feathers are always popular. But glitter works too. And glued-on hair is more common than you'd imagine.

• **Bad artists believe that a bad painting can be turned around by the last-minute inclusion of a monkey or a poodle.** This happens often. In a crowd scene, a character in the background might be holding a poodle ("to lend the picture a certain Parisian air"), or there'll be a lone monkey standing off to one side looking confused, as if it was on its way to an organ-grinding audition and got off the bus at the wrong stop. In short, the artist will do whatever it takes to give the scene a lift. And by the way, if you think human hands are tricky, you've obviously never tried to draw monkey hands. They're scandalously hard. Seventy percent of the time the fingers come out looking like used condoms.

"Many of the works in MOBA," Lisa said by way of a conclusion, because all good things, even good things that are bad, must come to an end, "are done by people with incredible technique. I could never do it and you could never do it. But you just wonder *why* they did it."

Me, I'm still wondering.

The museum's slogan is "Art too bad to be ignored." A better one would be: "Walk fast and keep your eyes shut."

Nevertheless, this was a joyous experience and one I shall never forget.

THAT NIGHT I WAS SCHEDULED TO pay a visit to Cambridge to see something called the Annals of Improbable Research, which I'd heard was terrific. But I called up and canceled. I'd laughed *waaaaay* too much already, far exceeding my daily quota. Instead, I asked if I could bump the Annals to later in the week—which they readily agreed to—then, rather than waste the entire evening (something I'm quite capable of doing), I went in search of a library to see if I could track down an address for the elusive Museum of Dirt.

Public libraries let you use their computers for free, did you know that? Doesn't matter who you are, you can go in and log on and it won't cost you a dime. That way, I'm thinking, tourists and visitors can check their e-mail and poor people won't be denied access to porn. It's quite wonderful. But because the service is complimentary, inevitably a long queue of cheapskates and free-loaders builds up, eager to take advantage of a good thing.

It was a full thirty-five minutes before my turn came around. When it did, I leapt to one of the eight terminals and typed "Museum of Dirt" into Yahoo! Straight away it came up with something: a Web site, full of color and movement and things to click on. With the roar of victory ringing in my ears, I scrolled down the home page, looking for a "Contact us" button. But just as I found it and clicked, my mouse stopped working.

Over to my left, one of the library assistants, a smoldering red-haired hobgoblin with a scowl that would curdle milk, was already storming over.

"Excuse me. I have a problem," I said.

"It's nine o'clock," she shouted, ignoring me. "Time's up. Get off the computers. Come on. We don't want to be here any longer than we have to."

The others, clearly used to this kind of treatment, began winding down. A couple of them logged off and left. But not me.

"I think my mouse is broken," I persisted.

"It's probably dirty."

"No, the ball's jammed. Is there someone around who can help me?"

Everything stopped. A thunderous silence enveloped the room. Her face turned the color of borscht. Help? *Help you??* I thought she was about to have a seizure. "No."

"Look, I've been waiting for thirty-fi . . ."

But before I could begin the process that would inevitably lead to me compounding my universal reputation for bickering and this woman hating me forever, she leaned down, unplugged the computer, said "Go home!", and stormed back to her desk, hating me anyway.

CALL ME SLOW, BUT AROUND ABOUT NOW I began to realize after three days in this town what my friends may have meant when they said, "Boston? Oh yeah, great place. Shame about . . . er . . ."

The *people*.

Shame about the people.

Frankly, I don't know how the Bostonites could have been colder, ruder, or more aloof. Almost everyone I met or passed in the street had a deep scowl etched into his or her face; every waiter who served me was sullen and abrupt, every shopkeeper unhelpful. And of course they smoke compulsively, these guys, especially the young. Then again, if I lived among people as miserable and stuck-up as these, I'd probably want to die too.

The following day I took a brief walk along Joy Street (at least we can admire their sense of irony) and found myself a bench to sit on. As I approached, a young mother, no doubt fearing the onset of light chitchat, grabbed her child and left.

"Careful," she snorted over her shoulder. "There's a coffee spill."

"Where?" I leapt up.

But she didn't reply. Didn't need to. That look on her face spoke volumes: "The few words I uttered just now, they were complimentary," it said. "Do *not* ask for details. No special requests. Thank you." Then, desperate not to be considered in any way friendly, in case she was caught red-handed by one of Boston's Happiness Patrols and fined, she made a run for it, leaving me, by now thoroughly demoralized, to continue my walk, carving a rough diagonal across the Common in the direction of downtown.

Boston has the feel of New York City at its Sunday morning laziest. But whereas the Big Apple offers speed, danger, and a modicum of glamour for your money, the Big Lemon takes the cushier route, opting for a more cutesy Victorian-style atmosphere.

Beacon Hill particularly, on the far side of the Common, is like that: a bustling village of eighteenth- and nineteenth-century townhouses, antique stores with smart-ass names like A Room with a Vieux, and upscale restaurants nestling tightly together on slopes steeper than their prices. It's a charming little enclave, especially in the fall, when the air is nippy and suffused with the musty aroma of wood smoke and the alleyways are ankle-deep in leaves the size and color of Olympic medals that swish and scrunch and catch on your trousers as you walk. Everywhere you go, you're carried along on undulating red-brick sidewalks, like a low-key roller-coaster for extremely nervous people. It couldn't be more delightful.

At the same time, you can't help wondering if the Bostonites themselves have even the slightest clue what they have here. How captivating it all is, how sublime. And if they do, how can they allow themselves to be so goddamned miserable all the time?

I mean, it can't still be about King George taxing tea, can it? It's been three hundred years, guys; come on! Even the sulkiest of children usually come around by suppertime. Please say it's not a Revolutionary War thing. And even if it is, couldn't you tone down the outrage just a little for visitors—from bitterly hostile to merely seething and resentful? That would be a start.

Anyway, I spent most of that day in a state approaching depression, hiking around Beacon Hill, diving into cafes and grocery stores, trying to strike up idle conversation with strangers and failing. "Come on, *smile*, damn you," I thought. "Talk to me. Be nice. Just one person. Anyone." But nobody did. Not that day, nor for that matter any of the days that followed it. Pouts, scowls, moody glares, that's all they have on offer here.

And if you ask them why, they just walk away.

BOSTON COMMON IS THE OLDEST PARK in America. In fact, I think it may even date as far back as Historical Times.

Skirting its northernmost edge I came across a landmark equally as famous and every bit as enthralling as anything history has to offer: I'm talking of course about the *Cheers* pub, the bar featured in the opening credits of the sitcom. In real life it's called The Bull & Finch, and is instantly recognizable by its white half-moon canopies and staircase leading down to the basement, although when you walk in, the lively, bustling room is a lot smaller than you imagine and, the day I was there, was overrun with German tourists—something I don't remember from the show.

A guy on the door appeared to be taking luncheon reservations. So, since this was the place "where everybody knows your name," I deliberately didn't identify myself. I simply confronted him with an extra-perky "Hi," and waited for his face to brighten.

"*Cash Peters!* Is it really you? Oh my God, how's it going, buddy?"

But I could have stood there 'til the Twelfth of Never; he had no idea who I was. None at all. (And I'm on the radio, so what chance do the rest of you stand?)

I'm patient, though. Thinking he might be new on the job, I turned to the regulars hunched at the bar—Cliff, Norm, the rest of the guys (who look *very* different in the flesh, incidentally)— and tossed them a friendly wave: "Hello, everyone!"

And you know what? The darnedest thing! They didn't know my name either. Or maybe they did and they weren't letting on. Whatever, it was weird. Like suddenly finding yourself in chapter seven of a John Wyndham novel.

I don't want to alarm you, but something's wrong here. *Something* has happened to the people of Boston, I'm convinced of it. One assumes they started out like the rest of us: carefree, jocular, kind, courteous individuals, but then . . . well, some event must have taken place, some terrible, frightening encounter with a not-altogether-friendly paranormal intelligence that came down unannounced one night and turned every last Bostonite it could find into a humanoid—that is to say, an annoyed human.

It was totally perplexing, and I came very close to alerting the media with my story. Then I remembered: I am the media, and even I wasn't *that* interested. Nevertheless, thoroughly unsettled, I gave up trying to be friendly, left the basement bar, and headed upstairs to the street.

BY THE TIME I GOT BACK TO THE B&B, I was feeling miserable and washed out, and tramped wearily up the threadbare stairs, looking forward to a relaxing bath and a warm bed where I could let the troubles of the day evaporate away into dreams.

Unfortunately, the troubles of the day weren't over yet.

When I entered my room and turned on the light, I found everything exactly the way I'd left it—and I mean *everything*: trash unemptied, wet towels draped over furniture, pillows on the floor, sheets and blankets peeled back and rumpled. I mean, you expect your bed to be made at least, right? I don't know why that is; maybe because you're paying a hundred bucks a night for it, something stupid like that. But that's the thing about the O'Hares, they're minimalists, so you could never take attentive service for granted. In their world view, a guest's job was to cough up the rent promptly, then stay quiet and take what he was given for the rest of his stay. Anything over and above total apathy costs extra.

Grrrrrrrr.

"Don't let the sun go down on your wrath." Isn't that what they say?

Well, too late; it was already dark. And with my head full of trenchantly witty comments I was planning to lambaste the O'Hares with first thing tomorrow—"You lazy, selfish, money-grabbing bastards" being one of the cleverer ones—I dug a cave for myself under the mound of blankets, curled up inside, and within a matter of seconds drifted off into a deep, wrath-filled sleep.

NEXT MORNING, THE CHAIRS OPPOSITE ME remained empty for the whole of breakfast.

I looked around briefly for signs of a scuffle, but there was none, leading me to conclude that the Moussefs, unable to take the pressure of B&B life, must have checked out early. This was my second thought, by the way. My first was that they might have exchanged their bright double-room on the second floor for a somewhat darker, more cramped space beneath the patio!

After a while, Gerry came bustling into the dining room, bringing back the plate of fudge brownies from yesterday. He seemed in a better mood now that the troublemakers were gone, and even whistled as he worked. Taking advantage of this lapse, I stopped him before he could hurry out again. "Sorry to mention it, but . . . well, er . . . you forgot to make my bed yesterday . . ."

His whole body stiffened.

Clearly, not *all* the troublemakers were gone.

". . . but that's okay . . . I mean . . ." Oh God! The British hate conflict. We're hopeless at it. If we have more troops and fire-power than you we're fine; we'll happily march in and take over your country.[19] But if it's just head-on verbal sparring you're after, a war of words that we might lose, our courage evaporates. (Should anyone ask, this in a nutshell is how we lost an empire. Make a note.) "I'm sure it's . . . I mean, it's just an oversight, right?" I bumbled. "And . . . today it will be . . . well, if you have the time, of course, it will be . . . er . . ."

"Hey!" he shouted, raising a hand.

I stuttered to a stop.

Suddenly, I could hear every clock in the house ticking. Why

19. Historically speaking.

something wasn't thrown I'll never know. Yoplait. Stale brownies. A bagel.

"You ffffff . . . ," he began.

But the word fffffizzled on his lips. Swallowing hard, he turned on his heels and shot off along the passageway at high speed.

"Good," I thought to myself as the kitchen door slammed shut. "Now we understand each other."

6
Let's All Go Stare at
Barry Manilow's Dirt

The reason George Clooney drowned ◆ helping the homeless ◆ a
bright new slogan for Worcester ◆ lots of childish potty talk ◆ the
life of Thomas Crapper ◆ living with a schizophrenic ◆ the
toilet museum ◆ Jim ◆ beating the ghastly Lisa-a-a-a at her
own game ◆ an unscheduled visit to the Museum of Dirt

ID YOU KNOW THAT THE MAJORITY OF MONKEYS
are nearsighted? Or that the official state sport of
Maryland is jousting? What d'you mean no?? Where
have you been?

Well anyway, these are just two of the priceless nuggets—A
termite can live thirty years—*three* of the priceless nuggets I came
across in a bathroom trivia book at the American Museum of
Sanitary Plumbing.

This institution, a tribute to the domestic toilet, is located in
the nether regions of Worcester, Massachusetts, which is one of
the most depressing places I've been to in my life. Interestingly,
the town was used as the location for the movie *The Perfect Storm*,
which to my mind explains a whole lot. If you ever wondered why
the George Clooney character decides to go down with his ship at
the end of the picture, well, now you know. Apparently he'd
rather drown than return to Worcester. I entirely sympathize.

Breezing into the coach station, I asked the woman behind
the information desk for directions.

"The museum of *what?*"

A quick poll was taken among a small crowd of bus drivers
and passengers, many of whom looked like they'd been there
since 1972.

"A toilet museum?" they murmured. "Here? Are you sure?"

I had an address—Piedmont Street.

"Aaah!"

"I know that," someone pitched in. "It's in the unfashionable part of Worcester." (This may sound helpful, but it's not. As far as I can tell, every part of Worcester is unfashionable.) Though to get to where I was going, he said, would necessitate cutting through a very seedy neighborhood indeed.

"No problem," I grinned, and, slinging my backpack over my shoulder, I set off at a confident stride, as I'm apt to do when I'm out of my mind with worry and trying to hide it.

Back in England, of course, we have the original Worcester, a pleasant, middle-class university town nestling comfortably amid undulating hills of lush green pastureland. By contrast, parts of its American namesake are seriously working class and depressed, and Piedmont Street, I soon discovered, is right there at the heart of the beastly ghastliness. To reach it takes considerable courage and involves traversing half a mile of urban hellscape, a grim, twisting broadway of abandoned storefronts plastered with FOR LEASE signs, being careful as you go not to get mown down by hordes of teenage mothers pushing strollers at breakneck speed.

"Why all the rush?" I thought to myself.

"Hey, buddy!"

Ah.

Just ahead was what I took to be a hostel for derelicts. I'd already crossed the street once to avoid the bums loitering outside. Now, unable to take a hint, one of them came lurching over. "Buddy. Hey, buddy!" He had the kind of deep brown tan that proves once and for all that there really is a hole in the ozone layer.

"Spare some change?"

Quickening my pace from a march to a sprint, I brushed past without acknowledging him, the way you're taught to.

"Got a dollar for food?"

"No."

"Please? Hey, buddy, come on. A dollar. I haven't eaten in two days."

Damn my good-hearted nature! It's always been a weakness. I'm just too nice. "Sure, okay," I relented and, with a warm smile, dropped three pennies into his outstretched hand, which in Worcester, England, would be sufficient to buy a fellow the heartiest of three-course lunches, with a flagon of mead to follow and enough left over for a fine cigar and a hansom cab home, then scooted off up the street, humming cheerfully to myself, happy to have done my bit for the disenfranchised.

"Yermodderfockingnogoodstingygoddamnbastard . . ."

"My pleasure. Don't mention it."

In these conditions, when you feel you may be in mortal danger, half a mile feels like forty. At no point did I feel safe; not until, finally, Piedmont Street slipped into view. Hurrah! As it did so, a great promotional tag line for this town popped into my head out of nowhere. Dunno why, it just came. One of those catchy come-ons often used by tourist offices on billboards and commercials to pull in visitors.

"Bad. Worse. Worcester."

That's it.

Simple, but effective, I think.

Take it, Worcester, my dear old, grubby, downtrodden friend, it's yours.

THE AMERICAN MUSEUM OF SANITARY PLUMBING is not on the face of it what you might call an obvious tourist draw, though I suspect it's the very preposterousness of the concept that really sells it.

It was started in 1927 by local plumber and sano-visionary Charles Manoog, as a way of showing people "that sanitary plumbing saved as many lives as medicine." Not that most of us needed much persuading, I'm sure, but it never hurts to have the message rammed home in museum form.

At least three people a day, I'm told, stop by this place to take a look—four would be considered a rush—as well as many school and college parties, all of them hungry to explore the history of domestic sanitation in a safe, bright, and above all defecation-friendly environment. If you're similarly obsessed with this topic, and perhaps have been planning for a while to organize an excursion to Worcester to see the exhibition (the longer this sentence goes on, the more ridiculous it seems somehow), then let me prepare you for the experience by summing up the basics.

As far as I can tell from a cursory inspection of the exhibits, the history of domestic sanitation can be boiled down to a very simple time line, and it goes something like this: In the beginning there were no toilets, then, a little later on, there were.

Any questions so far?

Good.

Of course, you could always complicate it. You could add that the core design has been fine-tuned over the years. Or that the early squarer bowl, which was so large that George Clooney could have drowned in it, eventually made way for today's oval one. Or that flushing mechanisms have undergone many changes, becoming cleaner and more efficient. But why would you? It's a toilet museum! The faster you grasp the concept, the sooner you can be out of there and on your way, that's how I look at it.

MY TOUR GUIDE WAS A DELIGHTFUL, quiet-spoken woman called Janice.

Janice had been in the plumbing trade for over twenty-seven years, she said, although, astonishingly, to be a plumber wasn't always her dream. In her teens she treasured far grander aspirations. She wanted to be a surgeon. But times were tough back then and courses expensive, and many would-be surgeons saw their aspirations fall by the wayside for want of funds. Then, one day, quite by chance, Janice was bitten by the plumbing bug, and when that happens, I guess, it's a bit like losing a leg: there's no going back.

"So show me what you have," I said, my enthusiasm simmering like an anticipation casserole.

"Okay." First stop: Exhibit No. 1. "Here we have the very first water closet. This invention brought the outhouse *inside* the house."

I wish I'd taken photographs to show you. Basically it looks like a small metal salad bowl with a hole in the bottom. A simple enough idea. You sat on it, did your business, then a maid would take a pitcher of water and swill the poo down the hole.[20]

"Where did it go?" I asked.

"Into the cellar."

Interesting.

Next!

Exhibit No. 2: the Boston Pan Closet. Another salad-bowl device, only this time with a small flap at the bottom. This flew open with a clang, allowing the poo to drop freely away. A laudable advance in some respects, except for one thing: Nobody thought to attach a disposal pipe to it. So once again several more pounds of fecal matter would disappear into the cellar.

"Isn't there a danger," I asked, thinking this through to its natural conclusion, "that you'd just wind up with a cellar full of poo?"

"No, because the servants would clean it up."

How handy. "And if you didn't have any servants?"

"Then your children had to do it."

Gulp!

Anyway, *thankfully*—and already I'm feeling nauseous; is it any wonder there were plagues?—the switch from this primitive salad-bowl technology to today's fully flushable toilets happened quickly.

I'm guessing that one bright sunny day sometime around 1900 the poor servants staggered down the cellar steps as usual, with hands over their mouth and shovels over their shoulder, ready for their regular early-morning date with the master's droppings, only to find . . .

---

20. A technique still used by Parisians to this day, despite the hazards.

"Oh my Lord, what's happened? Where's the poo? It's disappeared!"

"P'raps the master's constipated."

"No, no. You know what I think? I think something's going on, that's what I think. Something sinister . . . and weird."

Honestly! People in Historical Times were such alarmists.

This sinister, weird thing they were so afraid of was a little something called Progress, and it arrived in the shape of the syphonic flush, invented by arguably the greatest plumbing legend of all time, Thomas Crapper.[21]

Crapper, an Englishman, was Queen Victoria's personal plumber. A year after she came to the throne, he was helping her empty it. And of course once Her Majesty had one, *everybody* had to have one. That's how things are in England.

This new and ingenious device was an instant smash. Almost overnight, the crude, insanitary conditions of old were gone. To hell with buckets. To hell with shovels. To hell with sick children running up and down stairs giving everyone cholera. Now all the maid had to do was pull on a lever or chain. This released several gallons of water from a refillable tank into the toilet bowl and, hey presto, the master's caca was swilled down a pipe into the sewer, bypassing the cellar floor altogether. In fact, come to think of it, to hell with the maid also; the master could now flush his own caca away!

But hey, listen to me, rambling on. Can you believe it? I'm sitting here explaining how a toilet works when, in truth, I don't care a damn. And if you're half the person I think you are, then you don't either.

Even though the roaring flame that is my newfound love of household objects continues to burn ever-brightly, the internal

---

21. Seriously, what are the odds that the man who revolutionized the workings of the crapper would himself be called Crapper? If you ask me, I think he should have songs written about him. If Dr. Scholl has them, why not this guy? With prize lyrics like "Crapper-di-doo-dah, crapper di-ay," for instance. Or "Ground Control to Crapper Tom . . ."

workings of the objects themselves don't interest me at all. Mechanicals and electricals remain as much a mystery to my limited mind as, say, how the planet Jupiter stays in orbit or why people buy Yanni albums. My only concern is that, when I flush the can, my "business" disappears down the hole and never comes back.

Speaking of which, before I wind up this subject, and it needs winding up pretty fast, I think you'll agree, I do have a very creepy lavatory experience that I feel pressured to share with you. So totally odd is it, that in my opinion it should be included in a future episode of *Tales from the Crypt*, or at the very least in a chapter about a toilet museum.

ABOUT FIFTEEN YEARS AGO, I LIVED WITH a schizophrenic. (I have also at various times lived with a nun, a manic depressive who made half-assed attempts to kill herself by jumping off a roof,[22] a writer who got high every night by sniffing warm emulsion paint, a cross-dressing lawyer, a bad artist, a multiple sclerosis victim, a crack addict, an ex-heroin addict who used to build life-size effigies of his landlord in the garden and run them through with spears, and a deaf-mute saxophone player.)

Of all of them, the schizophrenic was the nicest by far: a benign, funny blonde called Victoria, whom I grew quite fond of in the early days, mainly because at that point she hadn't told me she was being treated for schizophrenia. (I think she considered saying something, but was in two minds). There was no way of knowing merely by meeting her that this perky, delightful woman was secretly shot full of horse tranquilizers. However, on the odd occasion when she grew lazy and skipped her medication, it became obvious that something wasn't right. In a matter of hours, Good Victoria would turn into Bad Victoria, a freaky,

---

22. From what I hear, she deliberately waited until her elderly mother was walking directly underneath to break her fall. Only then did she jump, dropping like an anvil, putting the old dear in the hospital for eight weeks.

wild-eyed wacko who was so strange, so evil . . . well, she had Lizzie Borden on speed-dial, *that's* how strange and evil she was. Regularly she would see strange lights dancing over the Bible and hear voices in her head, voices that, for some reason, kept directing her to stab me in my sleep.

One day I was about to set off for work when she intercepted me by the front door with an extraordinary announcement: God had spoken to her during the night. (Oddly, God seemed to spend a lot of His time speaking to Victoria; it doesn't surprise me that the world is in such a mess.)

"The Lord," she informed me lindablairishly, "is going to punish you for your sins."[23]

"Oh yeah?"

Not only that, but He would shortly be sending me a sign to prove His omnipotence.

"Hm, is that right?"

And so, only slightly terrified out of my wits, I left the apartment and headed off to work.

At the time I was a reporter for a radio station in London. Our ground-floor newsroom was the tiniest of places, as was the bathroom next to it: a narrow shaft into which some logistical whiz had managed to squeeze a toilet, a sink, *and* a toilet roll holder. The first thing I did when I got in that day was go for a pee. But—and this is where it gets weird—while I was using the toilet I heard an odd gurgling sound from between my legs and, looking down, saw to my horror that the bowl was filling with soap suds. *Soap suds.* Imagine! Even as I watched, a foaming tide of lather rose steadily toward me, bringing everything I'd just done back up again.

"Oh—my—God!"

Panic-stricken, I dragged on my pants. But the suds were accelerating, coming and coming, faster and faster, until eventually they belched over the rim and onto the floor, covering my

---

23. And, believe me, that's a *lot* of sins. I'm surprised He has that much free time.

shoes. At that point, I ran to fetch help. Babbling like an idiot, I got on the phone and yelled for a janitor, the maintenance people, *anybody* to come quickly.

"In there . . . it's in there . . . be careful . . . it's huge . . ." I said as I watched John the maintenance guy edge forward and push back the restroom door, only to recoil at once as a wall of suds came pouring out all over him. It had been a matter of three or four minutes, no more, but already they'd reached the ceiling, filling every available inch of space with a dense suffocating white lather. It took hours for the room to be swilled down and made fully serviceable again.

Even now, I can't say whether this was God's hand at work or just some prankster with a packet of Tide, but to this day it remains one of the most terrifying moments of my entire life. Call me paranoid, but if the lock had jammed, or the handle had come off in my hand and I'd not gotten out of there when I did, I'm sure I would have died.

And that, my friend, is my creepy lavatory experience.

BACK, THOUGH, TO THOMAS CRAPPER.

"We have a picture of his toilet somewhere," Janice said, drifting away. "I wonder where it is." After rummaging around downstairs for several minutes, she returned empty-handed. "That's strange. We used to have one. I'm sorry."

I was devastated.

Anyway, the syphonic flush was certainly a historic watershed. Unfortunately it was a bit of a one-hit wonder, and the world of toilets never recaptured the same level of glamour and excitement again. In some ways the Museum of Sanitary Plumbing reflects that, I think. However, on the plus side, it's very informative and extremely well laid out on two floors. Zinc bathtubs, lavatory paper dispensers, cistern pumps, stainless steel plug-holes, copies of the Worcester Plumbing Code of 1885—whatever you're interested in, they've got it. Plus, as you can imagine, there's no shortage of places to sit. And if at any point you should tire of staring at toilets, I recommend a trip to the basement to see their lavish display of plumberabilia, a hundred years' worth of stop-cocks, spigots, widgets, and thingamajigs, which are like spigots only bigger.

For swiveling-diorama fans, they also have a swiveling dio-rama—yay! This was built to illustrate the evolution of prison toi-lets through the ages. And it was while I was busy with that, revolving the little turntable, turning a grimy Victorian toilet into a modern stainless steel one, and back again—going "Then . . ." swivel ". . . and now . . ." swivel ". . . then . . ." swivel ". . . and now . . ." swivel ". . . then . . ." swivel ". . . and now . . ." — that there came an ominous knock at the door.

"Who can that be?" I asked, following Janice up the stairs.

"Trick or treaters possibly," she said, in what is frankly the most ludicrous answer ever given to a sensible question.

Outside stood three people: two young men and a woman.

"Is the museum open?" they asked, their eyes alight with expectation.

I couldn't believe it. They were here on purpose!

"Oh yes." Janice was thrilled. "Is this your first time?"

"No," one of the guys said. "It's our third."

Third? Well, that did it for me. Leaving them to pore, mes-merized, over the Boston Pan Closet . . .

("Where did the poo go?"

"Down into the cellar!"

"Cooooooool.")

. . . I made to leave. First, though, in the name of fairness, I decided to give Worcester a second bite at the impressing-me cherry. "Is there anything in this town worth seeing while I'm here? Any points of interest?" I asked. In other words, something to brand upon my memory so that I wouldn't recall Worcester, Massachusetts, solely as the home of beggars, drunks, and the American Museum of Sanitary Plumbing.

"Er . . ." Janice gave the question considerable thought before coming up with the answer I was pretty much expecting: "No. I don't think so. Not close."

Well, at least I tried.

Thanking her for being such a good sport, I popped down-stairs again to use the restroom, then ducked out of a side door before she saw me go.

And d'you know something? To this day, I'm still not absolutely sure if it was the real restroom I used, or if I just soiled one of their more valuable exhibits.

INTO BOSTON ONCE AGAIN.

By now, the fact that I wasn't any farther forward in my quest to track down the Museum of Dirt was starting to bug me. Of course, I could drop it altogether; that was always an option. Frankly, the show could care less if I went back with five reports or six. All the same, "Why the mystery?" I wondered. "Why would anyone send me an invitation to come look at a pile of dirt, only to refuse me entry when I arrive?"

Also, and I may as well be totally honest with you, there was more than a little sour grapes involved. I so wanted to thwart Lisa-a-a-a's attempts to thwart my attempts to tour the museum. I couldn't let that ghastly woman win. I couldn't. That would just be too horrible. I had to do something.

So I put in a call to Jim, my producer at the studio.

You'd like Jim. He's without exception *the* most helpful man who ever walked the planet. I've known him for four years now, and in all that time not once have I ever seen him fazed or the slightest bit put out by anything. No matter how bizarre your request—"I need the Earth to start revolving in the opposite direc-tion; it's kind of important"—he'll take it on board with a "Hmm" and a "Leave it with me, I'll see what I can do," and by the end of the afternoon, *somehow* he'll have talked to the right people and made it happen. He's amazing. Always pleasant, forever on standby with a wave and a smile, never ruffled, never uptight—that's Jim. Indeed, I expect if you were to set a herd of rampaging bulls on him, then toss his gored body onto power lines, he'd still emerge at the end, bloodied and smoldering, to answer the phone with a cheery, well-modulated, "Hi, this is Jim."

"*Hi, this is Jim.*"

"Hey, it's me. I have a problem."

"*Oh yeah?*"

Since I was paying for the call I recounted the story with the minimum of embellishment: ". . . and basically I need the museum's address asap."

"*Hmm. You know what? I'm really busy right now. One of the hosts is going on vacation, so we're producing two shows this week, and I don't have the time . . .*"

"Oh."

"*. . . but if you call back tomorrow, I could do it then.*"

"What? So you're telling me you can make the Earth spin in the opposite direction, but you can't take five minutes to find me the address of a little museum?"

"*I'm sorry?*"

"No, don't apologize. It's fine. I understand. But just in case, I'm going to stay on the line until you've finished what you're doing. Then I'll be here when you're ready to give it to me. How does that sound?"

"*Hmm.*" (Sighing.) "*Okay. I'll see what I can do.*"

THE MUSEUM OF DIRT IS LOCATED in a low-rise office block in downtown Boston (thanks Jim!). In the end, strangely, finding the place turned out to be the easy part; getting inside—now *that* was hard. (Memo to other museum owners: want to deter people from seeing your exhibits? Bury them deep inside a building, put guards on the door, and install security keypads everywhere—that'll work.)

However, I'm resourceful. I managed to slip past the front desk, posing as a guy who was in too much of a hurry to explain where he was going or why, and took the elevator up a couple of floors. This brought me to a glass security door, which was locked. Peering inside, I found the company to be some kind of Web design service, the usual dot.com arrangement of desks and PCs and nobody sitting at them.

I buzzed the intercom a couple of times, but nothing happened.

Knocked twice. Still nothing.

Must have loitered on that landing for a good ten minutes in all, buzzing and knocking and buzzing some more and getting nowhere, until I was on the verge of quitting altogether, when, all of a sudden, the angels smiled on me.

A young guy with a shaved head came pounding down the stairs.

"Hey, how's it going?" I said. "Look, I'm trying to . . ."

Ignoring me completely—which is fast becoming standard practice for anyone under thirty—he jabbed a code into the numbered keypad, opened the door, and went in.

Grrrrrr.

This made me so mad. I'd like to tell you that I leapt out from my hiding place, rushed the kid from behind, reducing him with a shower of well-choreographed karate kicks to a crumpled heap on the floor, then, with my standard-issue .47-caliber Glock automatic raised at shoulder height, kicked in the door, tossed a couple of CS gas canisters across the carpet, and held the entire staff at gunpoint until they condescended to show me the Museum of Dirt.

At least, that's how it would be if I was, say, The Man from U.N.C.L.E. But I'm not. I'm more the "catch the door before it closes and tentatively slide inside" type.

"Can I help you?"

Spotting a stranger in reception, a female executive came running over. I must say she was extremely pleasant and helpful, so one assumes she was from somewhere other than Boston—oh yes, and deaf too, incidentally, because she was standing less than ten feet from the door; how could she not have heard me buzzing and knocking?

"I've flown in from Los Angeles to see the Museum of Dirt," I said, making it sound pressing, as if I'd tumbled off the red-eye and cabbed it straight to their offices. I laid the whole woeful story on

her up-front, about the trouble I'd been having fixing an appointment, and the Ice Maiden, and my run-in with Lisa-a-a-a-a . . .

"Ah yeah, she's quite something-g-g-g-g, isn't she? Hahahaha."
Damn it, her impersonation was better than mine! "But I'm afraid
it's true what she told you; most of the museum's packed in boxes.
We're moving."

"Really? Where to?"

"To the fifth floor."

"The fifth floor where?" It took a few seconds to sink in. "You
mean upstairs in this building?"

"Right."

Three bloody stories? *That's* why they wouldn't let me see it?
"Sonofabitch!"

Fearing that I might at any moment, in my fury, suffer an
unforeseen incrediblehulkian lapse, burst out of my clothes, and
start breaking things, she said, "Look, stay here, I'll see if I can
find Glen," and scurried into another room.

Nearby, a young blonde sitting at a desk caught my eye and
nodded hello.

"I guess you didn't hear me buzzing and knocking, then?" I
said.

She shrugged and made a face, as if English wasn't her first
language, nor answering the door her first responsibility, and went
back to whatever she was doing.

And *that* was when I spotted it!

The Museum of Dirt.

Or at least that part of the museum that hadn't been packed
away in boxes ahead of its highly complex move from this floor to
one slightly higher.

"D'you mind if I . . . ?"

The blonde who shrugged before shrugged again.

"Thanks."

It was arranged neatly inside a glass wall-cabinet directly
behind reception, and believe me, as dirt museums go, this one
doesn't disappoint. If jars filled with dirt standing on a shelf are
what you're looking for, that's exactly what this baby delivers. Jar

after jar after jar after jar after jar. Although the definition of what constitutes dirt seems to be fairly broad. I was surprised. I mean, soil gets in, natch! And grit. And who can say no to gravel? But there are bits of debris too, and small twigs, and grass, which personally I wouldn't class as dirt at all. As for the rest, well, the contents are either dark brown and not immediately recognizable, or they look like curry powder.

This project is the brainchild of a man called Glen. According to popular legend—one I think he probably started himself—Glen was in Palm Springs one day with a friend and found himself standing outside Barry Manilow's house.

"This is Barry Manilow's house," the friend said.

(Incidentally, for those who don't know, Barry Manilow writes the songs that make the whole world sing. Take it or leave it.)

Just for a laugh, Glen snuck a handful of little pebbles from Barry's driveway and, when he got home, put them in a jar, which he labeled "Barry Manilow's Driveway."

And that, for then, was that.

Over the next few months, he did even more traveling, and as he went along he decided to collect some fresh dirt samples— from Liberace's house, for instance, and Eartha Kitt's star on the Hollywood Walk of Fame, and Dyke Bridge, Massachusetts, which must be important for something, though I have no idea what; and that's when I guess he said something to the press about it—always a mistake—because word started to spread pretty fast.

Next thing you know, even more strange dirt samples are rolling in from locations as diverse as here and there: Gianni Versace's front step (twigs), Woodstock (twigs and soil), Graceland (something brown and unrecognizable), O.J.'s Rockingham Estate (sand), the Menendez Brothers' house (brown and unrecognizable), Pearl Harbor (curry powder), Atlantis (grit), Sonny Bono's grave (silt), Dick Clark's parking space (looks like peanut husks)— hundreds of them, often sent in by strangers, people Glen knows nothing about, other than perhaps that they have way too much time on their hands.

What a treat, he must have thought, as he very patiently cata-
logued these in jars too and labeled them, until . . . well, I guess
you reach a point where you have so many jars with dirt in and
labels on that you may as well start a museum. What else are you
going to do with them?

And that's how the Museum of Dirt came about.

So you'd think, given the range and curiosity-value of what
he's managed to put together so far that, viewed as a whole, this
would be a truly spectacular and engrossing affair, enough to keep
even the most demanding intellect occupied for hours. But it's
not. Indeed, if anything, it's almost as dull as the dullest place I've
ever been to, which just happens to be Eartha Kitt's star on the
Hollywood Walk of Fame.

To be fair, I don't know what else I was expecting. Glen promises dirt, he delivers dirt—what's to complain about? But . . . I just
find it so tedious. Jar after jar after jar after jar. Two minutes I'd
been there and already I was yawning. Jar after jar after jar. And I
was just staring at yet another handful of something dark brown
and unrecognizable that had been picked up "directly below
motion detector on fence at rear entrance of Mick Jagger's house"
when at long last the executive woman reappeared.

"I'm sorry for the delay, but Glen's stepped out for a moment.
He had a dental appointment."

("Thank God!" I thought) "Oh, what a crying shame."

"But here's his card, and this is his direct line. So why don't
you call him later."

("Not bloody likely!") "Sure. I'll do that," I smiled. "Thanks for
your help."

And without looking back, I hurried out of the door, past a
delivery guy jabbing furiously at the security buzzer, and down
the stairs into the street. Didn't even wait for the elevator. Just ran
and ran for three blocks until I reached the nearest Starbucks—
or "my little coffee hospital" as I refer to it—where I collapsed,
panting and dazed, with a latte and a scone and consoled myself
on a very near miss indeed.

7

'Thine Ignorant Pitlings Rile Me Most Hearty'

The greatest theme park in America ◆ the O'Hares do something useful for once ◆ Salem: a tour, a museum, and a waste of an afternoon, all in one ◆ witchcraft: what's up with that? ◆ another town, another Lisa ◆ a cellophane fish tells me I'm sick ◆ I have a run-in with an angel ◆ seven ways to turn your town into a tourist mecca ◆ local history reenactments—I volunteer to stone a witch for pleasure ◆ getting the hex on my life removed

ALTHOUGH MY STAY IN NEW ENGLAND HADN'T been the happiest of times, I'm pleased to report that it wasn't all bad news and there were after all a couple of high points, times when the clouds lifted and I came perilously close to enjoying myself.

One such instance happened midweek. Anxious to shrug off Boston's pall of gloom for a few hours I took a short rail journey, heading northeast out of the city this time, and half an hour later detrained (now the official term for getting off a railway car, replacing the infinitely more complicated disembarked) in one of the greatest theme parks in the entire United States of America: Salem, Massachusetts.

For the past three hundred years Salem has been a thriving seaport of enormous historical, economic, and maritime significance. Every watershed in America's turbulent growth as a nation has in some way impacted this cute little town, from the Civil War to the Industrial Revolution and beyond. The modern justice system had its origins here, the country's first millionaire came from here, the first Congregational Church was organized here, novelist Nathaniel Hawthorne wrote some of his greatest work here . . .

But really, who cares about any of that? Be honest.

I'd heard on the grapevine (well, Donna had told Gerry, and Gerry had told me, at the end of another of those long, oppressive silences that passed for lively breakfast conversation in the O'Hare Family Guest House) that Salem was also one of the few places around these parts that welcomes psychics onto its turf, meaning it was the only town for miles where you could go to get your fortune told. How fantastic, I thought. Because as we know, at this particular point in my own personal historical, economic, and maritime development, with years of failure behind me, no money in the bank, and very few career options ahead of me, other than maybe stowing away on a galleon bound for India, I was badly wanting for spiritual input, however unproven and spurious that input might be.

So the moment I got wind of this, I quickly reappraised my plan for the day—a trip to the see the Annals of Improbable Research, which I'd postponed once already—and postponed it again, because when your entire future's at stake you have to be flexible, and headed off to Salem instead.

WHAT A GREAT LITTLE TOWN! THE PEOPLE are friendly and obliging, the architecture cute but not nauseatingly so, and the sea air never less than invigorating. Also, being as this was October time, the trees, in the last throes of their autumnal opulence, were shedding leaves in a nonstop cascade of red and gold medallions that scrunched like crackers underfoot. Magical!

Unfortunately, in the ruthless new economy of the twenty-first century, friendly, obliging, cute, invigorating, opulent, and nonstop simply don't cut it any more. These days, to thrive as a major tourist destination you need something more: a gimmick of some kind. Doesn't matter what it is really, since tourists'll hand over good money to see virtually anything, but it helps if you have, say, for instance, the tallest something or maybe the widest something or the biggest ball of something, or if you can't manage that, then at the very least get yourself an oddity, a quirk, an unusual festival, a zoo, a house made out of beercans, an over-blown art gallery funded by some local eccentric with a single-figure IQ but heaps of cash, or a site of real historical significance—just *something*, is all I'm saying: a unique feature that, marketed correctly, will put some distance between you and all those boring old loser towns where nothing tall, large, big, odd, quirky, unusual, overblown, eccentric, or historically signif-icant goes on at all.

Well, as luck would have it, Salem can boast such a gimmick. Yes, sir. A Class A, totally original, top-of the-line gimmick that I imagine must be the envy of major tourist destinations nationwide, and it's all thanks to a brief but grisly period in the late seventeenth century when the local people hereabouts, for reasons best known to themselves, began killing each other indiscriminately.

ACCORDING TO HISTORICAL RECORDS, OVER A thirteen-month period in 1692 (there were thirteen months to a year in those days), fifty-six innocent citizens were put on trial, accused of practicing witchcraft.[24] Of those fifty-six, nineteen were found guilty and hanged, a couple were ducked—tied to a plank and dumped upside-down in a lake (if they drowned they were a witch; if they lived, they were ducked again)—and then there was this one guy who was considered such an out-and-out menace that hanging and ducking were simply not good enough for him. He had to be *pressed* to death, just to be on the safe side. Though historical records fail to fully explain what that involved, I'm guessing elephants.

In truth, there's probably never a *really good* time to be accused of being a witch, but the late 1600s were the very worst. Women suspected of practicing witchcraft were reviled, spat at, set upon by mobs, and stoned; some were even pulled off their broomsticks as they flew by. That, or rerouted to Kennedy. It all

---

24. That's how bad things were: The mere fact that you were *practicing* witchcraft was enough; you didn't even have to be any good at it.

got pretty ugly, and continued for a long while; that is until the governor's wife was herself mistaken for a witch. After that, you won't be surprised to learn, things took an immediate turn for the better. As usual, the rich and powerful will stand by forever, idle and without a care, allowing the poor to be abused wholesale; but the instant their own rights are adversely affected they're outraged and leap into action, instigating drastic change. And so it was in Salem. Minutes before the governor's wife was due to be dragged to the lake and drowned, the townsfolk had a change of heart. They decided that the practice of goading witches, though heaps of fun, was wrong on principle and didn't work, and it was promptly discontinued.

But, as with my trip to New England in general, this harrowing episode wasn't all bad news. The Witch Trials (1692[25]) did give birth over time to a couple of very positive social developments that we still acknowledge to this day:

- A new legal system—the very legal system currently used in American courts (and which, coincidentally, doesn't work either).

- The celebration of Halloween.

Halloween is a big event in Salem. How big, you ask? Well, they have it marked with a red circle on their calendar—*that's* how big.

The reason is simple: for eleven months hardly anything else happens here. If it ain't Halloween, and J. K. Rowling doesn't have a new book out, tourists tend to lose interest in witches and, by extension, the town that makes its living off them. It's a bummer, and something they're working hard to change. In the meantime, though, come the winter, many of the attractions put up their shutters, commercialism eases into neutral for a while, and Salem, like a proud but economically unviable polar bear, goes into hibernation. But then, before you know it October,

---

25. Nobody in Salem is able to mention the witch trials, not even in passing, without also telling you the date of them—1692. It's fun to begin with, and then you wish they'd stop.

which has been in short supply since last year, comes back around, and BOOM, the whole place is buzzing again. Simple as that.

Fortuitously, I blew into town about the same time October got there, and as a result found myself sucked into the vortex of their annual Halloween marketing efforts within a matter of minutes after detraining at the Scheduled Passenger Alighting Point (the replacement term for station).

FIRST THING I DID WAS PUT IN A CALL TO a local tourist agency, impressing upon them that I was an important person who needed to be given a free lunch, and fast. This is standard practice. Upon hearing that I worked for a radio travel show, Lisa, their PR woman, instead of thinking to herself the way everyone else seems to—"Radio?? But I thought he said he was important."—called up one of the finest restaurants in town and booked us in for an elegant four-course meal. What a wonderful gesture! Of course that was before she met me. Two minutes after "Hello," the plan changed drastically. This is standard practice also. Alarmed to hear that I couldn't care less about Salem's rich historical, economic, and maritime heritage and was only in town to have my fortune told by a psychic, she got on the phone, did some urgent reshuffling, and ten minutes later we ended up eating fish and chips at a local diner instead.

Mind you, this didn't stop her plugging the rich-heritage angle throughout the meal.

"People think there's a connection between the witch and Halloween, but there really isn't."

"Oh?" I said from behind a newspaper.

"Yes. Witchcraft"—pulling down the paper and peering over—"or Wicca, as it's known, is a contemporary religion. We have many witches living in Salem."

"Hm. Well, isn't that something!" Seeing she was unable to take a hint, I got out my pen and began doing the crossword.

Sorry, but I'm simply not interested in witches, period. My knowledge of Wicca and the people who practice it is sketchy at best. They cast spells, they make baskets, that's all I know about them. And believe me I have no urge to learn more.

"So which attractions would you like to see today?" she pressed, thrusting a brochure into my hand.

Among other things it gave a list of the museums located in Salem. And you have to admire their ingenuity, in taking what, let's face it, is an abominable glitch in their past and turning it around, cheerfully devising myriad ways to cash in on it. Scanning the leaflet, there was The Witch Museum, The Wax Witch Museum, The Witch History Museum, The Witch Dungeon Museum, The Salem Witch Village, the Witch Trials (1692) Memorial, and God knows how many more. So I agreed to a compromise: I'd walk around town, I said, asking reporter-type questions and generally behaving as if I was interested in witches, but then, the *second* I spotted my first psychic, that plan would be kicked into a ditch and I'd go get my fortune told. Agreed?

"Agreed," she said.

"Great."

And with that, we paid and left.

Well, just as we were coming out of the restaurant, what did I see across the street? *Only* a New Age gift store offering psychic readings. Very quaint and inviting it was too, run by a woman who claims to be both an angel and a medium, and also, perhaps most surprising of all, a qualified accountant.

"Don't let that put you off," Lisa said. "She has a good repu-tation."

Inside, the air was filled with gentle atmospheric New Age music, one of those relentless, feel-good, go-nowhere tunes that you're meant to meditate to, but which is so nerve-jarring it just makes me want to grab everything within a five-yard radius that's not tied down and smash it. Customer-wise, they couldn't have been busier. The place was teeming with people, all of them either buying New Age gifts, waiting for the psychic, or applying to have their star-sign changed—"I'm a Scorpio, but my husband hates that I'm so moody and secretive, and vengeful when I get angry, so here's ten dollars; from now on I'd like to be a Pisces please."—or whatever else goes on in shops like this, I have no idea.

While I went off and put my name down for the psychic (I forget her name; it was something like Mitsi, I think. Mitsi the angel), Lisa did a quick tour of the shop, returning moments later with an item she apparently found quite amusing: a piece of orange cellophane.

It looked like something a cat might choke on.

"What's that?" I asked.

"It's a fortune-telling fish."

"But of course it is, how silly of me."

Lay the tiny fish in the palm of your hand, said the instructions, and it reveals your fate.

Lisa balanced it in the center of her palm and straight away it curled itself into a tube. "Ooh! That means I'm passionate and will have romance in my life," she swooned, reading from the leaflet. "My husband *will* be pleased."

"Now it's my turn."

I grabbed the fish. But no sooner had I laid the thing flat on my hand than it became agitated and started wriggling and trying to escape, same way Jehovah's Witnesses do when I argue with them. Then, quite unprovoked, the cellophane did a back flip and flew off onto the floor.

"Oh my God! Did you see that?"

This was my very first encounter with the supernatural, and for a few creepy moments there I was absolutely terrified.[26] "What the hell does it mean, d'you think?"

"I'm not sure." Lisa squinted at the instructions again. "I think it means you're bipolar."

"Hm. I hardly need a small plastic fish to tell me that," I grunted and stuck it back in the packet.

---

26. Only later on did I realize that I'd been standing under a ceiling fan the whole time. This is not a new thing. According to recent research, it seems that 95 percent of psychic or supernatural phenomena experienced by human beings are caused by standing too close to a ceiling fan.

"Next!" a voice hailed us from the rear. I turned to find a small middle-aged woman poking her head out from behind some curtains and waving. The angel was free, apparently.

Now, please don't ask me what makes Mitsi an angel, because I have no idea. She just is, that's all, and when you've been a reporter for as long as I have, you learn not to question such things. Though I have to say that, at first glance, she looked no different from every other fortune-telling accountant I'd ever met.

Taking a seat in her dark, cramped booth, which was only slightly smaller than the butter compartment in my refrigerator at home, I decided to get the crystal ball rolling with a little interview; nothing too complex, just a few questions about the problems of running a successful business in a town that is basically shut for seven months of the year. Her answer went something like this: "Blah blah blah blah blah blah blah blah blah blah." I really wasn't listening.[27] Frankly, all I cared about was getting to the bit where she foretold my future. More than ever, my Boston experience had convinced me I needed to be out of radio and onto the next phase of my life as soon as possible. The field was wide open. All she had to do was give me a few pointers to what that next phase might be. But to my utter shock, not to say chagrin, she refused. Can you believe this? Her excuse wasn't terribly convincing either: She said she needed twenty minutes to "tune in" to the spirits (and I would only give her ten). Aside from that, she wanted twenty-five bucks for doing so (and I would only give her ten).

A brief standoff followed. I tried one last time, citing dire need as my justification, but the woman wouldn't budge—how do you get to be an angel when you're this bloody obstinate?—after which, and promising myself I'd never have my palm read by a qualified accountant ever again, I said good-bye, injecting a caustic edge into my tone, just to let her know she'd messed with

---

27. I think the gist was, "What are you talking about? We're not shut for seven months of the year." But I honestly couldn't say.

the wrong guy here, then ran away like a little girl before she could put a spell on me.

REMEMBER HOW I SAID BEFORE THAT every tourist trap needs a gimmick? Well, that still holds true; nothing has changed since I first mentioned it. However, a gimmick is not the only thing you need; it's just the beginning. On my travels, I've figured out seven other key features that your town must have before it can reasonably call itself a holiday destination.

1. **A catchy slogan.** One so bland that you'd swear it could only have been thought up by a team of overpaid PR executives on a weekend retreat funded unwittingly by taxpayers. Salem's is "The Bewitching Seaport," which isn't bad. There's also Minneapolis: "The Coolest Place on Earth" (though, having been there, I realize that this is more of a stern warning than a slogan); Albuquerque: "It's a Trip!"; and of course Boston's slogan: "How DARE You Come Here!"

2. **Museums and gift shops.** There's always at least one museum, even if it's of the clutching-at-straws variety. At one church I visited in New Mexico, they had a museum at the rear. On display was a bell, an organ, five chairs, and a stool, and very little else. Although they did have one extra something that I thought was cute. In a special glass cabinet, there was a collection of what were referred to as "Items found while walking in the garden." Ooh! What could possibly be more interesting than that? "Do any look familiar?" a sign said. Well, I should say so! The items turned out to be a teapot handle, a broken bowl, and a thin iron rod that looked like it had fallen off a lawnmower. (Memo to other museum owners: Go outside, gather up all kinds of useless crap off the ground, mount them prominently on a shelf, and pass them off as historical artifacts. It's a winner!) Incidentally, where there's a museum, there's always a gift shop, and since Salem has

around ten thousand museums, it is not surprisingly Gift Shop Central. There are *so* many gift shops actually, that in the future, to avoid duplication of merchandise, they might like to consider carrying just one gift each.

3. A visitor center. Handy for three things: i) using their bathrooms; ii) picking up leaflets with the town's catchy slogan printed on them (because someone might stop you and ask); and iii) visiting the multimedia theater—a plush two-hundred-seat auditorium out back where tourists who are exhausted after walking around town all day can sit down and take a nap for an hour. While they're asleep, a series of static drawings, sketches, and photos will be projected onto a screen, explaining the town's past in the most agonizing detail, beginning around 2300 B.C. Because their budget doesn't run to making a real movie, they instead resort to letting the camera zoom in and out constantly to suggest activity. All of this is accompanied by a soundtrack of nerve-jarring lute and flute music, over which an out-of-work Shakespearean actor reads a medieval narrative in the kind of exaggerated plummy tones that suggest he will continue to be out of work for some time.

4. A sight-seeing trolley. The mood on board the trolley varies between eager anticipation (which means they're just setting off) and depression (meaning the tour's almost over; by this time 50 percent of the passengers are feeling like human slaves in *Planet of the Apes* and are secretly wishing they'd walked).

5. A heritage trail. You follow a red or yellow painted line on the sidewalk, trekking mindlessly from one point of interest to the next, until they cease to be of interest at all. It's rooted in the bizarre principle that you have to see historical landmarks personally *with your own eyes* in case they're not really there. Or in case the city has a change of heart about its noble past and, next time you come, the site is a parking lot. My advice: Save your energy, buy postcards.

6. Local history reenactments. Increasingly popular is the replica seventeenth-century village, a clutch of thatched cottages and wigwams inhabited by drama students in period costume who, by the time you arrive, will have stubbed out their Marlboros and switched off their Game Boys and either be grinding corn, clumsily pumping the treadles on a spinning jenny, or out in the farmyard making like they have the first clue how to milk a goat. As with actors in foam costume, they are under strict orders to stay in character and speak like peasants the whole time. However, since most of them have no real clue what peasants spoke like three hundred years ago and can't be bothered to learn, and anyway they only took this stupid dressing-up job in the first place to help pay their way through college, they'll usually respond with some weird, convoluted peasant-speak of their own devising.

SAMPLE CONVERSATION WITH
SEVENTEENTH-CENTURY DRAMA STUDENT

ME: Excuse me, which way to the bathroom?

STUDENT: Insolent cotswain! Be gone, knave, lest I begroddle thy swank with my jerkin.

ME: Er . . . I'm kinda desperate, actually. Could you . . . ?

STUDENT: Forsooth! Thine ignorant pitlings rile me most hearty. Shall I compare thee to a moddled codling?

ME: Look, just tell me where the bloody toilet is.

STUDENT: [*Picking up a Wal-Mart broom and shaking it*] Ye gods, this festering shotspith offends mine eyes. Be gone, afore I smite thee hip and thigh.

ME: What the hell is the matter with you? *Just tell me.*

STUDENT: Guards! Guards! Pray, cuff this addle-pated clod

and escort him 'twixt this place and yon, where he shall
be . . . *Oooph!*

I'm a man of peace. I don't advocate punching anyone. But you
have to end this absurd exchange somehow. It also has the added
benefit of giving you time to run and hide before a platoon of art
& design students waving plywood muskets[28] rushes in to mock-
arrest you.

SOLDIER: Verily, sire, with trigger a-cocked, I demand thy
wizen-most surrenderment, lest . . . *Ooph!*

ME: Now, shut up!

Etc.

FOLLOWING MY ABORTED ATTEMPT TO HAVE my fortune
told, Lisa and I took to the streets to look for someone a little less
angelic and more obliging. En route, we ran across a young,
comely wench in a bodice and frilly bonnet loitering by the Old
Town Hall. You can never be sure in these places whether this is
a drama student pretending to be a historical figure—someone
you should, but don't, recognize—or just some hospital inmate
released prematurely into the community. Regardless, I walked
right up to her and demanded, "Who are you? Where are you
going? What do you want?"

Alarmed by the suddenness of my approach, she blurted out,
"Hullo—yes?"

"Who are you?" I said again, repetition being the mother of
comprehension.[29] "Where are you going and what do you want?"

Turned out she was part of the touring company of a show
called *Cry Innocent* (touring Salem, that is). You *have* to see this,
by the way. It's a total crowd-pleaser.

During the performance a woman called Bridget Bishop is
arrested right there before your eyes and tried for witchcraft. Once
she's in custody, members of the public form a jury to decide her

---

28. And for anyone unfamiliar with medieval weaponry, in essence a musket is a
clarinet that kills people.

29. and, coincidentally, the half-sister of annoyance.

fate, delivering up a verdict of guilty or not guilty. (Though since this is a regular event and since Bridget is arrested four times every day for the same offense, the court must *surely* have some idea by now.)

"So is she really a witch?' I asked the wench. I had a train to catch, so I didn't want to waste time on a foregone conclusion.

"We do not know," she replied, in that clipped tone unique to drama students charged with pretending they're from a bygone era.

"I bet she is a witch."

"I do not know," she said again.

"Will she be dragged through the streets?"

"Yes, there is every chance she will be dragged."

"Maybe I could get some stones and throw them at her as she goes past."

"No, she must be held for formal trial. This is a grand jury proceeding to determine if she should be held over for trial."

"Then what? Do we duck her?"

"There is no ducking in Salem."

No ducking?? But everybody ducks witches. Witches *expect* to be ducked. What self-respecting town with a history of persecuting religious minorities *doesn't* duck its witches? Punishing people indiscriminately is far more entertaining than trying them fairly, everyone knows that. It's the thrill of hate-filled mob violence we're after, not a bunch of starchy lawyers mumbling case-law at one another.

"Come on, let's throw stones at her," I said, turning vigilante. "I want a sense of closure."

"I do not think that is very nice."

"I don't care. I'm going to get some rocks anyway, just in case."

"Alright, you do that," she snorted, dropping her medieval tone for as long as it took her to half-walk, half-run away.[30]

"Poor girl, she's completely muddled," Lisa laughed as we watched her go.

---

30. Oh, and to everyone who wrote in to the show saying that this was a poor imitation of a Monty Python sketch, bless you for that. The only difference is, this really happened!

Good, I thought. Another resounding victory for the non-costumed guy!

Anyway, *Cry Innocent* is a smash with tourists. By two o'clock that afternoon, a jeering horde of bystanders had assembled in the center of town, ready to be addressed by two fresh-faced adolescents kitted out like extras from *Beau Brummel.*

"Many troubles have come upon our village as well as our town," shouted one.

"Many of our houses have been touched with the smallpox and many children and adults have been lost," shouted the other.

"Look—a witch!" shouted somebody in the crowd (possibly me).

Sure enough, just then, quite by scripted chance, the very cause of everyone's troubles, young Bridget Bishop—who, frankly, must be a bit dim if, after being arrested four times every day for the past month, she still insists on walking through the town center at scheduled show times—came strolling along and was immediately set upon by actors who escorted her (crying "I'm innocent!" to justify the title) toward the courthouse and an uncertain future.

As Bridget was dragged by, I hissed to Lisa, "Should I shout 'She touched my butt'?"

"I *dare* you," she giggled.

So, waiting for the right moment, I yelled, "SHE TOUCHED MY BUTT! STONE HER!" I even had a handful of rocks at the ready in the event of a pelting frenzy. But it was all to no avail. Nobody took me up on it. In the end, *very* reluctantly, I was forced to let the matter drop and allow boring old justice to prevail.

I'll tell you this for nothing: People are no—I repeat, NO—fun!

IT WAS ALMOST TIME for me to leave Salem.

At this point, Lisa, having realized that, true to my word, I was never going to be interested in witchcraft or, by extension, anything else Salem had to offer, and no doubt regretting the eleven bucks she'd wasted on fish and chips, made the excuse that it was time to collect her son from nursery school, and with a flustered good-bye departed at speed, leaving me to complete my tour of the sights alone.

By this time I was close to giving up on ever having my fortune told. For a town notoriously bursting with psychics, psychics were a bit thin on the ground, I thought.

But then, at the eleventh hour, just as I was starting to make a beeline for the Scheduled Passenger Alighting Point, I spotted a sign that said PICKERING WHARF and immediately knew I was saved.

If you recall, earlier on I gave a list of seven key features that must be present before a town can consider itself a tourist destination. You may also recall that there were only six of them. Well, let me rectify that right now by adding an extra one:

7. A historical wharf and marina. No coastal town with a proud maritime history behind it can ever let you forget the fact. So it's a good bet that somewhere down the line, a committee with big ideas and access to millions of dollars will have proposed building a wharf and marina development, including plans for three super attractions:

a. A full-size replica tall ship in dry dock. I've never understood the appeal of this. If they stuck the ship inside a full-size replica bottle, *then* I'd be interested.

b. A man-made lagoon. Filled with hundreds of bobbing sailboats that never seem to go anywhere, unless of course there's a freak tide overnight, in which case by daybreak 90 percent of them are lying upside-down on the promenade with their masts snapped.

c. An eerily quiet harborside village arranged in the shape of a neck brace. Made up of a dozen cute little stores, including a wool shop, a souvenir shop, a fishing tackle shop, a gallery selling the work of local artists (and in most cases, they're local for good reason); a cafe that's trying to claw back its astronomical rent by selling coffee

at $12.50 a cup and scones that are homemade, though
not necessarily recently; and a "world-famous fortune-
teller" nobody's ever heard of, called Mystic Sue-
Melinda or Tarot by Trish or some such nonsense, and
who surely can't be *that* psychic or she wouldn't have set
up her business in this godforsaken windswept hole in
the first place.

Salem's heyday as a thriving maritime hub ended many
years ago. This was principally on account of the depth of its
harbor, which was too shallow to accommodate more modern
vessels. Up to that point, I guess, ships would try to come into
dock, but at the last minute hit the seabed and fall over, which
killed any hope Salem had of perpetuating its glorious past.
Undaunted, however, and by way of a lasting tribute to its once-
great seafaring tradition, they've turned the seafront area into
Pickering Wharf. Oh, and what did I spy moored up alongside
the wharf? *Only* a three-masted replica tall ship! And what was
that close by the ship? *Only* an eerily quiet harborside village of
cute little stores arranged in the shape of a neck brace.

Now, in midsummer, when the ocean's an uninterrupted
plane of Wedgwood blue, the sun's burning down on the boardwalk, and the tinkling giggles of mischievous infants echo along
the parade of pretty white storefronts, I imagine this must be quite
the place. Charming, uncomplicated, a quiet corner where you
can noodle, amble, and unwind. But of course this wasn't midsummer. Nothing like. This was a bleak, gray, late-October afternoon. For most of the day a pelting rain had lashed the streets,
gusting in on the back of an Atlantic wind strong enough to pluck
your eyebrows and carry away any senior citizens not suitably
secured by harnesses. On days like this, I would venture to suggest, the Pickering Wharf harborside village development has all
the charm of a Siberian quarry.

Nevertheless, after taking a couple of photos to show people
back home (even the camera was shocked by how empty the
place was), I noticed that one of the shops did have a psychic,

who was bucking the no-customers trend by busily dispensing advice to a line of people craving spiritual rescue. Alas, the line was simply too long—a lot of public radio people must holiday in Salem, I guess—and so I couldn't wait. But then good fortune struck again. Walking farther on, I happened upon a thriving local herb-shop operated by a strong, vivacious woman called Terri, who I discovered, using an age-old journalistic technique known as barging in uninvited and asking, was *a real witch*. What a coup! And frankly, who better to help sort out my life at this point than a practitioner of the dark arts? So . . .

For the past twenty years, I explained to her, I've been convinced my life is cursed[31]—"*cursed*, I tell you! And so I thought I'd take this opportunity to find out why and, if possible, to get the curse taken off once and for all." I was even willing to pay whatever the going rate was for long-term hex removal.

But, like the angel earlier on, she just wasn't buying it. I won't bore you with the details of her diagnosis, but "You're a whiny little whiner" was the general drift of it.

If anyone had placed a curse on my career, it was me, she said. "You are responsible for your own life, Cash. Okay?"

Well, thank you, Deepak Chopra!

"But Terri," I pleaded, "my life sucks. It really does. I'm broke, my family hates me, my dad's cut me out of his will for reasons I won't go into, and, worst of all, my radio career's heading right down the toilet. *And it never gets any better.*"

I don't know what I was expecting. Sympathy maybe. Or if not actual sympathy, then certainly a spot of encouragement. But as always I was to be disappointed. In the end, she grew tired of my

---

31. I once interviewed a spiritualist in North London. Afterwards, invited to rate her psychic abilities, I said "medium," which, as old jokes go, must date back to Biblical times. Clearly, however, the woman was unfamiliar with Scripture. When she heard the report she was so angry that she placed a curse on me. That's my guess anyway. It was either her or one of a hundred other people I've inadvertently offended over the years. At any rate, life's been a living hell ever since, and despite countless attempts to get out of radio and into something that paid slightly more—say, playing a saxophone on the subway for pennies—I was still a journalist, with no obvious reprieve in sight.

complaints, concluding with a sigh, "Then go into television," and promptly turned to serve another customer.

Damn it. They have an answer for everything, these witches.

8

Life's Greatest Secret Revealed

The joy of watching boats capsize ◆ I try to save a drowning man ◆
Harvard University ◆ memories of my college days ◆ the Top Ten List
of Self-Evident Life Truths ◆ the Annals of Improbable Research ◆
an unexpected way to kill leeches ◆ the Free Stuff Experiment ◆
the Ig Nobel Prize Ceremony ◆ farewell, O'Hares!

WHAT A PROTRACTED EVENT THIS NEW England trip had been. Nine days in all, which is uncommonly long for me, especially since there was barely enough work to fill half that time, leaving me with four extra days of unremitting tedium at the end of my stay as I schlepped around downtown Boston in a drizzling rain with nothing whatsoever to do.

By this point, there was only one museum left on my list—the Annals of Improbable Research in Cambridge, which I'd already postponed twice, but which I'd heard was a hoot. Great, I thought. I'm bored out of my skull, I need a laugh, let's do it. So that's how I filled my final evening: I fixed an appointment with Marc Abrahams, the curator of the Annals, and went along to meet him.

TO REACH CAMBRIDGE FROM BOSTON, you must cross the Charles River. Luckily, the days when you had to swim it are long gone. Now there's a bridge.

This being late October, my visit coincided with the annual Head of the Charles Regatta. Consequently, I spent many happy minutes hanging over the bridge, watching a flotilla of pretty sailboats zigzag gracefully from bank to bank at the mercy of a high gale.

Now, heaven knows, nautical pursuits are not my thing. A psychic once warned me I'd die by drowning, so these days I won't even brush my teeth without a lifeguard in the room. But I have to confess, I do derive huge amounts of enjoyment from watching boats tip over. And they always tip over if you wait long enough.

However, if patience isn't *your* thing, then check out the windsurfers. They can't stay upright for half a second.

Crisscrossing between the sailboats that day, a dozen valiant surfer-dudes in brightly colored Spandex cat-suits did their best to impress bystanders with a spectacular array of tricks ranging from wobbling precariously and teetering dangerously, all the way down to losing their grip, dropping off, and crying for help. How splendid.

"Bravo!" I shouted, clapping. "More!"

There are few pastimes quite so absorbing, I think, as watching one of these swarthy athletic types, stripped clean of his dignity, trying to scramble back on his board after it's capsized. Indeed, I became quite entranced by one highly entertaining chap as he thrashed about in the water, making one feeble attempt after another to get his sail up. On and on he went— almost up, then down again; almost up, then down again. Twenty minutes later, he was still there, and his energy was starting to wane.

"Oh my God! He's going to die!" I thought, glancing around to see if anyone else had noticed him. Apparently nobody had. This was down to me. All my instincts were telling me to take decisive action. Dither now and a human life might be lost.

And so, with my pulse racing, I grabbed my cell phone and dialed 9-1- . . . then stopped.

I was forgetting something.

I didn't have a long-distance phone plan.

It may sound crass or even cruel, but in America roaming charges are prohibitively expensive. If you place a call on the East Coast when your mobile is registered on the West Coast the cost can be astronomical. And one *so* hates to ask for reimbursement. Wouldn't the drowning surfer-dude, placed in the same position, have felt the same way? Of course he would.

"Besides, this is Boston," I reasoned out loud. "He won't be expecting anyone to help him."

So, with a sympathetic smile, I waved back, silently sending him lots of old-fashioned luck, and without a second glance strode off along Massachusetts Avenue for my appointment at the Annals of Improbable Research.

THE WALK FROM DOWNTOWN BOSTON to Cambridge is deceptive. On the map it's about four inches, but when you actually try to get there it's a helluva lot farther!

No need to ask for directions, though. Just follow your nose. Eventually you'll find yourself pushing through a heaving mob of glum-faced adolescents with bad haircuts and stripy scarves. That's when you know you've strayed too close to Harvard University and are about to be made to feel totally inadequate.

I've heard a lot about Harvard, mostly from magazines, and also from Matt Damon, who seems to be forever talking about his college days. But it's quite another thing to go there in person.

Founded in 1636, the university claims to be the birthplace of higher education, and, frankly, who has the energy to argue? Clearly the students believe it, though. Oh yes. You can tell they've bought into the whole prestige and self-importance thing, because so many of them walk around with a peculiar disdainful look on their face, a look that says, "Quiet! I'm thinking important thoughts." In fact, anyone you meet in Cambridge who doesn't have that look is probably a tourist, a cleaner, or planning to rob the place.

Wisely, to keep their sacred institution exclusive, the college elders years ago hid the campus on the other side of a high wall; then, with a level of stupidity that bucks all logic, they went and put gates in the wall, meaning that almost anyone can walk in.

Once inside, you'll be simultaneously impressed by the sweep of the tree-lined quadrangle, flanked by three-hundred-year-old halls and terraced cottages, and also crippled by the thought that every one of these pimply youths milling around

you will someday be richer and more successful than you could
ever dream. Being better than the rest of us is their birthright;
that's what they're here for. Indeed, they're so bright, I'm surprised their heads don't glow. Strolling along the leafy walkways,
I realized I was probably the dimmest person there, and maybe
the oldest, and undoubtedly the fattest. It was very intimidating.
At some point I stopped and began taking photographs with a
ten-dollar disposable camera—my cardboard Canon, as I call
it—but quickly gave up, convinced I just looked like some
jealous old fool trying to compensate for a misspent youth.

Which in retrospect is not far from the truth.

MY OWN STUDENT YEARS CARRIED NONE of the Harvard
cachet, alas. I went to Kingston-upon-Hull in the north of England,
a red-brick-but-mostly-concrete university based in an old fishing
port that I believe was recently twinned with Purgatory.

It was cold, dismal, and gray in Hull, as I remember it,
raining almost nonstop. And whenever the wind blew in off the
North Sea, which it seemed to for twenty-three hours out of
every twenty-four, we were enveloped in the pungent stench of
freshly landed haddock, forcing us to run for cover with hand-
kerchiefs clutched to our mouths, the way Japanese actors do
from Mothra.

The three years I wasted there felt like thirty. I was sick constantly with strange inflammatory ailments I've never suffered
from since, and my studies, in law, have served no purpose I can
think of other than to wreck my eyesight and convince me that
most lawyers are entirely unnecessary and could be replaced with
a one-page leaflet to be handed out to clients, saying, "For Christ's
sake, stop blaming other people for your problems and sort them
out yourself."

That's all I recall about my ghastly college days, which is why,
though I'm not an envious man by nature, I nevertheless felt the
green-eyed devil rise up within me as I roamed around Cambridge, Massachusetts, for the first time.

Damn, how I wish I'd had the intelligence, the money, the

influence, and the necessary immigration papers to attend Harvard! Just to be welcomed as an equal in these hallowed halls, to have the assurance of knowing up front that you're a cut above everybody else; that doors, closed and barred to lesser folk, will open effortlessly to you, and life from here on in will be a smoother ride simply by virtue of that logo'd sweatshirt you're wearing—how wonderful must that be? How freeing.

It's certainly not an experience that anyone who attended Hull University in the 1970s will ever know, that's for sure.

But, as with all things worth having, there's a downside.

Education in America is a costly business and so must be taken very seriously. In my day, you went to college for three reasons only: to get drunk, to get laid, and to get away from your parents. Now students *actually study*, can you believe that?

Bumming up and down the narrow streets, I lost count of the number of young men I saw scampering along like well-trained spaniels at the heels of their father. In every case, Junior seemed to be a smaller, trimmer version of Dad; same haircut, same V-neck lambs-wool sweater, same sandy-colored Oxfords, same tasseled loafers, altogether the very models of decency and restraint, and exactly the opposite of what a student should be. All they needed now was a bar code stamped on their forehead and we could call them a robot to their face rather than merely thinking it.

Even so, you've got to smile. These guys have been primed for greatness since they walked their very first step. Such is the investment they have in winning, coming out on top, being viewed as successful, both in the eyes of the world but more immediately in the eyes of their parents, that I guess they never stop to ask themselves why? Why am I doing this? What's so great about being a winner anyway? Why does it matter so much to me to be the best and to have it all?

FORGIVE ME IF I DIGRESS FOR A SECOND, but the most important discovery I ever made, and this ultimately is why I'm glad I didn't go to a university as prestigious as Harvard, came to me regrettably late in life, after years of study and toil, trying to acquire all the various trappings of success and failing abysmally. What I discovered—and by the way, you may want to get a pen and write this down; pin it to your refrigerator or something, because it's very important—was this:

NOT EVERYONE IS MEANT TO BE SUCCESSFUL

I'll pause for a moment to leave room for gasps, because in America that's not something you'll hear very often.

We can't all be special. We can't all be champions and revered for our excellence. It stands to reason that some of us are, by our very nature and despite our best efforts, destined to be average and ordinary. But that's okay. We make our contribution in other ways. We drive buses, or serve in restaurants, or go on the radio and say stuff. We were built to lag behind the rest, to fall short of expectations, to sit for hours in Starbucks sipping foamy hot lattes, eating scones, and snickering quietly at our own unspoken observations on what passers-by are wearing. Not only is that how we're made, but—and this is an even more mind-blowing discovery, so hang onto your hats!—*it's perfectly okay to be that way.*

That's why I love the journalistic profession. Journalists live vicariously through others. They don't do anything themselves, they merely stand back and comment on what everyone else is doing. To me, life doesn't get any better than that. Okay, maybe I never achieved very much over the years, not by American Dream standards at least; I don't have the money, the big car, the meteoric career thing going on. Equally, I don't consider myself a failure. No way. Quite the opposite, in fact. Despite all my gripes, I feel I've been an unbeatable success at what I've done: i.e., nothing. What's more, as with any committed professional, I'm always on the lookout for new ways to hone my skills. Example: I don't only sit around in coffeeshops any more; I sit around in sandwich bars too! And, with all due respect, I hardly think the good old boys of Harvard University, even with all their authority, credentials, and resources, are able to foster quite *this* level of dedication in their students.

MY APPOINTMENT WITH MARC THE ANNALS GUY was set for 7:30 P.M. outside the metro station in Harvard Square. A chancy encounter, given that neither of us knew what the other looked like. As it is, I'm easily recognizable. I have a sissy red-and-blue backpack that I take everywhere, and a habit of tripping over curbstones. This is usually enough to single me out from the crowd.

I was in a thoughtful mood that night, as I recall. My mind is never still. Most times it's laden with a mass of scattered ideas that don't make sense even to me. Therefore, in order to bring a little discipline to bear, I deliberately force myself to Think Useful Things. That way, I may waste time, but at least I'm wasting it constructively. Winnie-the-Pooh hit on much the same idea. So, marching briskly along Massachusetts Avenue that cool, damp October evening, and farting to the beat of my own footsteps (it's a gift!), I began compiling in my head a list of what I'll call Self-Evident Life Truths.

These are lessons learned over a lifetime. Lessons that, given half a chance, I would hand to today's youth on a plate, thereby saving them the bother of finding this crap out for themselves. As a matter of fact, I was surprised by how fast and easily they came — bam bam bam, one after the other, like idea-bullets from an Uzi thought-rifle. It's astounding. So here they are now, my Top Ten Self-Evident Life Truths listed in no particular order, other than maybe numerical:

1. People who drink and smoke are more interesting than those who don't.

2. Doctors know less than you think they do.

3. Any food billed as "an acquired taste" was never meant to be eaten.

4. Adults under five-foot-one are in general extremely cut up about being short and will spend their entire life making everyone else pay for it.

5. In any crisis, you already know what to do.

6. Some folk enjoy conflict. They love to fight and are con-

stantly engaged in battles. That way, they don't have to focus on how screwed up they are or how lousy their life is. This applies to nations too.

7. There is no sauce, no dip, no condiment, paste, spice, or herb known to man that could ever make artichokes interesting.

8. Most people feel frightened or uncertain most of the time; some just disguise it better than others.

9. We start out in life full of confidence and convinced we know everything, then become steadily more and more unsure.

10. The louder and more vocal someone is in defense of his beliefs or principles, the less likely it is that he fully believes them.

11. The more outraged or disgusted someone is by your lifestyle, behavior, or cause, the more he secretly wishes he could participate in it.

12. Ninety percent of news is not news at all, it's merely dust kicked up by reporters to justify their paychecks and disguise the fact that they have nothing better to do. Has it never struck you as odd that very little news seems to happen at the weekend? That's because most journalists don't work weekends.

13. Macy's in New York has more than one Santa Claus.

14. Each person's life-experience consists of the same four or five basic scenarios repeated over and over again until they die.

15. There is no specific identifiable point in life where you can say the clouds suddenly part and things become clearer. It's all confusing, it's all uphill, and the hill gets a whole lot steeper around about the time your ankles start hurting.

16. Some types of pork sausage contain pig snouts, but it's hard to know which ones.

17. Men are born liars. First they lie to themselves, then, once they're convinced, they set about lying to you.

18. There's no such thing as a good toupee. Hairpieces are either "very obvious" or "less obvious," but never good.

19. Journalists are the only people in the world to use the word "pooch."

20. If you have the time to comment on or interfere in someone else's life, you're not doing enough with your own.

21. Some individuals were born to win. It's not fair, but it's how it is, so leave them to it. Don't waste precious time trying to keep up, or longing for their destiny in preference to your own; that will only make you bitter and envious. You are you for a reason; your only duty is to find what that reason is and embrace it unreservedly.

22. Bitterness and envy are justified sometimes.

23. Attending college is a waste of time unless you really need to or want to. If you have dreams that don't require a four-year layover in an institution of learning, then have the courage to stand alone. Create something, do something, be something. History is littered with examples of people who dropped out and made good. I can't think of any right now, but it is.

24. There is a God. It may not seem so on occasions, but that's only because He's busy yakking to Victoria the schizo-phrenic. Otherwise, He's on the case; never doubt it.

25. The most important word in the English language is "no." Closely followed by "donut."

26. If you believe it, then it's probably true (see 24 above).

27. Your body should be treated as if you have only one hundred Health-and-Looks Units to last you a lifetime. One hundred is all there is, then that's it, it's over. So you must go easy. Pace yourself. Spread them wisely throughout

the years. Most people use up 50 percent of their allotted units before they're thirty, then when they reach sixty they wonder why they're falling apart.

28. Bad deeds are boomerangs. It may take a while, but every wrongful act, however miniscule, rebounds on you. You never get away with anything.

29. Good deeds also return to you, but never straight away and seldom in kind.

30. It's better to be happy and healthy at any age than beautiful, witty, clever, cool, popular, thin, knowledgeable, stable, wealthy, competent, powerful, influential, athletic, successful, "on the team," "one of the in-crowd," "part of the set," "top of the class," or any combination of the above.

31. If you keep on telling people you're wonderful, eventually they will start to believe you.

32. The meaning of life is: a) to have fun; b) to loosen up; and c) to unlearn 75 percent of the things you learned as a child.

And there you have it—my personal Top Ten List of Self-Evident Life Truths.

I'd probably have carried on adding to them too, had I not just then spotted a man in a gray duffle coat loitering by the metro entrance, and had I also not, in my rush to get his attention, tripped over the curb and plunged headlong into him.

I LIKED MARC ABRAHAMS INSTANTLY. It's hard not to. He's a congenial, super-sparky intellectual with a quick wit and, far less importantly, a degree from Harvard in applied mathematics. The American Medical Association once called him the "Puck of science," which, if I knew what it meant, I'm sure I'd be inclined to agree with.

Early on in his career he ran his own business developing Optical Character Recognition Computer Systems (including a reading machine for the blind) or OCRCS (IARMFTB) for short.

Then, in 1990, he became the editor of something called the *Journal of Irreproducible Results,* and, when that folded, a new magazine, the *Annals of Improbable Research.* To my ears this doesn't sound a whole lot different from the first one, but apparently readers can tell which is which, and the *Annals* has since become a true phenomenon.

Eager to know more, I followed Marc across campus into a modern building teeming with people who were half my age and had twice my IQ. This I assumed to be the home of the *Annals.* For some reason I was expecting all kinds of kooky nonsense: two hundred years' worth of stupid surveys, dumb experiments, and wild, pointless statistics gathered together in a small, dusty library, and possibly guarded by a troll.

But not so.

After sticking his head around a couple of doors at random, Marc led me into an empty lecture theater and sat down.

"So where are the *Annals?*" I asked, glancing about.

At which point he leaned over to one side and produced them from a bag.

Contrary to what I'd imagined, the *Annals* isn't a library in the singular so much as it is a bunch of magazines in the plural, meaning that there's nothing to tour around, only something to flick through and laugh hysterically at. On the plus side, it also means there's no gift shop, which is always a blessing.

A.I.R. is "the journal of record for inflated research and personalities," he explained. Its professed aim is to chart in detail the history of goofy scientific experiments, or, when that doesn't work, of valid, ingenious experiments that just sound goofy and which deserve to be laughed at hysterically anyway. Examples:

- "Is Barney the Dinosaur Really a Dinosaur?"
- "Cooking with Poo"
- "Does Prune Whip Reduce Laxative Usage in a Skilled Nursing Facility?"
- "Oral Injury Caused by Fellatio"

- "The Evolutionary Advantages of Being Stupid"

All these topics were naturals for the *Annals*.

The sole criterion for inclusion in the magazine is that you must have conducted an experiment that "could not or should not be reproduced."

A team of Norwegian researchers, for instance, won their place in *Improbable* history thanks to a paper they published in the *British Medical Journal* called "The Effects of Ale, Garlic, and Sour Cream on the Appetite of Leeches." I don't want to give too much away, but I will say this: Exposed to garlic, leeches die (why does that not surprise me?); exposed to beer I believe they lapse into a lingering stupor interspersed with the occasional medley from *Jesus Christ Superstar*. But dip a leech in sour cream, and bingo! He'll eat that crap forever.

Now, ask yourself: Who wouldn't want to know stuff like this? It's priceless.

Other researchers have made a similarly powerful impact, including the authors of such papers as:

- "Farting as a Defense Against Unspeakable Dread"

- "Optimizing the Airborne Thermal Detection of Possums"

- "Adder Bites in the British Army 1979–1988"

- "Coffee Enema Drawbacks" (I'm guessing there are hundreds.)

- "Distinguishing Between New and Slightly Worn Underwear: A Case Study"

Wow! You understand already, I'm sure, why such a movement would be gathering pace. Then again, you might be thinking: "It's not much fun, though, is it, if there's no building or library to visit and I don't get to see these experiments for myself."

Hm. You're right. The *Annals* are now so extensive that there probably should be an *Improbable* museum. Maybe you could be the one to organize a petition and get the ball rolling. Consider it homework.

In the meantime, there is a way you can participate.

As well as publishing the magazine each month, Marc and his pals stage a boisterous shindig once a year. It's called the Ig Nobel Prize Ceremony, an intellectual hootenanny performed to an audience of people with glowing heads, and you, too, if you feel like buying a ticket. During the course of the ceremony cheap statuettes—statuettes that are handmade and usually fall apart within three weeks, he tells me—are lavished on experts in any number of fields who, in the opinion of a panel of judges comprising "fifty distinguished scientists and a convicted felon," have mined a scientific nugget that deserves to be recognized, though not, and they hasten to add this in case you should try, emulated.

In past years, Igs have been handed out to:

• The guy who designed the pink plastic garden flamingo.

• Members of the Taiwanese Parliament for brawling.

• A man with an almost unpronounceable name from Lithuania, for setting up a Communism-based theme park called Stalin World.

• A Scot called Gordon McNaughton for co-authoring a report entitled "The Collapse of Toilets in Glasgow."

• John Keogh of Australia, the man who patented the wheel, only he waited 'til the year 2001 to do it.

• George and Charlotte Blonsky for coming up with a device that helps pregnant women give birth by spinning them around very fast.

• The Pepsi Company of the Philippines for a wondrous contest they organized some while back, in which a million dollars would go to the lucky customer who popped a special winning bottle cap. Unfortunately, Pepsi, in a moment of madness, went and printed hundreds of these special winning bottle caps, then, in a second moment of madness that easily overtakes the first, when hundreds of winners stepped forward to claim their million dollars each, refused to pay up, sparking riots in the streets, during which cars were set alight and several people killed.

And finally there's my personal favorite. A guy called Jeff Van Bueren of San Francisco received a prize for a study he conducted known as the Free Stuff Experiment.

All he did—and you'll kick yourself for not having had the same idea—was dump household items one by one in the street outside his home with a sign saying FREE—PLEASE TAKE, then retire a safe distance to see how long they'd sit on the sidewalk before someone ran off with them. Truly, this is science in action. The results were fascinating, albeit in an "I really couldn't care less" kind of way. Here's a summary:[32]

- A new pair of shoes—1 hour
- An old, beat-up pair of shoes—4 hours
- A pair of 1970s maroon bell-bottom trousers—4 hours
- A Scotch tape dispenser—2 hours
- An Easter basket containing shredded packing material—3 hours
- A new rubber ducky—2 hours
- An old rubber ducky—2 hours
- A rusty filing cabinet—16 hours
- A plastic cast of a human skull—30 minutes (a man picked it up, accidentally dropped and broke it, then ran off)
- Cookies on a tray—1.5 hours (someone dumped the cookies and took the tray)
- An old stained blanket—not removed (item eventually withdrawn)
- A live lizard . . .

At this point, the experiment was terminated by officers of the Department of Public Works and Environmental Health; which

---

32. Marc wants me to remind you that this material is copyright the *Annals of Improbable Research,* so please don't go reading it to your friends and charging them for it, or selling it on to *Vogue.*

is a shame because it was going so well, and Jeff had so many other interesting objects on standby, including:

- A dented camping pot;

- Some bent bicycle handlebars; and

- Artwork of a human face, with floppy disks for eyes, a Slinky nose, and a wire mouth, mounted in a frame made from glued walnuts.

But what the hell! He'd proven a point: that people are cheap (particularly the guy who swiped the Easter basket filled with shredded packing material—shame on you, you miser!), and for this he was awarded a statuette that falls apart within three weeks.

Bravo!

I'd applaud him heartily, only I'm typing.

THE *ANNALS OF IMPROBABLE RESEARCH* MAGAZINE is one of those things that, like a good joke, or antiperspirant, is better experienced firsthand, so I recommend you buy yourself a copy and read it. You can subscribe on the *Annals* Web site.

Getting your hands on an Ig Nobel Prize, however, takes greater ingenuity.

Strolling back in the direction of the college gate after our meeting, I dropped a hint to Marc that I'd quite like to win one myself someday if that could be arranged.[33]

"Ah," he said, smiling. And that was the end of that.

Obviously, he thought I was kidding.

Well, I'm sorry, I wasn't. As incredible as it may seem, my self-esteem was badly in need of a fillip at that time, and some tacky trophy that falls apart three weeks after you're given it, but awarded at Harvard University, would at that point have meant

---

33. And that's not as far-fetched as you might imagine. I once devised a new system of handwriting analysis that, among many other things, connects the way you write the letter "v" to how good you are in bed. I'm serious. Over the years I have expounded upon my research in three extremely popular books, including *Love Letters* (Kensington Publishing), and on TV. If that doesn't qualify me for some sort of cheap trophy I really don't know what does.

fifty thousand times more to me than the Bachelor of Laws degree I gained after three years of arduous, haddock-tainted toil at Kingston-upon-Hull. Call it what you will—sad, pathetic, I don't care; but that's how I felt.

"Well . . ." he began, but what I thought might turn into an "okay, then, since it's you!" quickly dribbled to nothing. And that's when I knew it was never going to happen. Or perhaps it might, but posthumously. Or maybe Jeff Van Bueren will leave his award out on the sidewalk someday with a sign saying FREE—PLEASE TAKE and that's how I'll get one.

Either way, thanks for nothing, bright guys.

ON THE FINAL DAY OF MY STAY, everything at the O'Hare B&B changed. Black to white. Minor to major.

Donna, whom I'd not seen since the first night, deigned to pop her head around the kitchen door with a hearty "Good morning" as I came thundering down the stairs at 8:01 thinking I'd missed breakfast. But today for once the rules had been relaxed and it didn't seem to matter. Shortly after, Gerry breezed in with hot tea, toast, and the same plate of brownies I'd been avoiding all week, being remarkably loose and pleasant. Conversation was upbeat. We laughed, we chatted, and he even told me a couple of his best Nightmare Guests Doing Strange Things in Rooms stories, which were a hoot.

"They left their blinds open *and* draped wet towels over the furniture . . ."

"Nooooo!"

"I swear to God."

And d'you know what? For the first time on this whole trip, I suddenly felt okay about these people.

More than that, I wondered for a moment if I hadn't made a mistake and misjudged the Bostonites. Perhaps they weren't hostile after all, just wary. Not rude, merely distant. Their carpets not threadbare, merely comfortably worn in.

One of the little signs in my room told me: "Check-out is at 11:00 A.M. Please return your key or there will be a *penalty*. Thank you." But my bags were packed long before eleven. With my free airport shuttle bus parked outside, I returned my key and said a last-minute good-bye to Donna and Gerry. And as I did so I noticed a small hesitation. Loitering side by side by the dining room door the couple looked lost for a second, as if unsure how to end this.

"Oh my God," I said to myself, taking in their empty faces, "they're actually reluctant to let me go. They like me and want to embrace me." So without further ado, because ados take up valuable time and aren't very British, I stepped forward and gave Gerry a kind of part-squeeze, part-tweak. "Thank you so much, it's been great."

Donna was next. Clutching her shoulder, I planted a saliva tattoo on her right cheek. "Thanks for the breakfasts."

It was all very sharp and quick. When I pulled back, however, I sensed that something had changed. Maybe I'd clutched *too* tightly, because her eyes were on stalks, as if she'd just sat on a branding iron. And poor Gerry was in shock.

"Fine," was all he said, backing away. "That's great."

Seems I'd read the signals all wrong. Isn't that so like me, though? They hadn't wanted to embrace me at all; they couldn't care less if I stayed or go-ed. They were just on the scrounge, I figured; expecting a tip, or at the very least a small gift of some kind, a token of gratitude for the many small, and I have to say predominantly invisible, courtesies they'd shown over the past few days.

"Tell your friends about us," Donna shouted after me, realizing that the tip was never going to happen and resorting to the next best thing: PR.

"Oh yes, I'll tell them," I thought. "You can bet on it!"

"And be sure to sign our guest book."

Jeez! The shuttle driver was honking his horn. I didn't have time for this. Besides, I hate signing guest books, I really do. On the one hand, I want to be absolutely truthful and say what I think; on the other, I don't want to hurt anyone's feelings. It's a constant dilemma. So, under Donna's watchful eye I grabbed the pen and, instead of transcribing what was really on my mind, wrote something true but cryptic:

"I will not forget this place in a hurry."

With that, and after scribbling my name in such a way that nobody would ever recognize it, I slammed the door and, like a vacationing version of Nelson Mandela, escaped to freedom.

9

A Stopover in Bloomington, Minnesota

The promise of a farm tour ◆ what's to be done about screaming babies? ◆ I'm overcome with a strange uneasy feeling ◆ the Museum of Questionable Medical Devices ◆ the link between cancer and jazz ◆ suitable appliances for the rectum ◆ dinner with Twee or Twa or Twerp ◆ a visit to Stuffopolis ◆ the Land of Enchanted PVC Cushions on Sticks ◆ more uneasy feelings ◆ the Farm Tour Debacle ◆ at last we find out how Minneapolis–St. Paul got its name

LOOMINGTON, I DISCOVERED AT THE VERY beginning of my stay, means literally "Blooming Ton," which, as I discovered by the end of my stay, means literally nothing at all.

I was in town because the Convention and Visitors Bureau had thrown me a bone: "Come to Bloomington, and we'll take you on a farm tour," they said. No other details were offered, since that would only have served to put me off.

Despite being clueless as to what a farm tour might entail—though, out of all the possible options, a tour of a farm seemed the most likely—and even though I have not a grain, nay, a nanospeck of interest in anything even vaguely outdoorsy, the invitation was all the more tempting. It might be worth going, I thought, if only to find out if something as dull and hokey-sounding as a farm tour could possibly live up/down to expectations.

Also, to be perfectly honest, I was hoping in secret that it would involve a surprise visit to the Gibbs Farm Museum in St. Paul, Minnesota, another one of those pioneer villages that sets my teeth on edge, but of which I evidently can't get enough.

THE STORY BEHIND GIBBS FARM is fascinating. I looked it up on the Internet.

In 1833, when she was only five years old, Jane DeBow was kidnapped by missionaries,[34] and, to cut a long story short, later married a guy from Illinois called Heman Gibbs. The end.

Hm.

Okay, lengthening the story just a little . . .

Eventually, Jane was freed by the missionaries. (Don't ask me how or why they let her go, they just did. Perhaps she made a run for it during Evensong.)

The next sixteen years of her life are a little lacking in detail, so we'll leapfrog over those until we reach 1849, which was when she and Heman bought a parcel of land in Minnesota. Straight away, they excavated themselves a dugout sod house[35] to live in and started up a farm. In those days, I believe, the labor laws were strict on quotas, demanding that 80 percent of the workforce be drama students in period dress. But that didn't faze the newlyweds. Determined not to be waylaid by such piddling obstacles, they continued to work hard and apply themselves dutifully to the task of doing what they were doing, whatever that was, and in the fullness of time made good.

Knowing this story, I'm not quite sure what's so great about the Gibbses that they deserve to have an entire tourist attraction dedicated to them. So they started a farm and ran it—big deal! But anyway, for right or wrong, the Gibbs Farm Museum now stands in splendid testimony to their efforts, offering an authentic reconstruction of the original dugout sod house, as well as an impressive rural setting of barns and outbuildings that look exactly as they did in those heady post-kidnap days 150 years ago.

---

34. Kidnapping is only one tiny part of a missionary's job, but a vital one.

35. Traditionally, a kind of fancy igloo made of earth. Not to be confused with Dutch filmmaker Dugout Sodhouse, director of such avant-garde classics as *Heeri Hoori, Ooody Neeri Oooo* (1964) and *Rupidu Pidu* (1974).

Needless to say, if a visit to Minnesota also included a tour of Gibbs Farm, I would be more than delighted. So fingers crossed!

IF ANYONE EVER ASKS YOU WHAT THE WORST part of being a travel reporter on public radio is—and if you're not one, I can't imagine why they would—tell them that the worst part is being forced to fly Coach.

I mean, they wouldn't fly Barry Manilow Coach, would they? Or Dugout Sodhouse. God, there are times when I *hate* being a nobody. It's so unfair.

On the flight to Minneapolis, I was forced to sit between a woman who couldn't stop sneezing and some extremely over-weight guy who kept getting his tray table caught on his nipples. To make matters worse, the three of us were wedged in directly behind the Screaming Baby Row—midplane, right by the movie screen—and you know what a nightmare *that* can be. Really, is it asking too much that children under two years of age be banned as carry-on items and stored in the hold? Come on, it's the twenty-first century, people; let's start thinking outside the box!

All of which meant that by the time I'd landed in Minneapolis and taken the free shuttle to my hotel,[36] I was totally frazzled, and far from ready to serve yet more time in one of these mid-range penitentiaries. Not that the hotel was bad or anything, but it wasn't exactly the Waldorf-Astoria, and right then my body was crying out for a Waldorf-Astoria. Just a tiny one. Or a Ritz-Carlton. Somewhere luxurious. With fluffy white monogrammed bath-robes, and towels so large that they would break your fall if you used them as parachutes, and French windows leading to a private balcony with an uninterrupted view of the New York skyline. That's what I wanted.

---

36. As I recall, it wasn't *my* hotel's free shuttle, but rather one from a different hotel. I'm great at faking helplessness. I have a quite remarkable Lost-Little-Lamb face that I can turn on in a second (closely allied to my Sad Clown face—think Bela Lugosi in *Chandu of the Magic Isle*) which generally has complete strangers rushing to my aid, lest I either burst into tears or fall down dead of despair. Using this foolproof technique I persuaded the driver of the other hotel's shuttle bus to take a seven-mile detour to mine.

Instead, what I got was the Country Inn & Suites.

Now, to be fair, this was Bloomington, so if the hotel *had* had an uninterrupted view of the New York skyline they could have tripled their room rate.

All the same, as I understand it, Minnesota is the Land of Ten Thousand Lakes. *Ten thousand.* That's a lot of lakes, right? In fact, as far as I can tell, if you discount Minneapolis and its neighboring towns, the state is just one enormous bucket. So would it have hurt them, d'you think, to put a single one—and all I'm talking here is just one measly lake—outside my hotel window for me to stare at? A trivial request, but it would have made all the difference. Instead, my room overlooked the parking lot and, beyond that, a busy road, then a monstrous thirty-foot wall that seemed to go on forever, which for the purposes of this book I'm going to refer to as The Mall of America.

But more about that in a little while.

THE FOLLOWING DAY WAS A GOOD ONE: sparkling bright and very warm.

It was August, ten months after my Boston trip, and Minnesota was enjoying a seasonal window of opportunity known locally as summer.

Winters in this part of the world are scarily, flesh-searingly, subarctically harsh, lasting anything up to nine months. And since this tends to be followed by a rainy spell lasting a further two months, which is then supplanted briefly by a kind of gray three-week interlude when the weather dithers slightly, as if unsure what kind of misery to inflict on people next, there isn't much room left for a decent summer. Instead, you get a quick burst of blazing heat, much as might happen if you slung a cup of water into a deep fat fryer, enough to singe your eyebrows and scorch the ceiling, then it's over.

I, of course, had miscalculated, the way I always do. Hearing how cold Minnesota could be, and after the Chicago experience when I'd not taken enough clothes with me, this time I'd stuffed my bag with thick socks and knitted sweaters and heavy-duty jeans, the kind worn on North Sea oil rigs in January, which unfortunately meant that, with temperatures unexpectedly kissing ninety degrees every day, I was basting in my own juices from the second I stepped off the plane right up to when I stepped back on again and left.

After breakfast on day one, a tall, charming young man called John from the Bloomington Convention and Visitors Bureau stopped by the hotel to pick me up and escort me to a place they're very proud of around here, called the Museum of Questionable Medical Devices.

As we motored into downtown Minneapolis, the sun was abnormally hot and the conversation unusually slow. So, sweating like a turkey roast, I stuck my head out of the car window to get a breeze on my face, leaving John babbling away next to me. I don't remember what was said, only that his main preoccupation seemed to be: "Don't forget to say that the Mall of America is in Bloomington, not Minneapolis."

Promising him that I wouldn't forget, which I promptly did, I took this opportunity to drop in a quick mention of the farm tour, at the same time thanking him for organizing such a thing at short notice and saying how much I was looking forward to seeing it.

"Farm tour?" He broke off briefly from telling me that the Mall of America was in Bloomington not Minneapolis for a moment, and frowned. "Sure, you *could* go on a farm tour if you really wanted to."

"Oh. Okay," I said.

Still a little puzzled, John then went back to talking about the Mall of America's location, and how it was in Bloomington, not Minneapolis.

And at that moment I was struck by a strange uneasy feeling. You know the kind of feeling I'm talking about? It's like a premonition. Almost as if, all of a sudden, I suspected that no farm tour had been organized at all and that I'd traveled three thousand miles for nothing. That kind of strange uneasy feeling.

I know, I'm an idiot. I should have said something. After all, the show had splashed out at least a grand on sending me here, which may not sound a lot, but in public radio terms it's equivalent to what NASA spent putting a man on the moon, and Jim, I knew for sure, would broil me alive if I went back to Los Angeles without milking something, feeding something, or at the very least sitting on something until it threw me off. But as always, being the mild-mannered Brit that I am and not wishing to kick up a stink, I stayed quiet, stuck my head back out of the window, and let the feeling pass.

THE MUSEUM OF QUESTIONABLE MEDICAL DEVICES has got to be one of the most interesting and entertaining places I've ever been to: a large U-shaped room devoted exclusively to "quackery, fraud, deceit, and deception" in the field of medicine, and run by everyone's favorite skeptic, Bob McCoy.

His idea, I gather, was to bring together in one place a bunch of bizarre machines that, according to the inventors, performed medical miracles, but which, according to Bob—whom, frankly, I tend to trust a little more—were total shams.

In a world obsessed with homeopathy, reflexology, and every other form of opathy and ology you can think of, this collection is a sobering reminder of how disgracefully willing we are as patients to suspend our disbelief and, where necessary, all common sense and logic too, if it means getting quick relief or achieving some extraordinary medical outcome with the absolute minimum of effort.

I know this to be true, because I am one of these people! (I believe the technical term for us is "suckers," but you might want to look it up.) For example, I watch TV infomercials as if they're regular programming. I do. Not only that, but I enjoy the reruns just as much as, and often more than, the originals. I am *dying* to whip out my credit card and hand over three easy payments for something big and bulky with lots of accessories that does very little and which will, the moment it arrives, go straight into the back of my closet unopened. As with the True-Air kitchen smell remover, I don't need it; but just knowing I have it brings me comfort. I was never like this before Chicago, by the way. But once I'd been exposed to the International Housewares Show and discovered the joy of owning heaps and heaps of junk that I don't want and will never use, I was as good as born again. So it's not surprising that, with people like me in the world, the trade in quack remedies has thrived for almost two hundred years.

Take, for example, phrenology machines.

These were very popular in their day. You sat in a chair and wedged your head inside a spiky-half-globe-dome-metal-hair-dryer-like thing that, according to the instructions, could read the landscape of bumps on your scalp and from this identify thirty-five of your most prominent personality traits. These included intelligence, chastity, and suavity (who among us hasn't at some point wished we knew what our suavity level was?). It would also rate your personality on a scale of 1 (deficient) to 5 (superior), and was even willing to stick its mechanical neck right out and suggest the perfect vocation for someone with your particular arrangement of bumps.

"Okay," Bob said, switching it on and pressing the spiky-half-globe-dome-metal-hair-dryer-like thing down hard over my head. (And here's an insider secret: The spikes are sharp and they really hurt.) "I want you to look straight ahead."

"Ow! OwowowowOWOWOW," I replied. "OW!"

Two minutes later a strip of ticker tape came snaking out of a slot.

"So let's see . . ."

When Bob unraveled the printout, the results were amazing. My personality ranked a meager 2, it said, falling somewhere between "deficient" and "sadly lacking," which is about right. No mention was made of my suavity level—a massive disappointment, this—but the machine was absolutely positive that I couldn't keep a secret, and that's entirely true. Also, I'm useless with money, which is true too. As for my ideal vocation, well, this took a while longer to arrive at, but finally, based on all available data, the recommendation came through loud and clear: "You are most suited to becoming . . . a zeppelin attendant." And really, who can argue with that?[37]

Next to the phrenology machine stood another mechanical wonder, Dr. John Kellogg's Vibratory Chair. And before you ask, yes, it's that Kellogg. Dr. John Kellogg—the cornflake guy.

Back in the late eighteen hundred-and-somethings, Kellogg—who was a bit of a flake himself, by all accounts—took the job of superintendent at the Seventh Day Adventist Western Health Reform Institute in Battle Creek, Michigan, which later became the Battle Creek Sanitarium, and began tending to hundreds of sick people,[38] employing a raft of innovative and quite radical new treatments he'd just thought of, each one designed to restore his patients to the peak of health.[39] One of these treatments was this awesome vibrating chair. Made of a dark wood and with a high back to rest your head against, it looks totally safe and harmless from a distance. But switch it on, and man!

"Sit down here and put your wrists on the armrests," Bob said. Then he flicked a switch.

WHIRRRRRRRRRRRRRRRRRRRRRRRRRR.

"Woah! Ow! Ow! Owowowowowwwww! Switch it off. Switch it OFF!!"

Goddamn! This thing rattles and shakes and bangs around like a road drill.

The museum is packed at every turn with fun items just like that, and Bob's gleeful enthusiasm for every last one of them

---

37. You may already have noticed that traveling by zeppelin is a recurring theme in my life. Yet strangely, you wouldn't get me up in one even if Dr. Scholl personally sat in the seat beside me and held my hand (if he were gay, that is).

38. One of whom was a guy called Post, who went on to start a rival cereal company and, from what I hear, did rather well at it. This was, of course, many years before General Mills left the army and began his own phenomenal rise to success.

39. You may remember, his story was turned into a movie by Alan Parker called *The Road to Wellville*. If so, you may also remember that it was really terrible. Stuck for something to rent? Try *Evita*. It has songs, drama, and Antonio Banderas dancing in a fountain. But leave *Road to Wellville* on the shelf.

means it never gets boring. Painful sometimes, yes. Boring, no. One machine I tried resembled a handheld cake mixer. Apply it to the Achilles tendon and it cures hemorrhoids (honest!), although for some reason I have yet to understand, Bob skipped my Achilles tendon altogether and decided to drill it into my chest. The effect was similar to being punched repeatedly and very fast by squirrels wearing knuckle rings.

"OwowowowowowowowowOWOWOWOWWWW!!"

I swear I cracked a rib.

Astonishingly, some of these early devices were conceived with a genuine expectation that they would actually cure something. The fact that they didn't is neither here nor there.

Take Dr. Ruth Drown, for instance. She was convinced that jazz music caused cancer (I've been saying the same thing for years, but does anyone listen?). In order to battle this groovy but insidious menace she came up with a clever device called the Homo-VibraRay. Of course, earplugs would have worked just as well, but Dr. Drown wore a white coat, which to all intents and purposes made her a scientist; not for her the easy or straightforward solution. Instead, the Homo-VibraRay used a technique called radionics, which was very big at the time. During the session, patients would be bombarded with bolts of radiation for many minutes. This, she assured them, would gradually remove the buildup of carcinogenic crotchets caused by listening to all that hazardous jazz music, and replace them with healthy ones.

"O—kaaay. And did the Homo-VibraRay work?" I hear you saying.

I have no idea—although I'm willing to take a guess! More likely it was a placebo, a psychological shot in the arm to convince Dr. Drown's patients that she had the power to heal, when all she really had was the power to swindle a gullible public out of vast sums of money.

My other favorite device is the Co-etherator. At first glance it appears to be nothing more than a wooden box with a lightbulb inside, but on closer inspection, if you pull it apart and start examining the components, you quickly discover . . . that it's nothing more than a wooden box with a lightbulb inside. It does have a pedal and a dial on the exterior, however, but these were just put there to look nice.

The Co-etherator was invented by Dr. Heil Eugene Crum, a master of deceit.

To begin with, he would demand a sample of the patient's saliva. "Here, spit on this!"

Pth!

"And again."

Pth! Pth!

"Oooh, Herr Doktor," the patient would coo, wiping her lips, "such a fancy machine you have there. It has a pedal, a dial, a lightbulb, and *everything*."

"Ja, sit still. I vill now insert your saliva into zis receptacle here . . ."

"You mean the trash can?"

". . . vhatever—so zat my machine can diagnose your illness."

Light from the bulb would then shine through a tiny hole in the box onto a piece of paper on which had been printed the standard alphabet A to Z.

"My goodness, how clever—the alphabet!"

Now here's where it gets complicated.

Whichever letter the machine picked out on the paper was the first letter of the disease you'd contracted. T for tuberculosis, G for gout, A for arthritis, etc. Do stop me if I get too technical!

Quite naturally, the patient was very impressed. "So this throbbing in my left ear is really a form of lower back pain, you say? Dr. Crum, you are a *genius!*"

But that's not all. According to Crum, who clearly needed the money, once it had pinpointed what was wrong, his small wooden box with a lightbulb inside it and a fake dial on the front could be programmed to emit a blast of healing rays so strong that they would, over time, cure any ailment. Good-bye blindness. Cheerio, leakage of the heart. Arrivederci, varicose veins and tumors. The Co-etherator had done it again!

Additionally, he said, the same rays could be used to fertilize fields, kill dandelions, and cause amputated fingers to grow back! I mean, is that cool or what? Admit it, you want one. Well, me too. That's how good these quacks were at peddling their ingenious little scams. And also how dumb I am.

Above all, for a bogus device to dupe the maximum number of people, it had to have a convincing name, something that looked good in a catalogue and provoked awe when dropped lightly into conversation at dinner parties, but which was in reality completely unfathomable.

Bob has a slew of such devices:

• The Nap-a-Night Anti-Fatigue Device. According to the leaflet, it made "two hours sleep equal eight." How it did this is not entirely clear, although I suspect it employed the same technique that Woody Allen uses in his movies and which also makes two hours feel like eight.

• The Tibetan Electric Rheumatism Rings.

• The Trilton Nose Straightener.

• Dr. Young's Rectal Dilators.

• The Prostate Gland Warmer (basically a lightbulb, a length of cord, and a quite disgusting-looking black probe).

• The Rectorotor (same orifice, different purpose).

• The Anti-Paralysis Electric Hairbrush.

• The Foot-Operated Breast Enlarger. I tried this. It's a funnel with a tube attached. You connect the tube to the faucet and the funnel to your breast, pump water into it, and bingo: bigger breasts. Probably. And when you're done with the water, according to the manufacturer, you can use it to wash dishes. These guys think of everything.

• The McGregor Rejuvenator. An iron lung-type device that, it was claimed, would help you live 'til you're two hundred years old, invented by a guy who didn't.[40]

• The Solar-Powered Necklace, which apparently helps fight depression. (I mean, how can you possibly find the time to be depressed when you're busy showing off your solar-powered necklace to people?)

• The Radium Ore Revigator, a water jar with a large radioactive rock inside. "For *every* home!" screamed the advertisement. Yeah—right. The aim of the rock, according to the brochure, was to revitalize "tired and wilted water." As a bonus, there was also the possibility that it would strike you down with liver cancer, succeeding triumphantly where jazz music failed.

• And finally, Grove's Tasteless Chill Tonic. Not strictly a device, this, but it's in the museum anyway, and takes credit for having an advertising pitch even more tasteless than its tonic: "Grove's Tasteless Chill Tonic—makes children as fat as pigs."

As you can probably tell, there is no aspect of this subject that doesn't thrill and enthrall me. I love things that do nothing whatsoever, but pretend to. Maybe because they parallel my own life.

Anyway, I'd just about wound up my tour and was getting ready to leave—actually, I was busy fiddling around with Dr. Young's Rectal Dilators and wondering if I had any use for them—when a group of inner-city kids on a field trip came

---

40. Along similar lines, if ever you're in Houston, Texas, try visiting The Orange Show, a weird sculpture playground built by a bizarre man called Jeff McKissack as a tribute to his favorite fruit, the orange. It's the most pointless waste of space I've ever seen. The centerpiece is a hand-painted map of Florida (home of the orange) but which is shaped like a large cucumber, bearing little or no resemblance to the real Florida. There's a homemade ship in a waterless pool; a viewing gallery with nothing to look at; a refreshment bar serving orange juice, if you're lucky; and an amphitheater in which McKissack planned to give lectures about the health benefits of oranges to an organ accompaniment, but later changed his mind. And anyway, the organist never showed up. Clearly, the guy was obsessed. At some point he even wrote a book claiming that if you eat an orange every day of your life, as he did, then you'll live 'til you're one hundred years old. Unfortunately we'll never know if his theory was true, since he died when he was seventy-two.

bursting in through the door, accompanied by a pair of bored-looking teachers. So Bob said his good-byes to me and drifted over to begin his "hello and welcome" speech to them.

Many of the students didn't seem interested in anything he had to say. One or two were listening to CD players. Several others staged a protest at the back by sitting down and chatting, evidently pissed off at being brought out to a museum where, God forbid, they might actually learn something.

But Bob has been doing this a long time. With a chuckle, he directed their attention toward Dr. Kellogg's Vibratory Chair.

I was already out of the door by now, but I lingered on the steps just long enough to hear him ask for volunteers. "Great. Now sit down here and put your arms on the armrests."

WHIRRRRRRRRRRRRRRRRRRRRRRRRRRRRRRR.

I swear I would lay down my life for a man like that!

THAT SAME EVENING, I WAS EXPOSED TO an isolated strain of St. Paul-style hospitality. It came via a friend of a friend—a retired college professor with a weird name: Twer, or Twee, or Twar, something like that. Nice guy, as a matter of fact. Agreeable, intelligent, and very pleasant company. So pleasant, in fact, as to be instantly forgettable. This was *my* problem incidentally, not his. I'm sure there are hordes of people all over Minnesota who know and revere this man, but for some reason, that's not how it was for me. In fact, only a week later, if I'd been asked to pick Twig out of a police lineup, I couldn't have done it.

"He was just some old dude with glasses," I'd have had to tell the officer in charge, "and white hair, and a gray suit . . ." The rest is kind of fuzzy. "And now you mention it, I couldn't vouch 100 percent for the glasses, white hair, or suit."

"But his name was Tworn, you say?"

"Or Twurn. I'm sorry, I just don't recall."

Even so, it was good of him to stop by and take me to dinner.

By way of a treat, the restaurant he chose was on an elegant riverboat that reminded me of the Battle Creek Sanitarium with paddles. It was moored on the banks of the Mississippi, a broad twist of inky blue that plays the unenviable role of cultural referee between, on the one hand, Minneapolis, the go-ahead, swinging metropolis with a skyline like a box of isotopes, and on the other St. Paul, its dowdy, flatter, and far less exciting neighbor, which unfortunately can't stay up too late or hang out with its homeys on street corners throwing Dr Pepper cans at police cruisers, because it's the state capital and has responsibilities and a reputation to maintain.

Though both places are pleasant enough and clean enough and vibrant enough to warrant a second visit, neither of them — and it pains me to say this, because they try so hard — really possesses the kind of stand-out personality that sticks in the mind. I don't care how many street parades they have, or how many statues of Charlie Brown they've stuck up all over town (and it must be dozens; someone went crazy!), or that Minneapolis was recently voted second-coolest city in America, with St. Paul coming in a very close 1,976th, in the final analysis when the chips are down and all's said and done, and not only has the fat lady sung but she's stormed off the stage and caught the last bus home, downtown Minneapolis is no different than downtown L.A. or downtown Houston or downtown any-other-big-city-you-can-name. You've seen one, you've seen 'em all. And even one's one too many.

To put it another way, if you were at the grocery store and you met Minneapolis and St. Paul in the frozen food aisle and, while you were chatting to them, Chicago happened to walk by pushing a cart, you'd immediately lose interest in Minneapolis and St. Paul and run after Chicago, trying to strike up a conversation. That's just how it is. In much the same way that I had problems afterwards recalling certain small things about Twie — his height, hair color, skin tone, demeanor, clothing, and gender, for instance — I don't remember much about Minneapolis either.

By the time dinner was over,[41] it was growing dark. A thrilling

---

41. Something tells me it was the restaurant's opening night, because they'd forgotten to line up a dessert menu and the waiter, who was new to waiting, broke our wineglasses, then promised to bring new ones but forgot, which meant we quickly became new to waiting too. Other than that, nothing sticks in the mind. How *very* Minneapolis!

pink and orange sunset brought merciful release from the pizza-oven oppressiveness of summer, inducing an assortment of neighborhood kids to collect at the water's edge, strumming lazily on guitars and singing folk songs sotto voce.

To walk off the meal, Twerp and I took an easy stroll along the towpath, making innocent chitchat and dodging swarms of tiny bugs, the type that otherwise get sucked into your mouth and up your nose and remain there.

"So what exactly do you do for a living?" he asked.

Years ago I used to be embarrassed by what I did. I'd tell people I was a plumber. That way I would avoid the usual question: "And how long have you been visiting kooky museums?" and so prevent the SS *Self-Esteem* from running aground on the jagged rocks of personal humiliation. But it didn't work. In the end I was getting inundated with so many flush- and drainage-related inquiries that I had to give that up. So:

"I'm a travel reporter for public radio."

"My, but that's wonderful. I bet you fly everywhere first class and stay in the best hotels . . ."

"Hm."

"What's wrong? You don't like it?"

I get asked the "you don't like it?" question a lot. To anyone who may have chained his or her wagon to a fire hydrant, a career as a freelance radio journalist must seem attractive. And sure, it's good in spates. But the rootless slacker existence is not always a bed of roses. Sometimes it's even more depressing flying under society's radar than above it.

"I've been doing it ten years too long, that's all. I need a change. Right now I'm trying to get into TV."

"Oh? To do what?"

"Travel reporting, I guess. Anything. I haven't thought that far ahead."

Since the fall, when Terri the Witch had planted the idea of becoming a national celebrity in my brain, I'd been extending a few feelers, and, phrenology machines aside, who better to advise you on your next career move than a witch? So I had put in some calls. I spoke with a producer at Fox News who was enthusiastic at first, but then said she thought my body language was all wrong and I was too animated for TV. Then I tried an editor at CNN. He thought I was wrong too, though for a whole load of different reasons. But he invited me to go in anyway, as a guest on one of their afternoon debate shows, offering a Brit's-eye view on America.

"Perfect!" I cheered. "Exactly what I'm looking for."

Then he canceled at the last minute, saying there'd been some breaking news.

"The Pope's going to walk down a flight of stairs," he said, "and we have to cover it live in case he trips."

Damn!

Other than those two, and a few extra odds and ends that looked hopeful for about a millisecond then fizzled away to nothing, no openings had so far presented themselves. Therefore, stuck for a viable alternative, and for money also, I'd drifted back into radio again.

". . . but I haven't given up. I'm still out there looking."

"Good for you."

By now we were approaching the car and I realized as we crossed the parking lot that I'd droned on about my lousy career for so long that we hadn't talked about Twock or Twix or Twitch or his interests once. How incredibly selfish of me. (Maybe that's why I can't remember anything about him: I don't *know* anything about him.) But, being the generous, hospitable man he is, he didn't seem to mind, or even to be concentrating.

"Can I interest you in a quick sight-seeing trip around Minneapolis–St. Paul?" he said, changing the subject.

"A sight-seeing trip? Oh, er . . ."

It was getting late. The farm tour was scheduled for the next day, and since more than likely it would involve a spot of hay-baling, I wanted to be good and rested for that. However, it was obvious that Twap's offer was founded on a genuine desire to entertain a first-time visitor, and—as this was Minnesota—on having nothing better to do with his time, so . . .

"Sure. That'd be fun," I said, and ten minutes later, we were bouncing across town, crisscrossing first one of the twin cities, then the other, then, surprisingly, a third, with Twig providing a running commentary on what we were looking at, which, as far as I could tell, was very little, and me going "Oooh!" and "Oh, *really?*" and "My God, that's *sooooo* fascinating!"

Back at my hotel, we shook hands the way old friends who've just met for the first time do, telling each other what a *great* evening it had been, which it had, and promising to keep in touch. Maybe I could return later in the year, he said, and we'd go up to his lakeside cabin in Northern Minnesota together, how about that?

"Wow—thanks. That sounds excellent. Let's do it."

"Good. It's a date, then," he shouted as the car moved off.

"You bet!" I called after him.

"Stay in touch."

"I will."

"Bye."

"Bye. Thanks again."

And of course we've never spoken since. I am *sooo* L.A.

EXCELLENT NEWS REACHED ME FIRST THING next day: The farm tour was on! Yay!

John called from the Convention and Visitors Bureau to say a bus would pick me up after lunch and the whole thing would last about two hours.

The tour wasn't until the afternoon, though, which left me with the whole of Minnesota (the Nothing-to-Do-But-Visit-the-Mall-of-America State) at my disposal. So, rather than stay in my room, I took the hint and set off to explore the concrete leviathan across the road.

IF SHOPPING MALLS WERE CAKES, THE MALL of America would be a three-tier double-chocolate fudge with chocolate cream filling and chocolate icing. Oh, and chocolate sprinkles too. And extra chocolate wedged in wherever there's a space. And a fancy message on the top written in piped chocolate, saying, *"Jeez, have you seen the size of this frickin' place?"*

Nothing on its bland exterior offers even the tiniest clue to the spectacular goodies that await you inside: the seven-acre amusement park, the fourteen cinemas, the aquarium in the basement, the wedding chapel, the QVC broadcast studio, the stage for live performances, the university,[42] the restaurants, the nightclubs, and hundreds upon hundreds of stores, way too many to count (although I counted them and there are 520, which come to think of it isn't that many; I bet there's a mall in Japan with more). All the same, it swallows you whole. And once you're in its belly there's almost no reason to leave, except maybe to go home, and very soon even that will be redundant. You see, plans are under way to build condos right there on site, enabling the consumer of tomorrow to be born, educated, amused, entertained, grow fat and satiated, and die, all within spitting distance of a Banana Republic.

For the first few minutes I felt lost, cast adrift on an ocean of noise and glitter. I wandered up escalators and down again, marveling open-mouthed at the sheer razzle-dazzle of it all: the Ferris wheel, a stuff-your-own-teddy-bear emporium, a woman selling aphrodisiacs, a store specializing in cookies that can be eaten by dogs *and* their owners, a pool with a shark in it—it's overwhelming, and then some.

The only disturbing side to the Mall experience, I found, was meeting Minnesotans. Not that they're not nice or anything, because they are. It's just that . . . well, some of them are so . . . how can I put this tactfully?

So bloody *fat*, is what I'm trying to say.

There is no way of putting it tactfully.

To say Middle America is overweight is like saying Madonna's slightly well-known. Or Alf might be a puppet. In fact, the more you travel through the Midwest the more obese everyone seems

---

42. One can only imagine the excitement of walking into a job interview armed with a law degree from the University of the Mall of America. Nobody else need apply.

to be. Guts hang over belts, butts spill out of chairs, and 30 percent of them have a chin collection that could someday end up
behind glass in the Smithsonian. As a time zone it's two hours
ahead of Los Angeles; in health terms it's a hundred years behind.

Like one vast herd of life-size Gummi Bears, I watched folk
from all over the Midwest waddle around the Mall that day, insufferably fat parents trailing behind insufferably fat kids, with a mus-
tard-drenched hot dog in one hand and a fistful of shopping bags
in the other. Shocking. I think it's high time someone filmed it
and put it on The Discovery Channel.

And, naturally, they smoke (I hear there are parts of Minnesota where the smell of Camel Lights is considered a cologne),
and drive everywhere instead of walking, and drink ketchup
straight from the bottle,[43] and spend hours with their feet up in
front of the TV, gorging on chocolates and take-out pizza and
popcorn and cookies—in short, dedicating their lives to a deadly
regime of laziness, gluttony, and sedentary indulgence.

"It's time to wake up and smell the Slim-Fast, Minnesota," I
felt like shouting down the length of the Mall, "or I won't be
responsible for what happens to you."

But it's no use. They won't listen. And anyway, I'm not responsible for what happens to them, am I? So why are we even dis-
cussing it?

That aside, though, I had a great time that day, and wore
myself out.

But then, just as you're exhausted from being razzled and you
have a migraine from being dazzled, and you're thinking it can't
get any better than this, it does. It gets a *whoooole* lot better.
Because, dare to wander upstairs, if you can tear yourself away
from the stuff-your-own-teddy-bear emporium and the woman
selling aphrodisiacs, and you'll come across something quite
extraordinary, something I like to call General Mills' Cereal
Adventures.

---

43. Probably.

SO GREAT IS THIS ATTRACTION THAT, IF THE MALL burned to the ground, the GMCA would—assuming it escaped the blaze—still be a crowd-puller in its own right.

As far as I can tell, it's a theme-park/corporate brainwashing exercise aimed at showing kids how Cheerios, Wheaties, and a bunch of other General Mills products make it to the nation's breakfast table, stressing the good, wholesome cereal grain side of things while placing somewhat less emphasis on how much processed sugar they contain. The noise inside is deafening, the primary colors almost blinding. There are chutes to slide down, games to play, silos of wheat to wade through, large glass tubes filling and unfilling with cereals the whole time, and machines all around that gurgle and go *boing!* and *fzzzzzzz!* and *wheeeeeeee!!*

And best of all, it's educational. You learn so much along the way.

For instance, did you know that wheat grows in fields?

You did? Oh.

At some point also, you get the chance to meet Lucky the Leprechaun.

Now, because I'm a journalist, I'm not free to walk around these places and meet leprechauns by myself like an ordinary person might. Companies insist that I'm chaperoned at all times by a fully authorized PR officer, the way geriatrics are in clinics, in case something untoward happens and I cause a scene.

My chaperone that day was Lisa. But for once, and in contrast to the many other Lisas I'd encountered, this one was no corporate android yes-bunny. Far from it. She was fabulous; a wild-eyed, fun-lovin' twenty-first-century gal with a mind all of her own. And, although she took her chaperoning job seriously, she sure wasn't about to let work get in the way of a good time. When my tape recorder was on and I was interviewing her, her demeanor was demure, respectful, and proper; but the second I switched it off— *wham!* She'd hitch up her skirt so as not to trip over it and would be ready to rock 'n' roll.

Climbing a staircase to the second floor she stood before three cylindrical openings, each one the entrance to a different-colored kids' slide, and was truly stumped as to which one to choose. "Oh, I don't know, I don't know—how about we go with . . . PINK!"

And, with a little help from a uniformed attendant, away she went, arms flailing, skirt up, laughing madly.

More than once, I flopped down on a bench like a jaded parent, listening to her tortured squeals somewhere in the distance as she plunged headfirst down a long curly tube into a giant cereal bowl. That done, she'd return up the steps smiling and breathless, ready for another go. Or maybe not another go, maybe something else had caught her eye. "I know. Let's take a trip to the magical forest."

"Sure, why not?"

When we got there, the "magical forest" turned out to be a bunch of PVC cushions on sticks.

"It's just a bunch of PVC cushions on sticks," I said.

(One should never be afraid to state the obvious.)

"They're not PVC cushions, they're clovers. This is Lucky the Leprechaun's magical forest."

"And who the hell . . ." (Being foreign, I'm totally out of the loop, cereal-mascot-wise) " . . . is Lucky the Leprechaun?"

But by sheer good fortune—hey, let's call it luck—the answer to my question happened to be standing right outside the door.

L. C. Leprechaun has been the face of Lucky Charms marshmallow breakfast cereal for decades. On the box, Lucky is small and impish and looks like Jiminy Cricket with a hangover, whereas in real life, he's a man in a ridiculous green pixie outfit and a big plastic head who's paid to hug you and pretend he's pleased to see you, when in reality he can barely make out who you are through the holes in his costume. And of course, as always, he's been told he can't speak to anyone, which is the most infuriating thing of all. You'd think, just to help out the radio guy, they'd let him say *something*, even something muffled. But apparently it's written into Clause No. 1 of the Actors in Foam Costume

Rulebook: "Never help out the radio guy," so he just stays quiet and mimes.

As we loitered in Lucky's blind spot (which looked to be roughly 359 degrees around him), I let slip to Lisa about my long history of angry run-ins with mute costumed characters.

"Really?"

"I even got into a fight with an avocado once."

"*Really?* You're serious?"

Immediately, there was a change of plan and, seconds later, to prevent an incident, Lucky was spirited away through a staff entrance and, to the best of my knowledge, never reappeared.

Frankly, he doesn't know how lucky he was.

AS YOU'RE LEAVING THE PARK, FLAGGING WITH delight and with your ears still ringing from the machines that go *boinggggg!!* and *fzzzzzz!!* and *wheeeeeeee!!*, you get the treat of your life: a chance to have a real box of cereal made especially for you. Tiger Woods has done it, and Michael Jordan, and the Wright family from Michigan, so why not you?

First, you choose what kind of cereal you want and also the box design—I picked Wheaties—then an assistant comes along and takes your photo against a plain green backdrop. Altogether, I had twelve photos taken (in the first eleven my tongue was sticking out), and that's really all there is to it. A few minutes later, thanks to some hidden technology which I'm guessing is a damned sight more complicated than the Co-etherator *and* the Anti-Paralysis Electric Hairbrush put together, a cereal box drops from the ceiling with your picture on it.[44] This makes an excellent

---

44. I was very proud of my personalized box of Wheaties. It's rare that I take a good photo, but this one was a dazzler. General Mills should use it on all their Wheaties boxes—they'd become collectors items, I'm sure. When I got back to L.A., I took it into the studio to show everyone. "Wow, that's great!" they said. "You look quite handsome." (I used to be "fairly cute." Since turning forty, I'm now "quite handsome." Soon I'll look "pretty good for my age." Then I'll die.) Sadly, that same afternoon, while my back was turned, someone took the box and I've never seen it since. Damn! It's a hassle sometimes, being quite handsome. Everyone wants a piece of you.

keepsake to display prominently in your home as a reminder of the day you spent in General Mills' Cereal Adventures, trying to convince yourself that a bunch of PVC cushions on sticks was a forest.

OUT IN THE STREET AGAIN, BLOOMINGTON was a furnace. Beneath a vindictive midday sun I hurried back to the hotel, sheltering under the Wheaties box the whole way to prevent my hair catching fire. When I got up to my room, I took a quick shower, changed from one sweater into another just like it that was less damp with sweat, and emerged once again to find John waiting in his car, ready for the farm tour.

"Get in," he beamed.

"Why? I thought the tour bus left from the Mall."

"It does."

"Okay." And, a little confused, I sat back and let him drive me back to the Mall of America again, which as I've already said was located directly opposite the hotel.

Nine seconds later we arrived.

We could have walked it in eight.

As we pulled into the parking lot, the tour coach was preparing to move off.

Actually, that was the first surprise: we were going on a full-size bus and not the stifling little minivan I'd been expecting. Evidently I'm not the only city boy fascinated with working farms. About forty other people had paid ten bucks each to accompany us on our quest to find something utterly pointless to do on a long, hot Minnesotan afternoon.

"Hello, everybody!" As we rumbled out into bright sunlight, the guide at the front grabbed the mic. "Welcome to the tour. My name is Margaret Thatcher."

Across the aisle, John chuckled.

She comes out with it right up front, to get the cheap laughs out of the way. In fact, her name is really Margeet Thatcher, and she's Swedish. You know who she reminded me of actually? That relentlessly cheerful blonde who's always popping up on TV infomercials, frothing and foaming over fig dehydrators (I own one of these) or vacuum-packing devices (two of these) or those special extendable rods with a sponge on the end to help small people paint their own ceilings. (I'm 6 feet tall, but hey, who can resist?) Well, Margeet has a similar knack. She managed to sell me something I wasn't the least bit interested in—Minnesota— but in such a slick, clever, bouncy way that I didn't even realize I wasn't interested until long after it was over.

"Welcome to our tour this afternoon of Minneapolis–St. Paul," she frothed, as if the Twin Cities were just one enormous fig dehydrator, before going on to alert us to the numerous heady delights to come, including a visit to the Minne-Ha-Ha Falls.

By now we were heading at speed in the direction of Minneapolis, which got its name, Margeet said, after early settlers discovered the St. Anthony Falls in 1680. *Minne* being a Dakotah Indian word, meaning "of the waters." And *polis* being Greek for "city."

Oh really? How interesting.

Just then the high-rises of the downtown area slid into view, and as they did so something stirred inside of me. A strange uneasy feeling not dissimilar to the strange uneasy feeling I'd had the day before in the car. "Welcome to our tour this afternoon of Minneapolis–St. Paul." Isn't that what she'd said?

"Oh my God!" I grabbed John's arm. "We're on the wrong bus!"

He turned and looked at me as if I was insane. "No, it's the right bus."

"But this is a city tour. We want the farm tour."

"Farm tour? What farm tour? What is this farm tour you keep talking about?"

Uh-oh!

Just as I'd expected all along, a terrible, *terrible* mistake had been made.

When the Bloomington Convention and Visitors Bureau had invited me to come to Minnesota for a farm tour, apparently they hadn't meant a farm tour at all. There was a typo on the fax. What they were offering was a *fam tour,* fam being short for familiarization. It's one of those new tourism industry *buzzwords* (I'm making funny little rabbit-ears in the air with my fingers to indicate quotes), and relates to a free bus ride around the city tailored to the needs of journalists, giving them a quick, all-over view of what the place has to offer. Frankly, though, even if the city has nothing at all to offer and it's as barren as the surface of Mars, that's unlikely to stop them; a tour will be organized anyway, and that tour will be fam.

But here's the rub. The Minneapolis–St. Paul fam tour was a moment by moment, monument by monument, repeat of the same journey I'd made the night before with Twee or Twoo or Twipp. Over two arduous hours, we took in the sixty overhead skyways that enable Minneapolites to scurry like rats between buildings in winter without having their lips freeze to their teeth; the statues of Snoopy, the parks, the cathedral, Betty Crocker's birthplace (1921), the intersection where Mary Tyler Moore once threw her hat in the air on the credits of the *Mary Tyler Moore Show* (1970) . . . and on and on and on. It was like sitting through every episode of *Roots* twice in the same day.

However, as I said before, Margeet has this strange knack for making the tedious come alive. Somehow she sucked me in with her perky commentary about local industry, weather, sports teams, and also agriculture, including the news that a hundred years ago at least forty kinds of apple were grown in this area.

"Oh *really?* How interesting."

Along the way we took a couple of rest stops, to allow older folk to go pee and everyone else to take photos. Standing on a bridge overlooking the Minne-Ha-Ha Falls—a rush of rapids that, on the scale of impressive water spectacles, ranks just above garden hose—I grabbed the opportunity to corner Margeet and quiz her about her years at the forefront of British politics, and in particular about her reasons for closing Britain's coal mines and breaking the back of the print unions in the '80s.

The reaction was not good. The look on her face said, "That's not funny, now please step aside," thereby confirming what I'd feared all along: that she was indeed just a Swedish tour guide, and had never been prime minister of Great Britain at all, not even once.

Before stepping aside, however, I went on to challenge her theory about the derivation of the name Minneapolis. It was not, I suggested, a fusion of the Indian word *Minne*, meaning "of the waters," and *polis*, the Greek for "city." Rather, it had come about as follows: One hundred and thirty years or so ago, an enterprising apple farmer from hereabouts was negotiating with the Dakotah Indians, hoping to sell them large quantities of his crop. "Hm, I wonder," he asked himself, "what the Indian word for "many apples" is?" And from that day on, the name stuck, eventually becoming linked with its glowering neighbor across the Mississippi which had suffered a similar fate. And together they came to be known as the twin cities of Manyapplesis–St. Apple.

The rest, I need hardly add, is history.

Without saying a word, John turned around and walked away, leaving Margeet to take over the job of staring at me like I was insane. Insisting quietly that her version was most definitely the correct one, she extricated herself with great dignity from the conversation, the way only a true career-politician can, and strode off in the direction of the coach to speak to someone less annoying.

IT HAD BEEN A DAY OF HIGHS AND LOWS. On the way back to the hotel, I talked gravely to John, telling him how disappointed I was that there'd been no farm tour. He was genuinely apologetic. It was a typo; it could happen to anyone.

"I'm sorry to let you down."

"It isn't only a letdown for me," I said, with my head out of the window. "The show's spent all this money to bring me here and I don't have a report to take back. Everyone will be angry with me. Jim the producer will be angry with me. The head of the company will be angry with me. It's going to look so bad. They may even ask me to refund the cost of the flight and the hotel, and I can't afford that. What am I going to do?"

Panicking, I pulled my head back in the car and stared at him. There had to be a last-minute way of making this farm tour happen. Even a trip to the Gibbs Farm Museum would be okay. There's always a way.

"What d'you say, John? Is there?"

"Hm." Something could have been arranged, he said. Given more time. But with my flight booked for tomorrow there was nothing he could do. Not now.

Then, taking his eyes off the road for a moment, he turned his face toward me, looking genuinely, deeply apologetic, and added in a doleful voice: "You will remember to say that the Mall of America is in Bloomington, won't you? Not Minneapolis."

10

If It's a Cow, It's Not Free

*The American obsession with weather forecasting ◆ Diana Ross causes
me to miss a meal ◆ crutches: really, who can say no? ◆ a brief history
of mental illness (concentrating on the fun parts) ◆ the Glore
Psychiatric Museum ◆ how the Victorians treated their shop-window
mannequins ◆ patients are a virtue ◆ all alone in Kansas ◆ another
brief history, this time of barbed wire ◆ the Kansas BWM*

I WANT TO SAY SOMETHING ABOUT WEATHER FORECASTS.
Recently, Channel 7 in Los Angeles made a huge splash
about some incredible new radar technology it had just
installed in its news studio: Live Doppler 7000—the very
latest, up-to-datest, outer spacest rainfall-tracking system known to
mankind.

It's bad weather's worst nightmare, a meteorological sniffer-
dog so new, so cutting edge that it makes licking your finger and
holding it up in the wind seem positively primitive by comparison. That's as I write. By the time you pick up this book, Live
Doppler 7000 may be history, replaced by the much-vaunted Live
Doppler 8000, which I have no doubt will be the fanciest, advan-
ciest, nothing-left-to-chanciest innovation of all time, capable not
only of tracking rain, but of actually making it. *That's* how sophis-
ticated this crap's going to get very soon. And so impressed is
everyone by the software and the flashy graphics that the question
"Are you absolutely sure we need Live Doppler 7000, since we
hardly get any rain in Los Angeles and it's sunny most of the
year?" doesn't even get asked.

Weather forecasting has become an obsession across America.

In the Midwest particularly it ranks higher than "What's for supper?" as *the* hot topic on everyone's lips. And you can see why. I mean, if you're an arable farmer in Oklahoma and there's a chance of a fine drizzle by late evening—well, so what? You could probably care less. But if a freak storm system is heading straight for you, you *definitely* want to know about that.

That's why weather forecasts are vital. Given ample warning, you can take steps to minimize damage. You'll have time to round up the chickens, tie down your vegetables with string to stop the rain washing all your crops away (most of my farming knowledge is derived from the song "Patches," so it's a little limited, I'm afraid, but I assume that this is what happens), and pack your family safely indoors with paper bags over their heads, ready for when the tornado hits.

The reason I mention all of this, in case you were wondering what the hell I'm rambling on about, is because on my first night in Missouri we were beset by a thunderstorm of near-Biblical magnitude. For three solid hours, fork lightning convulsed operatically about the heavens. Coiling twigs of fire skewered the horizon every fifteen seconds, uniting earth and sky in a high-voltage blue blaze, followed each time by a roll of earsplitting bangs violent enough to rattle windows and doors and send normally laid-back rural types, the kind of guys who wouldn't break into a run if their crotch was spitting flames, sprinting for cover. Finally, on the back of a tumultuous driving wind, squalls of warm summer rain rushed in to dance with the trees, lashing the cornfields for miles around amid a *son et lumière* display so precocious, so utterly majestic and bestial, that, quite frankly, even Jerry Bruckheimer would be agog. All of which—and here's where we get to the point finally—had been predicted hours before and with eerie accuracy by the local weatherman.

But of course who knew?

Thinking it was just a huge exaggeration, a ruse, a ploy, to get viewers interested, I chose to ignore everything he said. I even saw the little dark cloud symbol that drifts across TV screens in the Midwest ahead of any meteorological cataclysm, and thought, "Huh, yeah, right—there you go again, scamming us with your fancy talk of gale-force winds and tying vegetables down. Well, I'm not one of your back-road hicks, mister. You're fooling with the wrong guy here!" And, smiling smugly to myself, I grabbed the remote and flicked over to a *Rugrats* marathon on Nickelodeon, perfectly contented. That is, until the time came for me to leave the hotel and go get something to eat, and I found I couldn't.

"God's on the rampage," the concierge told me, saucer-eyed.

It's a long story, but apparently around midafternoon the Lord had gotten testy, and like some vast cosmic Diana Ross, started making loud noises and throwing things. It was quite frightening at times. The result being that I was forced to spend the rest of the evening locked up in my room listening to shutters bang and trees fall down, cursing myself for ignoring the warnings on TV.

BY THE FOLLOWING DAY, TO MY RELIEF, BUT also to the relief of the concierge who overnight, by all accounts, had started building an ark, Tropical Storm Diana Ross grew weary of tormenting us and moved on. Now the sky was a deep spiritual blue, the air crisply energizing, and you could see for tens of miles across open country.

Relieved that my trip wouldn't be interrupted after all, I began drawing up travel plans over breakfast. This time, for once, my assignment was a bit lacking in focus. Canter briskly through Missouri, I'd been told. Noodle your way from St. Joseph down to Branson, stopping off at points of interest along the way.

Now, I guess to some, this measure of personal freedom must sound like heaven. Go anywhere, do anything, take your time, don't hurry back. But not to me. I'm hopeless at choosing points of interest. Hard to say why that is. Unless it's because very few things interest me at all. Come to think of it, yes, that's probably why.

For once, though, I was blessed. After breakfast that first morning, the perfect starting point was laid at my feet by one of the waitresses in the hotel dining room, who told me of a fascinating psychiatric hospital just north of where we were that came with a museum attached, and very possibly a gift shop.

"Hm, a psychiatric hospital . . ."

"*And* it has a collection of crutches," she tagged on with great excitement.

"Hm, crutches . . ."

I tried to suppress my enthusiasm, but couldn't. There was something about a psychiatric museum, maybe its capacity for boring the ass off me, that made it irresistible. So with little more than that to go on, I rented a car[45] and sped away in the direction of St. Joseph, Missouri, happy at the thought of spending several happy hours among the mentally ill.

THE STIGMA ATTACHED TO MENTAL ILLNESS is not what it was. Nowadays, it's considered quite chic to be out of your mind, but back in 1874 they would lock you up for it. *Forever.* It was like the medical equivalent of subscribing to the *Reader's Digest.*

Just east of St. Joseph town center stands one of the finest nuthouses in the country, although perhaps in this age of political correctness we shouldn't call it that. Instead, let's refer to it by its official name: State Lunatic Asylum No. 2.

Or "The Booby Hatch" for short.

"This hospital used to be a dead end," Scott the curator told me as we walked around. "If you dropped someone off at our front door, we'd say, 'Bring them in the clothes you want them buried in.' We have a cemetery on the grounds with 1,753 graves in it. A lot of people did not leave here."

Gulp!

But that's how things were back then.

From the very first day it opened, State Lunatic Asylum No. 2 was a hit.

---

45. How simple those four little words, "I rented a car," make it sound. In actual fact, it took me hours to pluck up the courage to do it, and hours more to fill in the paperwork. When I walked in, the man behind the desk at the rental company stared me up and down in apparent disbelief, as if to say, "*You?* Drive a car?" and, even after the deal was done, seemed most reluctant to hand over the keys. I was quite hurt.

To begin with, the hospital had 275 beds. These filled almost immediately.

So 120 more beds were added. These filled almost immediately.

So they added 350 extra beds, making 745. These filled almost immediately.

So they added even more beds. These filled almost immediately.

Seemed like everyone for miles around wanted in on the crazy-relative craze and began dumping their loved ones at the asylum with the same nonchalance you or I might deposit a sack of soiled underwear at Goodwill. In consequence, the place kept right on expanding, until, by the 1950s, the hospital offered multiple facilities on four floors—qualifying it as a full-blown insaniplex—with a staggering 3,500 beds.

And d'you know what happened to those 3,500 beds?

Yup, they filled almost immediately!

Fast-forwarding to 1967 now, here's where George Glore enters the picture. A bright, enterprising man with a gift for building dioramas—always a plus if you're thinking of opening a museum—George was a forty-one-year veteran of the Missouri mental health system, though not as a loony, more on the admin side. Over the course of his career he'd managed to accumulate an attic-full of vintage psychiatric instruments and fascinating historic artifacts, the kind of stuff that causes experts on the *Antiques Roadshow* to go, "Oh my!" and "This was part of a pair; d'you have the other one?" and "The last time I saw something like this, it was in a psychiatric museum."

"How great would it be," old Georgie thought to himself, "if I put all this junk on display for everyone to see? We could have life-size sets and dioramas and *everything!*"

Which is how the Glore Psychiatric Museum came about.

At first the collection was housed in what had once been the old medical wing of the facility. Glore bought a number of shop-window mannequins to stand in for doctors and patients, then filled each room with authentic period psychiatric memorabilia,

everything from full-size sixteenth- and seventeenth-century treatment devices to surgical instruments and—yes, the waitress at the
hotel was right—a collection of crutches that must be the envy of
crutch-collectors everywhere.

They're on a rack.

Together.

Lots of them.

And . . . well, that's all I have to say about crutches.

TREATMENTS IN VICTORIAN TIMES WERE HIDEOUSLY
brutal. For a start, there seemed to be a bizarre consensus among
medical professionals of the day that if you locked a crazy person
in a dark cabinet for long enough, then he was bound to see the
error of his ways, give up on this silly madness thing, and take up
a different hobby.

I can certainly see how that might work. But sadly, it didn't.

Any patient who insisted on remaining nutty after Stage I of
the treatment would then move on to Stage II, which might
include one or more of the following: being straitjacketed, abused,
assaulted, probed, beaten,[46] cut open, pressed as a witch, half-
drowned in a freezing cold bath, lobotomized, lobectomized,
bled with a razor, made to stand in his own excrement for days, or
even—and this was their pièce de résistance—being placed on a
swing and revolved at 90 mph, the theory being that if rapid spinning takes the water out of lettuce then *surely* it must remove
insanity from a human being.

Duh!

To digress for a moment, if you're interested in seeing other
examples of medical barbarism and you're planning a trip to

46. The Victorians were great believers in remedial violence. There was no ailment,
disease, injury, or affliction that in their view couldn't be reversed by clouting the
patient thirty or forty times with the back of your hand. It's precisely because of this
that I don't trust doctors. Who's to say that, in a hundred years' time, we won't be
wetting our pants with laughter at today's medical practices—the very notion that a
broken leg can be fixed by putting it in a plaster cast, or that long-term care and
attention from qualified professionals can help nurse a patient back to full health. In
fact, it's sounding more and more ludicrous even as I write it!

Baltimore any time soon, allow me to recommend the urology[47] exhibition in the William P. Didusch Museum at the American Urological Association, a place that goes out of its way to make diseases of the female urinary tract and the male reproductive organ seem enthralling. To that end—and it's really only "that end" they're interested in—it has collected together more catheters, rotating rectoscopes, transurethral prostatic surgical devices, gallstone removers, cystoscopes, and techniques for combating bladder tumors than you ever had nightmares about, along with a wide and captivating range of sharp, pointy instruments designed specifically for rapid insertion up the human ass.[48]

The Glore Psychiatric Museum, by contrast, is nowhere near as unsettling.

Mostly it involves walking between a sequence of small rooms and looking in on shop-window-mannequin patients as they're being cured of their disease by shop-window-mannequin psychiatrists. The faux patients are made to sit in sweat cabinets, lie in metal crates, and stand in horribly cramped vertical coffins, dutifully acting out the most advanced treatments of their day.

By the way, I'm not entirely sure where Glore got his dummies. My guess would be a close-out sale at Saks Fifth Avenue. There's just something about their chichi, coiffeured demeanor, their suavity if you will, that puts them so hilariously at odds with the peril they're in. For instance, it's not uncommon for a mannequin to be smiling enigmatically, the way she might if, say, she were modeling Versace evening wear, while at the same time struggling to escape a straitjacket. And the fact that in their witch-

---

47. Many people confuse urology with astrology. The main difference between them, as far as I can tell, is that Urology doesn't predict the future and Astrology won't help you pass a kidney stone. Otherwise they're identical.

48. And if this doesn't cause your spirit to wither, then uncross your legs and hop on a train to Philadelphia, where you'll find the educational but gruesome Mütter Museum, an institution preoccupied with human abnormalities to an almost unnatural degree. Among other things, they have two floors of brightly lit display cabinets packed with objects so gross you can only look at them through your fingers, including enough tumorous facial growths, bubbling syphilitic hands, and other terrifying deformities to make you wish you'd stayed in Baltimore!

craft diorama the shop-window mannequin witch who's about to be burned at the stake looks like she's largely indifferent to her fate and can't wait to go to Hell made me want to leap over the velvet rope and light the fire myself.

All in all, it's quite an experience, and one I shall never forget. Yet, as we neared the end of the tour, quite inexplicably I became listless. My interest in dummies demonstrating mental health treatments was starting to wane. And I guess Scott picked up on this because suddenly his face lit up and he turned all mysterious.

"Come with me," he said. "There's something I want you to see."

Oooh!

IN RECENT YEARS, THE HOSPITAL COMPLEX has been split into three.

First, there's the museum end of things, which we've done to death, I feel.

Then comes the Psychiatric Rehabilitation Center.[49] And my, how things have changed. Treatment of the insane has altered radically in recent years, moving away from the bludgeoning and harassing methods of a century ago, toward the less-likely-to-kill-them approach of rehabilitation and light vocational training, which is where the profession is at today. Gone are the oppressive sardine conditions of the 1950s when 3,500 inmates roamed these corridors. Now the place is more comfortable and better furnished than 80 percent of the hotels I get to stay in, and the number of patients is down to a more manageable 108. Furthermore, if things ever got tight in the future, I'm sure they could always start admitting mannequins again. They're far less trouble than real people, and, should beds be in short supply, won't complain if you stack them in a cupboard.

The third part of the complex stands behind a tall, intimidating perimeter fence. This is the psychiatric prison, which is

---

49. If you decide to go visit, be sure to take a member of staff with you. For some reason they don't like tourists mingling freely with the patients.

like a huge brick humidor used to preserve criminals that society has judged to be maniacs, the ones you can't trust to go to McDonald's for a burger because you just know that the moment your back's turned they're going to start massacring people. The real crazies, in other words.

"This way." Grabbing a large bunch of keys, Scott led me to an abandoned underground tunnel that connects the prison to the hospital.

Booooooooooooooooooom–oooooom–oooooooom!!!!!

With a startling alcatrazian clang, the closing of the door reverberated along the passageway, a spookily dark concrete artery speckled with puddles, leading eventually to a metal gate. Beyond the gate was the prison. Approach it, Scott promised, and armed guards would appear out of nowhere and . . . uh, well, I have no idea what they'd do then. Wave their guns theatrically probably, and order us in stern voices to return to the hospital.

Our footsteps chimed like buckets in a gale and every whisper was multiplied a thousand times over in echo, becoming a chorus of phantom voices that boomeranged back and forth about our heads.

"Hello!"

Ello-ello-ello-ello-ello-ello-ello-ello-ello-ello-ello . . .

"Ping!"

Ing-ing-ing-ing-ing-ing-ing-ing-ing-ing-ing . . .

"In the old days," Scott said, stopping halfway along, "this is where patients would come to have sex."

Ex-ex-ex-ex-ex-ex-ex-ex-ex-ex-ex . . .

He pointed to a recess in the graffiti-covered walls, a space barely large enough for one, much less two groaning bodies to writhe around in. It was certainly not ideal, by any means. On the other hand, I bet you've done it in worst places. I know I have.

"THE . . ." Not sure why, but I started to sing.

The-er-er-er-er-er-er-er-er-er-er . . .

". . . SUN'LL COME OUT TOMORROW. BET YOUR BOTTOM DOLLAR THAT TOMORROW . . ."

. . . row-row-row-row-row-row-row-row . . .

My words galloped like music-horses into the darkness. Who knew that insane asylums could be so much fun? I even wondered if I shouldn't take up singing show-tunes to prison inmates as a sideline.[50]

". . . THERE'LL BE SUN!"

. . . un-nun-nun-nun-nun-nun . . .

Scott made a move to go, signaling the end of my tour. Any minute now, he said, Security would come running.

Well? So what? I've never had much respect for authority figures waving guns. Sure, they *look* intimidating, but circumstances would have to be pretty extreme before they'd actually fire at you. Shoot an innocent civilian in cold blood, especially for singing songs from *Annie*, and the legal consequences could be truly epic, possibly leading to an extended stay in the very institution they're being paid to protect. Fear of the irony in this situation alone would, I suspect, be enough to neuter their enthusiasm.

Even so, rather than provoke a spat, I said goodbye to Scott and left the building, taking my buoyant mood and my lusty Broadway vocals with me.

MY NEXT STOP AFTER ST. JOSEPH was a town called Carthage, Missouri.

No, hold on. That's not true.

MY *IMMEDIATE* NEXT STOP AFTER ST. JOSEPH was a town called LaCrosse, Kansas.

Some bright spark at the studio—I forget who exactly, but let's call him Jim—while flicking through a guide to Midwestern towns, had hit on this place, LaCrosse.

---

50. When they come to make the movie, Dame Judi will love playing the insane asylum subterranean tunnel scene. It's so lighthearted. On the soundtrack, alongside the half-dozen hip-hop songs that seem to make it onto virtually every tie-in album, I'm hoping she and I will get to duet on an *Annie* medley. (Is it too much to hope that legendary filmmaker Dugout Sodhouse will step up to the plate and direct this little gem? Fingers crossed.) Actually, I met Dame Judi briefly at an Academy Awards party in Beverly Hills a couple of years ago and took the opportunity then to suggest the idea of a duet. But she walked right past me. Perhaps she didn't hear.

"It's a blast," he said. "They have a barbed wire museum filled with thousands of strips of barbed wire."[51] Plus, there were dioramas—*dioramas*, mind—documenting early barbed wire use. Already my pulse is racing; how about yours? Plus a theater showing videos of farmers talking about barbed wire, plus a Barbed Wire Hall of Fame, plus a research library charting the turbulent history of this revolutionary flesh-snagging product as it went about "transforming the open prairie into America's Bread Basket."

"Plus they have an array of antique fencing tools!"

"Is that right?"

Strangely, given all of that, the Begotokomugubu didn't care. Not even remotely. And remember, you're dealing with a guy here who'll stoop to almost any level of idiocy for a quick thrill. But barbed wire? Could there be a duller subject? Given a choice between visiting a barbed wire museum and gashing my throat with a rusty razor blade, I'd be dead within seconds.

But the sorry truth is that, on my noodling trip through Missouri picking out points of interest, the only point of interest I'd picked out so far was a psychiatric museum with a quite exemplary crutch collection, and I was starting to panic.

So, early next morning, under a flawless blue sky, I loaded up the car and headed due west across state lines, shooting for some far-distant horizon, until the combined high-rises of Kansas City were no more than a sparkling glass nipple in my rear-view mirror, before finally sliding away altogether.

For the next several hours, the wheels of my top-of-the-range beige Camry rolled across the open prairie like four quarters over a tabletop. Windows down. Cher's Greatest Hits blasting from the radio . . .

---

51. I know what you're thinking. "Hell, why didn't I come up with that? Snip a coil of barbed wire into a thousand small pieces, mount them in a display case, and charge folk to see 'em. I'd make a fortune." Well, sorry, bud, it's not that easy. They have a thousand *different* kinds of barbed wire, that's the secret (though admittedly they do look identical).

"If ahhh could turn back tahhh-ahhhme, I'd give it all too-oo-yoo-oo . . ."

I'd traveled all over the United States these past few years, but amazingly this was my very first excursion into America's Bread Basket, and I was shocked to find how empty it was. You'd think there'd be bread at least. But there was nothing. No bread, no people, no cycle cops, no signs of civilization for mile after empty mile, just cornfields and grassland and road signs pointing to Wichita and Tulsa, and other places Glen Campbell's always singing about, but which you don't really believe exist. And when you find that they do exist, you wonder why the hell anyone would write songs about them.

If you've ever flown from Los Angeles to New York and thought "Why does it take five hours to get there?" here's why. You have to traverse an immense wide-open vista of roasting hot wilderness called Kansas, where the molten road shimmers dreamily the way it does in car commercials, and on a still, clear night every star in the known universe seems to be blinking at you out of a moonless sky. This is in stark contrast to the night sky over Los Angeles, incidentally, where, if you look really, really hard, you might see eight.

Which, by sheer coincidence, also happens to be the total population of Kansas.

Many times that day, mine was the only vehicle on the highway. There was nothing ahead of me and nothing behind. I even drove on the left-hand side a couple of times to break the monotony; although I'm sure, if you were minded to, you could zigzag; or stop, get out and do somersaults; or even enjoy a four-course picnic with friends at the first intersection that catches your eye—and nothing at all would hit you.[52]

"Do you belie-heeeve in laaaaahfe aaahhfter luurr-urrrve . . . ?"

---

52. Having said that, if you try any of these things and something *does* hit you—even if it's a police citation for blocking a major highway and nearly getting yourself killed—I don't want to hear about it, okay? You're on your own.

Despite all the drawbacks, I took to Kansas (the State-With-Nothing-To-Recommend-It State) very quickly. Solitude is chloroform for the nerves, and by the time I reached the small, rural township of LaCrosse, which after five hours of blissful tranquility felt like a teeming metropolis, I was calm and rested and ready for barbed wire.

Oh yes. Very ready indeed.

STEPPING INSIDE . . .

". . . just like Jesse Ja-ames . . ."

No, the radio was off by this point. But stepping inside, I asked to speak to Ruby, the curator. Nice woman. Good fun. We'd enjoyed a brief phone conversation the week before, during which she'd offered to show me around the museum personally.

"So where is she?" I asked one of the staff.

"She's gone to her weekly bridge class."

"But she promised she'd be here!"

"Well, I'm sorry."

"But she *should* be here. I'm radio!"

"There's nothing I can do."

Hm. (Memo to self: Never use that "I'm radio" line again.)

Clearly, it was a lost cause. Then again, one glance at the exhibits told me her services were entirely unnecessary, barbed wire being, as it turns out, a very straightforward subject indeed.

JOSEPH F. GLIDDEN OF DEKALB, ILLINOIS, patented the very first barbed wire product in 1874, after being struck by a revelation: that if you put a wire fence around a field, cattle are unable to climb over it.

He also discovered that, if you go one step further and put sharp spikes on that fence, not only will the cattle not try to climb over it—not even the more agile ones, using crampons and pulleys—but if they try, they'll be taught a very painful lesson. Cows are made of leather; spikes are made of metal. It's a no-brainer.

"That'll tame 'em," Glidden said as he hammered the last of his wooden stakes into the ground. And he was right. Not only are cows poor climbers, but it turns out they also lack even the most rudimentary tunneling skills. So their fate was sealed. From this point on, never again would cattle and bison wander freely across the plains.

But this is America. Nothing resembling progress can ever take place without a fight, a public demonstration, a petition being signed, months of vitriolic mudslinging, or someone filing suit against someone else. It's such a waste of energy, but they never learn. Some trail-drivers, particularly those cheap bastards who'd grazed their animals for free up to now, even went so far as to go around cutting the fences under cover of darkness. But they were too late. As well as being hostile to change, Americans, paradoxically, also love anything new and glamorous; and barbed wire, or Beelzebub's Floss, as it was popularly known, caught on fast.

In the ensuing years, ranchers continued cordoning off large sections of the prairie, putting up fences faster than the fence-cutters could cut them down again, until, over time, the protesters grew weary of fighting and even the most strong-willed, rebellious cows became lazy, eventually resigning themselves to being on a prairie with roaming restrictions and, later, on a plate with fries and ketchup.

And that, in essence, is the tale told by the Kansas Barbed Wire Museum, only in their case they take an entire shed to do it in. Frankly, a small leaflet would have done just as well. I'm willing to take it on trust that there are over two thousand different varieties of barbed wire in existence; there's no need to go ahead and actually show them to me.

Thankfully, the whole experience was a short one, which is good because I almost dozed off standing up at one point. But hey, that's just me. You might be different. You might find rows and rows of glass display cases filled with short strips of metal absolutely riveting. If so, you'll also, I have no doubt, be entranced by the barbed-wire-twisting equipment (caution: the squeaking of the handle is so piercing it could make your ears bleed), and if that's the case then I'm sure you won't be able to tear yourself away from the Barbed Wire Hall of Fame or their comprehensive display of nineteenth-century antiseptic ointments.

I, on the other hand, am not ashamed to announce that I couldn't get out of there fast enough.

11

The Place Where Jesus Explodes

*Why I know nothing about Carthage, Missouri, and will continue
to do so* ◆ *"You've got hate mail"* ◆ *Samuel J. Butcher receives news
from the Lord* ◆ *the Precious Moments Chapel* ◆ *return of the actor in
foam costume* ◆ *the miracle of the singing bushes* ◆ *the world's largest
ball of twine* ◆ *a brief and not entirely accurate history of Branson,
Missouri* ◆ *Jennifer gets a national interview*

MY NEXT STOP AFTER ST. JOSEPH, AND THE minor detour to LaCrosse, was Carthage, Missouri. What's nice about Missouri, I discovered while motoring through it one muggy afternoon, is that it manages to be quaintly historical in parts—many key skirmishes of the Civil War were fought here, for instance—yet it doesn't ram the past down your throat with a clenched fist, the way some places do. (Salem comes to mind at this point.) Consequently I was able to drive into Carthage, stop, get out and walk around, dive into a supermarket to buy a Diet Coke and a bag of Doritos, then get back in the car and drive out of Carthage again, without ever finding out what important events had happened there, or when, or for what reason. It was very refreshing.

By this stage, you're in the Ozark Mountains, a heavily forested tongue of highland extending from St. Louis down to the Arkansas River. A beautiful part of the country it is, too— Missouri: the Very-Green-and-Surprisingly-Laid-Back-About-Its-History State—an undulating landscape of twisty lanes skirted by lush parkland.

The local people around these parts are absolutely charming, I found, and couldn't have been more pleasant to me as I traveled through. They're so friendly to visitors, in fact, that they make Bostonites seem gruff, rude, aloof, and miserable by comparison. Full marks for your sunny welcome, Missourilinos! I appreciate it.

Bearing all of this in mind, then, why is it, d'you think, that after I got back to L.A. and broadcast my report about the Precious Moments Chapel on the show (see below) that I received so much hate mail from this part of the world? More bloody hate mail than I've received about anything I've ever done in my life. They disliked the tone of the piece, they despised the fact that I appeared to be mocking Precious Moments . . .

"Mr. Peters, you are a disgusting human being. . . ."

"Mr. Peters, creatures like you shouldn't be walking the earth. . . ."

"You should be ashamed of yourself for saying such awful things. . . ."

. . . it was quite disturbing, though thankfully the authors did me a favor and stopped short of threatening to kill me, which I always look on as a plus. Thanks again, Missourilinos![53] And it went on for weeks. Every time I checked my e-mail, my inbox would be stuffed with them. So much so that, in the end, it became suspicious. This had to be an orchestrated campaign. *Had to be.* I mean, who gets this angry over a stupid radio report? And more especially over a stupid radio report about a museum full of saccharine, droopy-eyed dolls?

Well, although I didn't know it at the time, the clues to this mystery were right there all along, inside the museum full of saccharine, droopy-eyed dolls itself.

FOR ANYONE UNFAMILIAR WITH PRECIOUS MOMENTS, let me fill you in:

    a. They're cute porcelain kids wearing cute porcelain
       Victorian outfits, standing or sitting (which somehow

---

53. It's a matter of great pride that I have only received a total of ten death threats during my entire career, and guess where they came from. Boston! Surprise, surprise.

they also manage to do cutely) in cute porcelain settings. Keyword: CUTE.

b. They have oversize heads and about-to-cry eyes.

c. God advised on the design.

For years, artist Samuel J. Butcher would sketch these endearing balloon-headed figures for the amusement of family and
friends in Grand Rapids, Michigan.

"Wow, aren't they *darling?*" everyone would say. "You should
sell these commercially."

Of course, a lot of the time you can't trust family and friends
on anything. I struggled to master the piano for nine years—
nine dispiriting, key-pounding, knuckle-grinding years—after
family and friends convinced me I was a prodigy, when in truth
I am as adept at playing a musical instrument as I am at time
travel.

However, luckily for Sam Butcher, his folks were right on the
money, and in 1974 he set up a small business marketing greeting
cards bearing his scrumptious little characters. Then, five years
later, along came the mighty Enesco Corporation, offering to turn
his artwork into porcelain bisque figurines, which by now he'd
called Precious Moments ("because they spread love, caring, and
sharing in everyday situations"), and lo, these began selling by the
truckload, and an impregnable brand was born.

But that's not the end of the story—though I'm sure you were
hoping.

Then—oh boy, Sam Butcher hit on the best idea of all.

One day in 1989, he was divinely inspired to purchase a stretch
of rolling farmland in the Ozarks and build a theme park on it.

No, let me correct that.

Although it's a park and it has a theme, it's not a theme park.
The two Precious Moments PR women I spoke to—Lisa and
Lisa—were quick to assure me of this. It's more of a landscaped
devotional offering: a gift to the Lord, aimed at glorifying the Lord
and, I guess, at impressing the Lord, in case the Lord should drop
in for a look-see.

Now, obviously, putting together an elaborate three-thousand-acre park is an immense undertaking which takes a long while. So for the sake of kick-starting this story, because there's nothing magical or fun about construction work, let's pretend Sam completed it single-handedly in a weekend, and pick it up from there.

By the time he was finished four days later (let's also pretend it was the Memorial Day weekend), he'd built a chapel, a wedding island, a Resurrection cave, a musical dancing fountain, another chapel, singing flowerbeds, a lake, and numerous sculptures. Finally, the Lord, who I'm guessing was in a state of shock by this point that anyone would go to all this trouble just for Him — I know I would be — must have given him one last piece of inspiration: charge tourists to see parts of it.

So that's what he did, and lo (again), his Bible-themed non-theme-park was a smash. People came in droves. Others came in a coach. Very soon a million awestruck visitors a year were trekking through the place, and yet again the brilliant Sam Butcher had another success on his hands.

Praise Jesus. Yay!

EVERYTHING BEGINS IN THE VISITOR CENTER, a crescent of indoor gift shops. I'm guessing a team of elves came up with the initial concept, because the design is very fairy-tale retro: Toyland circa 1840. This is where the Three Little Pigs might go to buy gifts, for instance, or to pick up ideas for a house that won't blow down. It's also where you get your first glimpse of the Precious Moments themselves: There are drawings of Precious Moments, Animatronic Precious Moments, welcome videos narrated by Precious Moments, and even a full-size Precious Moment wandering around waving at people. But don't be scared, it's just another of those actors in costume again.[54]

---

54. In addition, they have a second actor in costume out in the park somewhere. He's called Timmy and he has wings because he's supposed to be dead. I think it must have been his day off when I was there because I didn't see him. And I'm very glad. I'd have *freaked out*.

I don't know why, but even though all she did was wave and hug and pose with children for photographs, I still wanted to knock her to the ground. The endearing globular head balanced on unassuming little shoulders, the nonthreatening, plaintive expression on her face, the sheer inoffensive pastel blandness of this creature, all brought out the worst in me. I couldn't help myself.

As I approached, she was perched on the edge of a fountain.

"Aren't you hot in that outfit?" I said, sitting down beside her.

No response.

"D'you do this every day?"

No response.

"Who's your favorite *Gilligan's Island* character? Mine's the Skipper."

No response.

"What do you think of the situation in the Middle East? Expecting more flare-ups?"

No response.

"Are you dating? Cuz if you are, I know this guy in a Jimmy Neutron costume. I could talk with him, maybe fix the two of you up."

No response. She continued to sit in silence, lazily waving a white-gloved hand at passing kids. Most waved back. The smaller ones retreated, unsure whether to laugh or cry at this maraca-headed freak.

I tried again. "Wanna fight?"

No response.

"This is so wrong," my conscience was saying. "You sick bastard. How can you pressurize an enormous pink child in this way? Look at her—she's close to tears."

But that's the point, she's always close to tears. She's a Precious Moment!

"Aw, c'mon. This is radio. Make a noise. Give me *something*," I pleaded, aiming my microphone at her eyes. This is where the holes are, enabling the actor inside to peer out and see who's bugging her. But by now she'd grown tired of my attempts to befriend her and walked away, which I guess is something. Even fear is a response, right?

Nevertheless, this awkward encounter reinforced one of the most important lessons of my life, one I should have learned years ago: Never try to interview anyone who doesn't have a working mouth.

So, giving up, I left her to her work and made my way out into the park.

LET ME SAY STRAIGHT OFF THE BAT THAT I HAVE a very high tolerance for mawkish sentimentality. I do. In the same way that the body converts carbohydrates to sugar, mine effortlessly converts saccharine to indifference. I put it down to my early Christian Science upbringing. So instead of finding the cloying sincerity of the Precious Moments park sickly or maudlin or offensive, to me it was entirely palatable; fun even. The staff members are adorable, the sprawling grounds clean and beautifully maintained, and the various attractions infused with a high-octane religious zeal that is as enthralling as it is scary. Here's what they have:

1. The Resurrection Cave. There's a deck. You walk to the edge of it and look down. Set into a wooded slope is a dark hole which, by some distortion of logic that I have yet to unravel, is meant to represent Christ's tomb. Standing guard at the entrance is a five-foot-tall Precious Moment angel. What he's waiting for is uncertain. If it's Jesus, then I have bad news: a) Jesus died in a different place a very long time ago; b) I'm no statistician, but even if the Lord is reborn in our time, I'd say the odds against His emerging from this particular cave must be fifty trillion to one; and c) well, that's enough. It's just too silly.

2. The Chapel. Not a place of worship (unless you worship Sam Butcher, that is, in which case you should take something to kneel on); rather, it's an elaborate, life-size, church-shaped display cabinet showcasing Sam's mural-painting abilities, which are considerable. Tour guides will walk you through, pointing out:

• Old and New Testament scenes in which Precious Moment figurines play a somewhat greater role than I recall their doing in the original Bible stories.

• A painting on the ceiling daubed with more Precious Moments. This is meant to remind you of the Sistine Chapel, and it does, in the sense that it's a painting and it's on the ceiling.

• An epic mural called Hallelujah Square. I think it's about children in Heaven, though the details are hazy now. Too much pastel affects my serotonin levels and I lose concentration.

• Stained glass windows. Like everything else around here, the windows were designed by Sam himself. And, when he had a spare minute between building chapels and sculpting angels and painting ceilings and overseeing a theme park that isn't really a theme park, he hand-carved the doors too. If my calculations are correct, this man hasn't slept a wink since 1987.

3. The Fountain of Angels. A magnificent theatrical presentation that's second only to anything you've seen that's better.

• On your way to the covered ten-story auditorium, the gardens alongside the pathway sing to you. This is *soooooo* neat. Either there are speakers cunningly hidden in the bushes or the world's smallest midget choir has been buried in a chamber under the lawn and is begging you in song to call 911.

• The show itself is camp and quite trippy, with multi-colored dancing water jets, deafening ethereal choirs, and a basso-voiced narrator: "TONIGHT, WE ARE IN THE PRESENCE OF THE MOST HIGH—GOD . . ." Oh, and there's a cameo from Jesus. I guess they uncovered some old video footage of him shot in Biblical times, because he appears unannounced from a shed, then walks serenely along a path, and, when you're least expecting it, explodes—not into bloody pieces, because that might distress the young-uns, but to become a glistening crucifix. Oh, and be warned: Audiences take this Jesus-coming-out-of-a-shed stuff *extra*-seriously, and even cheer when it happens. So make sure you cheer along with them. And feel free to weep too, if you have it in you.

• The fountain features what look like 250 child actors dressed as Precious Moments being hosed down with water. "Oh my Gosh!"[55] I exclaimed. "Are those *real* children?" But apparently they're cast, not from school auditions, but from bronze.

• Arrive early if you can, because you won't want to miss the pre-show entertainment, starring the best and only Christian boy-girl gospel foursome I've ever heard: the Precious Moments Singers. They're like Peter, Paul, and Mary, and then a Second Chick, and they exalt the Lord with uplifting tracks sung karaoke-style to soaring strings. You can't help wondering where Sam found singers of this quality. The Book of Acts perhaps. One note: It wouldn't hurt them to dilute the gospel stuff a little, maybe with a couple of Jackson Browne numbers, or even something by Aerosmith. Try it, guys, it might work.

• The presentation, which lasts about a half hour, took my breath away. Or at least I thought it did. In fact during the Jesus video, my fingers were clutched so tightly to my throat in utter disbelief that I almost choked.

---

55. Everyone in this neck of the woods replaces the word God with Gosh. It's kind of a quaint custom in Missouri. If you forget, and accidentally blurt out "Oh my God!" expect people to turn and glare at you, the way they do if you fart on a bus.

4. The Samuel J. Butcher Home. Could this be the same Samuel J. Butcher who built the park? You know, the Precious Moments guy? I have no idea. If it is, then he clearly doesn't live in this house. Rather, it's a fussily decorated storage facility in which he displays all the stuff he's picked up on his world travels. To my mind, it's the only truly dull part of the visit. I walked in, through, around, back, and out again without registering a single interesting feature. I don't expect Sam Butcher to sift through my holiday souvenirs, why on earth would I want to sift through his?

5. The Other Chapel. You'll find this on Wedding Island (closest neighbor: Hitchedville), and it's been wonderfully and affectionately realized. The chapel complex is to cuteness what Chernobyl is to uncontained radiation. There's a small country church, a bridal cottage, reception rooms, a honeymoon suite, and a heart-shaped Photo-Opportunities Jetty overlooking a lake. As I walked around, Lisa, one of the two PR women who went everywhere with me, let slip that she got married here.

"It was such a wonderful wedding. There were 120 people sitting in the chapel."

"Oh yeah? And were they people you knew?"

"Yes they were."

"And were they all dressed as Precious Moments?"

"No they were not."

"So if I came to your home—and I'm not saying I won't—but if I came to your home, would I find all your wedding photos had been taken here overlooking the lake?"

"Yes, you would."

"Were any photos taken of you after you fell in the lake?"

"I didn't fall in the lake."

"Because that *would* have been a precious moment. Hahahahahahahaha!"

We rolled around laughing at this.

Or at least I did.

As I was leaving the complex, I had an idea. I was still single at the time, so I thought, "What the heck?[56] I'll cruise the wedding area, picking on people at random, and ask them to marry me."

But believe it or not, every one of them turned me down, falling back on that hoary old standby, "You'll have to ask my husband," which was a little depressing.

But I'm nothing if not tenacious. Nor am I the kind of guy to take "For God's sake, I just told you, I'm *married*. Now, get your pawing hands off me or I'll call Security" for an answer. So I wandered into one of the function rooms, where a waiter was busy folding tablecloths, and proposed to him instead.

Alas, once again my offer was met by a refusal. "It's not legal here yet," he chuckled fruitily. "Come back next year."

Oh yeah?

I wonder what Samuel J. Butcher would think of *that!*

No, don't tell me; I think I can guess.

THE FINAL STOP ON MY JOURNEY FROM KANSAS CITY down to Branson was, it probably won't surprise you to learn, Branson.

Being a foreigner, I'd never heard of the place before, which, as I now realize, was a grave oversight. Apparently it's been the butt of jokes among Americans for decades, and seems to be spoken of in faintly derogatory terms by almost everyone you meet.

"If you're in the Midwest and you're looking for a good time," one friend told me before I left L.A., "Branson is where it's at. Especially if you don't have the money to fly to Las Vegas, which is where it's *really* at."

Someone should put that on a T-shirt.

"Don't forget, Branson claims to have the world's largest ball of twine," Jim said before I set off. "It's in Ripley's Believe It or Not. You should go check it out."

---

56. As well as saying Gosh instead of God, they say heck instead of hell. Puritans are such innovators!

At once I was sucked in. "Hm, twine," I thought. "That might be fun."

NESTLING ON THE SHORES OF LAKE PERRYCOMO, Branson was named after Reuben S. Branson, a settler in the 1800s who pitched camp in a forest at the water's edge, then just sat around doing nothing for *ever* apparently, believing that if he waited long enough someone would eventually name a town after him. (By the way, this wasn't an original idea. Nathaniel Chicago and Jeremiah Fortlauderdale did much the same thing years before him.)

Anyway, in 1903, fifty years after his death, things finally started to go Reuben Branson's way. A bunch of rough, tough, manly lumberjack types rode in across the hills and set about chopping down trees as fast as they could. In fact, that's how the town of Branson began: as a logging community. And for a little while there it had all the makings of a prime commercial and industrial metropolis. But that didn't last long.

Four years later, in 1907, a book called *Shepherd of the Hills* by Harold Bell Wright was published, which changed everything. Set on a farmstead in southwest Missouri (I don't have time to detail the whole story, but if you can imagine a shepherd wandering in some hills, I think you pretty much have the gist), Wright's narrative and the characters he created inspired a nation, pushing the book to the top of the best-seller lists. Not only that, but its beautiful setting pulled in large numbers of tourists to the area, something that was guaranteed to upset the loggers big-time.

"Tourists? Aw—no way!" they said. "Tourists are a bunch of sissies."

So on they went, pushing ahead with their original plan of turning Branson into a rough, tough, manly industrial hub. They opened boat factories and gasoline suppliers and other butch, aggressive enterprises guaranteed not to undermine the pioneer spirit of unfettered masculinity pervading the town. And it worked.

Those early days were boom times. Business was good and money rolled in. Things only started going awry when a resort of vacation cabins sprang up alongside the lake . . .

"Vacation cabins? Aw, Christ! Whose nancy-boy idea was *that?*"

. . . followed closely by stores and hotels. Then some of the townsfolk became imbued with a little too much good-time spirit and started organizing parades and street fairs, which naturally only served to pull in even more tourists, which in turn caused more attractions to open.[57] First there was an outdoor theater . . .

"Oh—my—God! What the hell is this? Thee-ater ain't *manly.*"

. . . and, well, you can guess the rest. Once you have an out-door theater, you simply have to have an indoor one too. And Branson, being Branson and a bit of a show-off, couldn't stop at just the one. It had to build forty of them, staging seventy shows at any one time. Then, before you knew it, someone had thrown in museums too, and restaurants, theme parks, roller-coasters, golf courses, and outlet stores; it was never-ending. By the time they'd finished, this insignificant, overly heterosexual logging town had been transformed into what it is today: the entertainment capital of Missouri.

"Aw crap!"

Exactly.

BRANSON IS DIVIDED INTO TWO PARTS. First, there's the old town area down by the lake. Here it was, I believe, that young

---

57. Which of course was but a tiny precursor to what later became America's tourist industry. Today, the only reason many towns exist at all is so that people from other towns can come see them. Increasingly, as time goes by, that's how it's going to be. We'll all just move around looking at other people's towns and spending money there. Then they'll come to see our town and spend money here. And so long as everyone goes to visit everyone else's town and nobody slacks off and stays at home watching TV or reading, the whole country will enjoy a level of prosperity previously unheard of. If you're interested, an expanded version of this blueprint for the future can be found in my upcoming book, *What a Dopey Idea*, available next spring.

Reuben first pitched his tent almost two centuries ago. And, since nowadays they refer to this as "downtown," here's where I chose to stay also, and in accommodation not much better than a tent: a motel.

I imagined that downtown Branson would most likely be the center of all things, abuzz with loud music, frenetic activity, and all the bright lights and ballyhoo you'd expect from a city that never sleeps, but I was so wrong. It's nothing like that at all. Far from being a city that never sleeps, it naps constantly, and by the time I got there had nodded off altogether. The place was dark and empty—nobody in the streets, nobody in the restaurants or cafes. It was creepy. Almost as if news of a raging brushfire sweeping in from the west, or a plague of giant radioactive soldier ants swarming through the drains and up into people's homes, had triggered a mass evacuation.

"Hey, what can I tell you? It's Branson," shrugged a guy at the tourist information office, throwing on his hat and coat and heading for the door. "They roll up the sidewalks at 7:00 P.M."

"But I'm here to see the world's largest ball of twine."

Turning the key in the lock, he looked surprised. "We have the world's largest ball of twine?"

"You're a tourist information officer; you're supposed to know that."

"Sorry." Scurrying off up the street: "We do have the world's largest banjo, though."

"Yes, *and* the world's largest ball of twine."

"Oh," he called out from some distance away: "Well, hey, man, good luck!"

"No, don't go—take me with you!"

Too late. He'd already jumped into a waiting car. Seconds later, he was gone.

REMEMBER EARLIER, HOW I TOLD YOU that there are two main parts to Branson? Well, I know this *now*, now that I'm back home, but at the time I didn't. I had no clue at all, and of course nobody bothered to tell me ahead of time. The result being that I wasted half my visit wandering around the quaint but largely uneventful streets of "downtown," searching for theaters, bars, miniature golf courses, museums—all the things Branson's famous for—only to discover hours later when I finally grew so bored that I collapsed into a coffeeshop and complained to the owner about how crappy and dull everything was around here, that I was in completely the wrong place.

The *real* Branson, he said, the part where all the fun happens, was about a mile and a half away.

Goddamnit!

"Well, thanks for your help. And for the coffee!"

"Hey—you didn't pay for that! Come back here!"

So, with only three hours left before I had to set off back to Kansas City again, I hurriedly checked out of my motel, climbed in the car, and headed for the real Branson. And guess what! En route, without even trying, I chanced upon Ripley's Believe It or Not, home of the world's largest ball of twine.

Despite the fact that Ripley's has a ton of amusing, oddball displays on display, you really can't miss the twine. At nine or ten feet in diameter, it dominates the room in a way that has you going, "Whoa! *Man*, that's some ball of twine!" I mean, it's colossal. A record-breaker. Really really huge. Like something Indiana Jones would run away from. In fact, it wouldn't surprise me if this was the very ball of twine that wiped out the dinosaurs.

What's strange, though—and here's the bit of the Believe It or Not I didn't believe at all—is how fast, having seen the world's biggest ball of twine, you lose interest in it again. Isn't that weird? I don't know how long you could go, but my attention span, twine-wise, seemed to be about four seconds. Another record-breaker! Once the initial fizz of excitement passed, I found myself thinking, "It's just string—get over it" and left.

So unless you have anything more to add . . .

Good.

THERE MUST BE TIMES WHEN MANY of the singers and dancers in Branson wish they'd become loggers instead. Obliged to participate every day in full-scale musical tributes to the heroes and veterans of World War II long after the world has moved on to embrace a whole new raft of bitter conflicts, they're living in a time warp. I swear to Gosh, it's the strangest thing. I mean, my father fought in WWII—well, I don't know if he actually fought, but he certainly put on a uniform and left the house—and as I write this he's approaching eighty. So how can it possibly make good business sense, when half your audience has one foot in the grave, if not both feet and an arm, to continue putting on a bunch of shows that reminisce about the Second World War?

But apparently it does and they do. The theaters are a kind of vaudevillian Costco, offering entertainment in bulk, which means several performances each day. Quite often, curtain-up on the first show is just after breakfast.

In case your mind drifted and you missed that, let me say it again:

Curtain-up on the first show is just after breakfast.

By 10 A.M., performers are expected to be not only out of bed with their hair brushed and their happy face on, but actually tripping across a stage, jitterbugging to jazzy wartime numbers for the benefit of three coachloads of blue-rinsed old codgers, or whoever else has wandered through the doors. Many look utterly bewildered, as if they only came in to use the bathroom and got lost. The day I was there it was an end-of-season crowd, and possibly not typical. Yet the show had to go on. And by God it did. What professionals they are, those young people up there on that stage, what troopers, for seeing this ordeal through to its finale. My heart went out to every last one of them. Isn't it about time someone put on a show saluting *them?* I think so. In fact, you know what? I've written it right here on my to-do list.

The variety of entertainment on offer in Branson is staggering, and it makes finding a suitable show feel like hunting for a needle in a haystack. Or for editorial content in *Vogue.* Luckily,

I'd had the presence of mind to download a brochure off the Internet before I left home, which turned up a host of irresistible delights, including:

- **50s at the Hop:** Starring The Hoppettes. Possibly my favorite nostalgic dance troupe of all time with a name ending in ettes.

- **The Incredible Acrobats of China:** Starring the Shanghai Circus. Apparently their act dates back to 500 B.C., so chances are you saw at least parts of it in a previous life. I'm not sure what the appeal of the show is. To my mind, acrobats are like windsurfers. The only time they even come close to being entertaining is when they fall off.

- **The Andy Williams Christmas Show:** "*Starring 'Mr. Christmas' himself—Andy Williams.*" In the listings, it said the show would run 'til December 10, then stop. Well, thanks for nothing, Mr. Christmas.

- **The Barbara Fairchild Show:** "*Barbara Fairchild salutes our veterans.*" This too was scheduled to run 'til December 10, then stop. What was happening on December 11, I wondered? Maybe Andy and Barbara had gotten wind of a potential attack on Branson (possibly by a band of veterans waging a new war: against outdated hokey entertainment) and were leaving town early.

- **The Baldknobbers Jamboree:** Er . . . no thank you.

- **The Buck Trent Morning Show:** (What? You mean THE Buck Trent?) "*Buck and his all-star cast,*" it said, "*will get your eyes open, your hands clappin' and your toes tappin'.*" Is that right? "Well," I thought to myself, "quite clearly they've never met *me!*"

- **Frederick at Waltzing Waters:** By all accounts, this is a heady patriotic mix of pianos and waterfalls saluting America's veterans and her allies. Nostalgia is a gold mine, and there appears to be competition among many of Branson's entertainers to see who can salute the veterans a little better and for that bit longer than anyone else. Frederick, by saluting not only veterans, but the allies too — a masterstroke, in my opinion — wins by a mile.

• **The Lennon Brothers:** *"Do you like swing music?"* yells the brochure. Actually no, I don't. *"Of course you do!"* No I don't. Not at all. In fact, I find it quite annoying. *"Then come and listen to the Lennon Brothers."* Hm. Feel free to start without me.

• **The Duttons:** *"As seen on PBS."* For that reason alone, I wouldn't go.

• **Mike Radford's Remember When Show:** *"Take a rollicking trip down memory lane to celebrate grandparents, patriotism and the best of the 20ᵗʰ Century . . . the best tribute to veterans."* I have two words for you: "no" and "way." The day he dumps the veterans and starts saluting jaded radio reporters — *"He's the Boogie-Woogie Journalist from a Company in L.A."* — that's when I'll get my ass along to see Mike Radford, and not before.

• **Jim Stafford:** *"Jim has it all — hilarious comedy . . . dancing chickens, flying saucers, a 3-D virtual thrill ride, and more."* Actually, I don't need more; that's quite enough. But I won't hear a bad word spoken against Jim Stafford. He's the guy who sang "I Don't Like Spiders and Snakes." Well, neither do I, Jim. I *loathe* them, as a matter of fact. Call me sometime, we'll talk.

• **The Promise:** *"Come and witness the story of Jesus."* The original Mr. Christmas! I guess, on the basis that everyone knows the *Titanic* sank but they flocked to see the movie anyway, the producers felt there was still life in the old dog yet. Or maybe they added a new twist at the end, just to keep it fresh. Maybe Jesus takes time out from the Last Supper to salute allies and veterans. I'd pay to see that.

With such a cornycopia of offerings on offer, including a show starring the remaining Osmond Brothers, the ones you can't name, I was so dizzy with choice that I went into momentary over-whelm and came close to giving up. But then, right at the very last minute, something magical happened. As I was driving around I spotted a billboard.

JENNIFER, it said in huge letters.

Hm.

Few stars in the world today are so big and so internationally well-known that they can get by on just the one name. Madonna, Cher, Prince, and Schwarzenegger come to mind.

And Jennifer.

I'm not entirely sure how Jennifer made the list. Her legend may span entire continents for all I know, but I for one have never heard of her.

Judging by the photo on the billboard, she looked to be a radiant blonde with pretty features. Publicity shots, though, can be deceptive. In Hollywood, it's not unusual for the pouting young brunette whose double-D's and peaches 'n' cream face tower over Sunset Strip to be, in reality, a pancake-chested great-grandmother with stretch marks like trampoline springs. The rest is clever lighting and six hours with an airbrush.

But Branson is not Hollywood. Maybe things were different here. So I decided to stop by and see Jennifer's show.

It was midmorning, and for all the reasons you know about, I'd arrived very late. But that didn't seem to matter, because a lot of other folk seemed to be late too. Indeed, from where I was sit-ting—right at the back in the darkness with my hands over my face so that I wouldn't be recognized—there looked to be more people on stage than in the audience.

But this gal's a true pro. She behaved as if the theater wasn't half-empty at all, strutting confidently across the boards, looking curvaceous and glamorous, and whipping my senses into a veri-table tune-frenzy with a string of standards from pop to country and back again.

Wow!

How can I describe when I only have mere words to do it this giant among entertainers, so bursting with rollicking, upbeat wholefulsomenessness and with a singing voice that could strip wallpaper? "You're *great*," I thought, applauding 'til my palms stung. Which begs the next question: So what the heck[58] are you doing stuck in Branson? How screwed up was the business they call "show" that a monster talent such as Jennifer whose fans are legion—or at least legionnaires—could be playing here all this time and yet be overlooked by the Industry Big Boys?

It was a mystery that had me perplexed, at least for a while.

In the closing minutes of her performance (actually, I was fortunate enough to arrive in the closing minutes, so this bit came around pretty quickly. Memo to all Branson performers: Put the end of your act on first, then skip the rest. The audience will thank you for it!), the pace slowed dramatically. The music became a lot quieter—*pianissimo*—and more somber—*sombrero*. A hush fell across the auditorium as Jennifer stepped to the front of the stage with an apology.

"Every single day," she said, addressing rows of wrinkly baffled faces staring up at her, "I come out to the buses and the lobby to meet with you folks. But not today. Today, I just found out I have a national interview after the show . . ."

Oooooooh!

Jennifer's being interviewed—*nationally*.

". . . so I'm sorry, but I'll have to do that instead and won't be able to meet you all."

Disappointment. Murmurs of dissent.

I was immediately curious. Who could it be? CNN perhaps? Or—oooh, oooh—*maybe* that nice Katie Couric from NBC.

But Jennifer wasn't saying. (Perhaps Katie had insisted on a publicity embargo. It's possible. That's how people are in television.) Anyway, having caught us off-guard with this startling admission, she stepped back into the spotlight and proceeded to do the same all over again, by quite unexpectedly launching into

---

58. See—I remembered!

a monologue about the relationship she'd built up with the Lord Jesus Christ.

Huh?

"He is everything to me," she said, going on to mention what a boon he'd been in her life and career thus far.

And as she was talking, that's when it struck me. Oh my Gosh, I thought. I know who she's talking about. I *know* the identity of the person who'd come all the way to Missouri to talk to her.

It was me!

Little old tape-recorder-carrying, microphone-pointing, has-no-clue-what-he's-doing me. *I* was the national interview.

A casual invitation I'd extended earlier in the day—"Would you have time to meet up afterwards for a chat?" (a request that most performers, once they find out who's asking, turn down without a second thought)—had for once come up trumps. I don't know how I didn't wet myself.

"Yes, I do believe in Jesus Christ," she told me as we sat together on a couch in her dressing room. "Yes, I am successful." (She was answering her own questions here. Expecting her to say no, I'd come completely unprepared. So we began with the Jesus thing.) "Yes, I do have Christ working dead-center of my life, and that's good for me."

Sure, but what about the audience? "Are you trying to convert them?"

"Well, I wouldn't mind if they were converted," she chuckled. "I'd think that's the next best thing since sliced bread. I would adore that."

"Well, maybe so," I felt like saying to her, "but sadly, my dear, this kind of zeal can cost you a flourishing career in Tinseltown, where the pace is savage, the language saltier than anything you'll hear backstage at a gospel show, or for that matter at a stevedores convention, and where wholesome country values are as passé as bobby socks, tinsel, and what's left of The Osmonds."

TO THIS DAY, I DON'T THINK MY INTERVIEW with Jennifer was ever heard nationally. I have no idea where she got that from.

On the other hand, meeting her did wonders for my spirit. Plus, it went a long way toward explaining why I received a slew of hate mail from Missouri following my report on the Precious Moments Chapel.

The Ozarks is a world away from the one I live in. I know that now. Its people have nothing in common with anyone I'll ever meet back in L.A. Kind, simple, good-hearted, uncomplicated folk don't last long in Hollywood. Most times—and it can often be within days of arriving—their lofty ideals are ripped apart, ground to a bloody pulp, and thrown back in their face. In the big-time entertainment world, not only do people not have Christ working dead-center of their life, but quite often they've actually invited Satan to lodge in their guest house. Whatever it takes to get ahead, basically.

"Mr. Peters, I've never heard of you, but I DON'T like you!"

"Mr. Peters, you are EVIL and a despicable person!"

"Mr. Peters, I would HATE to spend a day at the beautiful Precious Moments Chapel with you. Your sarcastic comments would SPOIL it for everyone!"

Earnest messages from small-town people with small-town mentalities who no doubt have Christ working dead-center of their lives, but not much else going on. One woman even condemned me to burn in the fires of Hell. "Oh yeah?" I felt like writing back. "Well, come to think of it, madam, that might not be too bad. If Heaven is full of mean-spirited gargoyles like you, then burning in the fires of Hell will seem like Club Med by comparison, and I can't wait to get there."

But I didn't. Because I don't really want to go to Hell. And anyway, the last time I defied a God-fearing woman, an entire bathroom filled to the ceiling with foam!

By the way, none of this, I hasten to add, has anything to do with the lovely, super-talented Jennifer. She's too pure and professional ever to become embroiled in tawdry muckraking.

Last I heard, she'd decided to take a year off from her Branson show "to allow time for my foot to completely heal."

Oh really? Did I miss something?

Perhaps she went too far during a particularly spirited rendition of "Onward Christian Soldiers" and fell into the orchestra pit.

According to her Web site, she's continuing to work toward her Doctorate in Education and aspires to open a Christian school someday with her sister. Hurrah!

But a year's a long time to be away from the stage, especially in Branson, I should imagine, where half your audience could be dead or in a home by the time you get back. Never underestimate the lovely Jennifer, though. She's smart. She's managed to stay in the public eye while her foot heals by co-hosting the morning show on KTXR in Springfield, Missouri, a position which, at the time of writing, she still holds.

"I love and miss you all!!" she declares at the bottom of the Web site.

Well, you know what? Right back atcha, kid.

12

Intermezzico

*Albuquerque ◆ questions arise about my masculinity ◆ the Drifter
mixes with real men and gets stared at ◆ the lure of Stampede ◆
finally, the future foretold ◆ looking forward to a life in Antarctica ◆
I see the face of an angel ◆ an awkward encounter with a world-famous
TV star ◆ the American International Rattlesnake Museum*

NEW MEXICO IS NOT LIKE THE REST OF AMERICA. Perhaps the best way to describe it is "a dusty, primitive, flat, barren wilderness." Unfortunately, there's something about that phrase that doesn't look good on a license plate. So a few years back, the locals, who I guess had grown tired of flying under the radar, tourism-wise, and not making heaps of money the way other states were, said to hell with that, and dumped the dusty, primitive, flat, barren wilderness angle in favor of something far better. What they came up with was a stroke of genius: The Land of Enchantment, which not only looks *great* on a license plate, but is also infinitely more attractive to visitors. And bingo, you should see New Mexico now! In some places you can barely move for tourists and the roads are choked with traffic; it's unbearable. Well done, everyone.

At least, this seems to be true in parts of Albuquerque.

Often referred to as the Duke City, after some guy called Duke who came here years ago and did something—check your local library for details—Albuquerque is an atmospheric remnant of the Old West. High winds roaring in across the plains send tumbleweeds bobbing along the street to greet you. The landscape is dotted with quaint adobe houses that look like something

Fred Flintstone might upgrade to, and every guy you meet tends to remind you of those gritty, tough, no-nonsense cowboys who are always diving behind troughs and being shot at in Westerns. Everything around here—the buildings, the restaurants, the stores, even the hotel I stayed at with its uncompromising view over a freeway off-ramp—everything seems to have been designed by he-men for he-men. No frills, nothing fancy, just practical and earthy and oozing raw machismo, same way Branson used to be before "them darned pesky thee-ater folk moved in."

Myself, I've never quite mastered machismo. I'm okay for a while, an hour maybe, but then I'm in trouble. The second I crack a nail or feel even the tiniest hint of a headache coming on, all pretense to ruggedness evaporates. And I think the people of Albuquerque picked up on that quite early. On the first night, I sat in a bar reading *Hollywood Wives* and sipping a strawberry margarita through a dinky red straw, and was glared at menacingly for a full thirty-five minutes by everyone in the room!

Later, after I'd left there in fear of my life, I wandered into a large clothing store in the Old Town that sells the kind of gear I think only desert-dwellers could wear and get away with. (Seriously, in L.A., if you turned up in a restaurant sporting a creamy white ten-gallon hat, spurs on your boots, and a suede jacket with foot-long tassels down the sleeves, you'd trigger a fresh round of riots!) But that's not all they sell. There's also a wide assortment of plaid shirts that might politely be called "jazzy," and, on a shelf by the door, some of the butchest colognes ever stuck in a bottle.

The New Mexican man, it seems, doesn't mess around when it comes to how he smells. Not for him some dumb-assed perfume with a pussy name—Joop! ("Yuck") or Giorgio Beverly Hills ("Yeuw!"). When you're diving behind troughs and getting shot at all day long, your cologne needs to be robust, craggy, and loaded with consonants: Canyon, Dakota, or, best of all, Stampede ("Yeeehiiiii!"). Something that sounds like it could be used to slap on your face after shaving or, at a pinch, to anesthetize a horse. Luckily for me, I smell like Stampede most of the time, which has saved me a fortune over the years. All the same, this came as quite an eye-opener and I frittered away the next thirty minutes or so happily squirting my wrists with one cologne after another and sniffing them until, slightly overcome, I had to stop.

MY ASSIGNMENT IN NEW MEXICO WAS to visit the American International Rattlesnake Museum. I'll be honest with you, it's not the best job I've ever had.

You know already how I feel about snakes. I loathe them. If something has legs, you can usually hear it coming. If it doesn't, then Nature has handed it an unfair advantage, in my opinion, and I don't like that. Worse, snakes not only sneak up on you when you're not looking, they also get pissed off when you step on them. Sometimes they even retaliate and *bite you*. Well! Living in Los Angeles, you come to expect that kind of behavior from people, but not snakes. Which is why, to my mind, they deserve no mercy at all. They're just long, thin, curly rats, and as such, total extermination is not only their fate, I feel, but also their birthright. Hey, and that's a Buddhist talking![59]

So there I was, ambling in the general direction of The Rattlesnake Museum, dragging my feet because I didn't want to go in, and looking for a distraction en route, when I ran across exactly that, in the shape of a cute little backstreet souvenir store. A card in the window invited passers-by to step inside and have their "spirit guide" drawn by a local artist. On top of that, she would also tell your fortune.

"Oh boy!" I thought. "That sounds *futuretastic*."

Of course, as you know, my history with angels and fortune-telling is not good. But these were extraordinary times. The "should

---

59. I was raised a Christian Scientist, but then switched to Buddhism when I found it took a lot less effort. As I understand it, the principles are simple: First, you have to respect all living things—which, with the exception of PR people, snakes, and big dogs, I surely do—check. Second, you have to eat a lot of vegetables—check. And, last of all, you must acknowledge freely that everything in the universe is impermanent. Nothing lasts forever (although Woody Allen movies seem to). That's it. The rest of the time, you just sit in a chair with your eyes shut and think about nothing. In that respect, it's tailor-made for someone like me.

I stay in radio or should I move into TV if anyone will have me?"
question had dragged on way too long—almost the entire book!—
and the lack of progress had gotten to be quite depressing. Back
in Amsterdam I'd promised Mandy faithfully that I'd only be
travel-reporting for one more year, tops, then quit. And I meant it.
But already it was close to eighteen months, and still no feasible
alternative had presented itself.

One thing was for sure: Decisions needed to be made. And at
times like this, who better to advise you on decisions you should
be making than a local artist working out of a souvenir shop?

So, credit card at the ready, and smelling of five different
kinds of cologne, I raced inside.

The local artist in question was a soft-spoken middle-aged lady
named Jo. "She's the real deal," one of the store's owners assured
me. "We searched a long time to find someone this good."

"Excellent," I said, sitting down with great eagerness. "Bring
it on."

It takes about forty minutes to draw an angel—thirty if you
leave off the neck—and it's a captivating process. With a big box
of different-colored chalks at her right hand, Jo gave the paper a
quick sweep with her palm, and another, and another, while she
found her spiritual bearings. Then, once the coordinates were
locked in, she got to work, making large overlapping swirls, sometimes in a relaxed way, sometimes busily, as if she were ironing a
pillowcase, but swirling, always swirling. And all the while, she
was talking about my favorite subject: me.

"I don't know if you believe in the idea of having lived
before," she said.

"Er . . ." I'm a Buddhist, and Buddhists firmly believe in re-
incarnation. But no.

"Because . . ."

And out it all came. My entire life story, dating back almost to
the Paleozoic Era. Apparently, I'm a very old soul. I have walked
this earth many times before. Thousands of years ago, in one of my
earliest lives, I was an aborigine in southeast Australia. One of the
first, in fact. An aboriginal. In those days, I was a very wise man,

a prophet, a counselor, bringing light and solace to the troubled souls around me, a gift that did not, alas, transcend the centuries. In this lifetime, I startle and annoy almost everyone I meet.

"Ever felt drawn to visit southeast Australia?" Jo asked.

"No," I said honestly. "Never."

"Oh."

And her thin, delicate hand began skimming the paper once again, swirling, swirling, as she tuned in to the inaudible voice of my guide.

Having breezed smartly over my Past—skipping from the Dawn of Man to the twenty-first century in a heartbeat—we then dallied briefly and unsuccessfully with the Present.

"You like jazz, don't you?" she said.

"No, I certainly do *not*. It causes cancer. There've been studies."

"Oh. Ever traveled to New Zealand?"

"No."

"Do you have a sister?"

"No."

"Or a close friend called Anna?"

"No."

"Or something that sounds like Anna—Hannah or Susannah or Joanna or . . . ?"

"NO!!"[60]

"Okay."

And so, having pretty much exhausted the Present, we moved on, lurching into my future, which, since it hasn't happened yet, and might never, was a much safer bet. It was also the part that concerned me the most. Keyword: TELEVISION.

There was a pause while Jo reached into the box and toyed first with a red stick of chalk, then a blue one, before settling finally on yellow, and began again.

Swirling, swirling.

I'm guessing my spirit guide talks nonstop, because he babbled on for a very long time, revealing all kinds of interesting

---

60. Unless she's referring to my friend Anna, in which case I suppose I do.

details about what was to come in my life.

"I can tell you," Jo continued when he finally shut up, "that you will not meet an untimely end in a plane crash."

Right on! Well, that's definitely good news.

"Also, I see you visiting France in the next six months."

"Oh! Okay . . . if you say so." I didn't tell her, but this wasn't very likely at all (and indeed didn't happen, I can now exclusively reveal).

"And within the next seven years you'll move out of California and be living in Antarctica."

Ah.

Swirling, swirling, swirling some more.

This carried on for another ten minutes at least. And I was just wondering if it was too late to cancel my credit card payment, when something weird happened.

And I mean truly weird. The kind of weird that causes you to stop dead in your tracks and, for a few seconds, question your own sanity. For, right there and then, looking over Jo's shoulder, I saw the face of a real angel!

I swear to God.

A cherubim or a seraphim[61] was hovering in the store, staring directly at me. It was as if he'd been sent from heaven personally to pay me a visit.

"Ricky Schroder!" I gasped. Because I recognized him instantly.

Remember Little Ricky Schroder? The actor guy: short, blond hair, blue eyes. He played that kid who sobbed a lot in the movie *The Champ,* and later on, when he grew up, a cop on *NYPD Blue?* It was him, in the flesh![62]

---

61. I've never been able to remember which is which. Aren't cherubims the ones that grow down from the ceiling?

62. Unless, of course, it wasn't. If that's the case, then, man, Ricky's in trouble! He has a doppelganger who's better-looking than he is by a *mile.* Also, I wasn't the only person who thought it was him. At the time, two cast members from a touring company of *The Taming of the Shrew* were standing in the store, and they almost fainted when they saw a *real* actor walk in.

In what was perhaps *the* most astonishing coup of my life, a guy who looked just like an angel strolled right in off the street during my reading and started asking me questions. Now, you can't tell me that's just coincidence.

"Is there anywhere I can get food around here?" he said.

I almost passed out. Oh my God. *Ricky Schroder*, a TV star, actually asked me, a non-TV-star, a question about lunch!! Could there be a better omen than this? Maybe it was telling me to move into TV. Perhaps on the Food Network! Or *NYPD Blue*.

Unfortunately, he'd arrived at a tricky juncture. At the time, I was engrossed in what Jo was telling me and worrying about certain practical matters—aren't igloos made of ice? If I move to Antarctica, how will I plug in my laptop?—so I was unable, on the spur of the moment, to conjure up the name of a restaurant. "I don't know," I muttered.

"You don't know?" And he threw me one of those nonplussed looks I've seen him use on TV.

"No."

It was a difficult moment. He should have taken the hint: I'm in the middle of a psychic reading, come back later. Maybe he wasn't aware of it, but Little Ricky had never come closer to having a tray of different-colored chalks thrown in his face.

"Sorry. I'm a tourist," I mumbled.

"Oh."

That seemed to do it. Without further comment, he exited the store, perhaps bursting into tears outside, I really can't say.

All I know is, he spoiled the session. He didn't mean to, but he left me feeling very edgy in case any more TV stars—the cast of *Everybody Loves Raymond* perhaps—should walk in and stand around asking me stuff. As it was, the remainder of the sitting went off without a hitch. A few quick pencil strokes by way of a garnish and the picture was complete.

"This," Jo said, holding it up, "is your spirit guide."

"Wow," I gasped, dodging this way and that, trying to get a grip on what I was looking at.

"No—*this* is his head," she said, pointing.

"Ah yes, I see. It's just . . . er . . ."

I didn't want to offend her.

"Just what?"

I really didn't.

"Well . . ." I began, "it's just . . ."

"Just *what?*"

. . . that my guardian angel was fat!

I mean, it's entirely possible that obesity is encouraged in the afterlife, and even considered attractive. All the same . . . well . . . I couldn't believe that my guide—*mine*—would be so . . . you know, *Minnesotan*. He resembled an overblown King Neptune figure, with a mane of flowing yellow hair trailing behind him, an enormous Roman nose, great bloated cheeks, and rods of light shooting like lasers out of his eye sockets. Think of the weather forecast symbol for Very Windy, he was a bit like that. Of course, the canvas probably puts on ten pounds. But even so, to think that this monstrous great dumpling was at my shoulder day in, day out, steering my life, guiding every move I made—well, no wonder I wasn't getting anywhere!

Why couldn't my guide look more like Ricky Schroder? Small and lean, and rugged in a New Mexican kind of way; the type of guy who probably smells nice the whole time and who's not afraid to interrupt someone's psychic reading and ask for directions to a restaurant. *That's* the kind of angel I want.

And in some strange way, it's the role he unwittingly performed for me that day.

Ricky's cameo in my life was a sign, I felt. Who knows why, but it seems that God, in a 180-degree about-turn that's likely to puzzle theologians for decades, had stepped in and endorsed the views of a witch, directing me to give up on reporting for public radio in order to pursue a career in television. Ricky, if you're reading this, you're the man. I will always be incredibly grateful.

At this point, I'm tempted to say "Praise Jesus—yay!" again, only I think I overdid it in the last chapter. So let's just leave it at that.

UGH! SNAKES.

Due to my unaccountable loathing of the subject matter, this was to be a whistle-stop tour. Arrive at the rattlesnake museum at 9:45 A.M. and be in and out of there and sitting in Starbucks with a scone and a steaming hot latte before the church bell struck 10. That was my plan. Staring at a bunch of dead snakes in glass tanks being, I figured, only marginally more interesting than staring at the same tanks empty.

Regrettably, the snakes aren't dead. That's the first bit of bad news. They're all very much alive. I lost count of how many the museum had altogether, but "lots and lots" sounds about right; enough to line the walls of two small, dimly lit rooms anyway. Like drowsy pretzels, they lie curled up in fine gravel at the bottom of tanks, their eyes permanently open, mouths ajar, staring at you with brooding menace as you go by, like a reptilian version of Minneapolis–St. Paul.

"Good morning!" one of the female assistants called as I walked in.

"Hi," I smiled nervously. "My name's Cash Pe . . ."

But the greeting wasn't aimed at me. She was reaching into a box and pulling out a length of brightly patterned green rope. It was the rope she was talking to.

"This is Sidney the ball python."

"Oh really?" I took a step back.

Sidney, who, if he's anything like me, would rather be woken up with a copy of USA Today and a pot of tea, slowly reefed himself into a knot around her neck and stayed there.

"Sometimes I let him crawl inside my shirt," she laughed. "Snakes are cold-blooded animals. They like to absorb our body heat."

"Nice," I said, and took another step back.

"He loves to be picked up." She unraveled him and shoved him in my direction.

"Er . . . you know what? That's okay."

"Oh come on." She took a step closer, lifting his head up. "He's non-venomous."

At times like this, if you recall, the reporter is expected to swallow any misgivings he may have, be a good sport, and participate. That's one of the unspoken rules of crap journalism. Grab the snake, kiss it, pet it, hold it like you don't care, then give it back, brushing off the whole horrifying experience by laughing in jocular fashion like it was all nothing, hahahaha!

Unfortunately, it wasn't nothing and I did care.

Cared a whole lot, as a matter of fact.

I'd rather stick my hand in a blender.

So, with a forced grin on my face, I went straight to the jocular laughing bit without ever touching the snake, then, resisting the urge to run screaming from the building, swiftly changed the subject.

"What do snakes eat?"

"This way. I'll show you."

Given that walking into this museum was my first big mistake of the day, here now was the second.

I was led through a door into a kitchen area at the rear.

Ssssssssssssssssssssssssssssssssssssssssss.

More glass tanks. More live rattlesnakes. The moment we entered, a dozen tails shot up in the air and began vibrating.

Ssssssssssssssssssssssssssssssssssssssssss.

Call me an idiot, but I always thought snakes hissed like cats, the way they appear to in movies. But that's a myth. It's their tails you hear rattling. Another myth is: They have fully functioning brains and you can reason with them. Well, you can't. A snake is one of the dumbest creatures on the planet. Dumber than a herring. Dumber even than the gravel it's lying in in most cases. Though probably not quite as dumb as a guy who thinks they hiss like cats. All the same, as a species, I'm told, snakes raise the bar for stupidity among all living things.

Ssssssssssssssssssssssssssssssssssssssssss.

Some of them also come heavily armed. That's not a myth; it's true. They bite. Knowing that, the warning rattle triggered a sense of profound fear in me the likes of which I've not experienced since seeing Jesus appear out of a fountain at the Precious Moments Chapel.

"Oh my God—what are those?"

The assistant had opened the door of a freezer and pulled out a Ziploc bag. "You asked about food, remember?" It was packed with ten or eleven small frozen white things. Fingering it, I was able to make out individual features: pink noses and claws, closed eyes, cute question-mark tails.

"Oh—my—God. No!"

Mice. Dead mice.

Micicles, the staff call them. Bred in a lab, then killed humanely by lethal injection—not by smacking them several times with a rolled-up newspaper, as you may have been taught in school—and packed in ice, twelve to a bag.

Ohmigodohmigodohmigod!

I was shaking.

Buddha would have had a coronary.

And me too, if I stayed much longer. "Take it away! Take it *awaaaaaaay!*"

My neck was sweating, my clothes were sticking to my body, and I was feeling distinctly wobbly. It's precisely because of this that I never watch nature documentaries on TV: I can't stand to see things eating other things. And really, that's all nature is when you get down to it: one thing runs after another, brings it down from behind, then kills it and eats it. Ugh! It's all so ugly.

Well, that was it for me. In deference to the fact that I was close to passing out, the micicles were stuffed back in the freezer and I was escorted out into the museum again.

"Now, over here . . ." the assistant began, walking toward a tank with a boa constrictor in it.

I failed to catch the rest of her sentence. It was drowned out by the slamming of the door.

13

Elvis Is Dead. But Don't Tell Anyone.

The disease-ridden history of Memphis ◆ mosquitoes: nature's death squads ◆ continental breakfasts ◆ the beautiful Nicole ◆ eating whatever killed Elvis ◆ the Sun Studio tour ◆ an old bag thinks I'm trying to pick her up ◆ Nicole gets drunk ◆ things don't go well

MY LAST-EVER TRIP AS A RADIO TRAVEL REPORTER happened in August of that year.

I didn't know at the time that it was my last, mind you; it just turned out that way.

On the day the decision was made I happened to be in Memphis, Tennessee—recently voted "One of America's top ten convention destinations" by *Successful Meetings Magazine*, which by coincidence I recently voted "One of the top ten magazines I've never heard of." I'd been dispatched there to cover Elvis Week, a tight bundle of festivities organized for and by Presley fans, culminating in spectacular fashion with a candlelight vigil on August 16, the anniversary of that terrible but significant day in 1977 when their hero died on the toilet.

The fact that my career died on the same date is significant also, but only to me.

FIRST OFF, THERE ARE THREE PIECES OF ADVICE I'd give to anyone thinking of visiting Memphis in August. In no particular order, these are as follows:

    A. Don't!

    B. Don't!

    C. Don't!

That's a lot of information to take in at one go, so let me deal with each one individually.

A. Don't! It's hotter than Hell.

This is the South, the world's largest outdoor sauna. Average summer temperatures frequently reach Scorching and Humid Fahrenheit (that's Sweltering and Uncomfortable Celsius). When I got there they were in the middle of a heat wave the likes of which they hadn't experienced since the same time last year. As a result, the instant I left my hotel—something I did with great reluctance—my body's control mechanisms went berserk. I began leaking fluids from every available crevice, including a couple I sometimes don't even bother to wash, they're so remote.

Many people, I noticed, had slung little white hand-towels over their shoulder to catch the drips, but really what's needed if you're going to do this properly is a couple of medium-size buckets, one in each hand.

I swear, it was the most uncomfortable I'd ever been in my entire life. There was no air, no wind, only this thick, humid cloud that hung over the city like a sagging mattress, leaving me paralyzed with lethargy. I tried valiantly to move about, do a spot of sight-seeing, get my bearings, the way I do on my first night anywhere, but the whole thing was a bust. I managed two circuits of the area close to my hotel—and I mean *real* close; about two hundred feet in either direction—until, sweating like a farm boy at harvest, I had to give up and haul myself back to my room, where I didn't even start to cool down until I had all my clothes off, a strawberry margarita in my hand, and both my ass-cheeks wedged in hard against the air-conditioning unit.

B. Don't! It's the noisiest damned place on the planet.

During Historical Times, Memphis was the gateway to the Western Frontier, a rugged, lawless river town positioned strategically on a bluff overlooking the Mississippi River. The early days were notably rocky and can be summed up as follows: war, disease, sanitation problems, slavery, gambling, more war, more sanitation problems, and more disease; followed by bankruptcy, a new bout of truly horrendous sanitation problems, an extra wave of disease, and finally, just as the townsfolk were thinking the worst was over and circumstances might be taking a turn for the better, complete social disintegration.[63]

Some by this point had even started to wonder if the universe wasn't trying to tell them something: "Move to L.A., guys! They have hygiene and doctors and *everything!*"

But then, miraculously, there was an unexpected turnaround.

Robert R. Church, a former slave trader and banker, strode into town amid much ballyhoo and, in a move thought by some to be rash and unwise, began investing money in this impoverished, filthy, illness-ridden Mississippi cesspool.

A lot of what happened next was dull, so we'll skip that. All I will say is that Church's bold (and yes, rash and unwise) initiative injected much-needed confidence into the Memphian economy, ultimately stimulating a full-blown revival. By the 1890s, a prosperous trade in hardwood and cotton began to fuel the town's return to the big leagues, drawing in a different breed of merchant altogether—mostly African-Americans from the north who installed themselves on a fifteen-block stretch of prime real estate called Beale Street, bringing with them their business, their money, and—in case you thought I was going to drone on about this history crap forever—their *music*. Yay!

That's how it all started.

Of course, Beale Street has come a long way since then. These days, it's exploded into a promenade of blaring, cacophonous sounds and dizzying lights that flood the senses, quicken the pulse, and make you wish you'd brought something other than fingers to stuff in your ears.

---

63. You can read a longer, fuller version of this in a nine-page handout published by the Convention and Visitors Bureau; although trust me, these are the highlights.

"Put your hands together! Naaaaa-na-na-naaa-na!"

Windows are thrown wide. Homespun rock 'n' roll, distorted by cheap amplification, blasts from every doorway, soaring like audible steam into the night.

"Do you like good music? Aaaaaaaany kind of music . . . ?

Stepping onto the main drag, your senses start to sizzle. Every color, every nationality, every creed and denomination comes flocking to this one teeming thoroughfare, eager to experience for themselves the bars and clubs which, for over fifty years, have played host to such household names as B. B. King, Elvis Presley, Howlin' Wolf, Little Milton, Jackie Brenston, Roscoe Gordon, and . . . I'm going to stop there, because I've not heard of half of these people.

On my first evening in town, as I said, the heat was oppressive. Initially, I didn't even step outside. I lay on the bed watching TV and fanning myself with an *Abercrombie & Fitch* catalogue. But you can't visit Memphis, Tennessee, Home of the Blues, the Birthplace of Rock 'n' Roll, and remain in your room all night. At some point you have to get out there and mingle. So, throwing on the lightest clothes I had, I took to the streets to see where all the noise was coming from and to ask those responsible if they could possibly turn it down a little please.

What I didn't know is that to request quiet in Memphis is like telling the pilot of a 747 to switch off the engines because you can't hear the in-flight movie. Playing music, and playing it at full volume, is practically all this town exists for. Indeed, I don't know for sure but I think "Memphis" may even be the Ancient Egyptian word for "tinnitus."

Between the bars and clubs, wherever there's a space, singers with tobacco-ravaged faces and voices you could grate cheese on, compete for attention, standing on the sidewalk with a smoldering Winston in one hand and a microphone in the other, belting out a repertoire of blues standards seemingly for their own personal enjoyment.

The amazing thing is, you don't have to be on Beale Street to hear all of this. The music is so loud and invasive that you can stand virtually anywhere in Memphis, or for that matter in Tennessee probably, and sing along. In fact, if you ever wander down there in the evening and the place seems eerily quiet and peaceful, chances are you've gone deaf. Which, believe me, will come as a blessed relief.

Certainly, this would be a great place to get your eardrums pierced.

It was all too much for me anyway. After only ten minutes, and with my ears ringing and my eyes stinging from cascades of perspiration dripping from my hair, I staggered back to the hotel, locked myself in, did that ass-cheek-against-the-air-conditioner thing I told you about, and didn't reappear for another fourteen hours.

C. Don't! It's mosquito central.

Memphis is where bugs go on vacation.

If this doesn't bother you, fine, but it's a huge problem for me.

Mosquitoes *love* my legs. To them, this pale European skin of mine is like fast food. McFlesh. So to walk around town in shorts for seven days was the equivalent of throwing a weeklong open house; every bloodsucking insect for miles considered itself invited and stopped by to have a taste. Result: The moment I stepped out into the open air, I was eaten alive from the ankles up. My arms itched constantly for the entire trip and my legs were soon pitted with bleeding sores.

Naturally, I became hysterical. The only thought in my head was, "I've contracted yellow fever and I'm THIS close to dying." (My first reaction is always overreaction. I find I get more attention that way.) But then a pharmacist I spoke to at a local drugstore, throwing me one of those pitying stares that Southerners reserve for men who cry like babies, told me it was nothing at all, just a few silly mosquito bites, and the sores would heal if only I'd quit scratching them so vigorously.

"But they're *annoying* me," I snapped.

"And you're annoying *me*," she snapped back, which I thought was a little harsh.

MY HOTEL WAS LOCATED SMACK IN THE MIDDLE of the action, a block away from upper Beale Street, with a commanding view of a local landmark: the Memphis branch of Gap Kids. It wasn't my idea to be this close. I'm not really a "smack in the middle of the action" kind of guy; I'm more the "stay at a safe distance and travel to the action by bus" type. But for once I wasn't the one who'd made the booking, so I was left with no choice.

"Why don't we give him a true taste of authentic Memphian nightlife?" some bright spark must have said in a meeting. "Let's put him in a place where the ambiance is so thunderously loud, it's like someone's repeatedly banging a tin tray in your head."

And no doubt everyone cheered.

I guess they couldn't know that if the noise level in my room rises above 1500 decibels I have trouble sleeping. Or that if packs of unsupervised children are allowed to roam up and down the hotel corridor at 1:37 A.M. rapping on doors and setting off the fire alarms, then the subsequent evacuation might also prove a little inconvenient, especially if it happens two nights in a row!

A message had been left on my phone, telling me that a woman called Nicole from a local tourist agency would be meeting me and greeting me next day at 8:30 A.M. sharp, ready to show me the sights. So, making sure I washed and dressed in good time, and, compiling a mental list of snippy comments about the hotel that I'd be landing on her shortly after "Hello," I slipped downstairs for breakfast.

Southerners are very proud of their breakfast, with its mountains of scrambled eggs, grits, ham thicker than the sole of your boot, sausages that would do untold structural damage if fired from a grenade launcher, hash browns, biscuits, and country gravy, all of it swimming in grease and seasoned with a light touch of nail varnish from the waitress's thumb. Fantastic.

Already salivating, I asked one of the receptionists for directions to the restaurant.

"I'm sorry, sir, we don't have a restaurant as such."

"As such? What does that mean?"

"It *means* we don't have a restaurant. Breakfast is served over this way, right around here." She pointed at a large coach-party congregating in the lobby. "See?"

"Thanks," I smiled.

But the smile faded quickly. Only as I drew closer did I realize what was going on; that breakfast was one of those awful continental things—a "you're only a paying guest, so we've slung a whole bunch of cheap sugary crap on a table and we're just gonna let you fight over it!" buffet, consisting of cheese Danishes, blueberry muffins, overripe bananas, and single-serving packs of Cheerios[64]—in other words, not really a breakfast at all, just stuff to stick down your throat 'til you're full. Worse still, there must have been forty people in the lobby, but only fifteen or so chairs to sit on, so I was forced to position myself in an unoccupied corner and eat my cheap sugary crap standing up. Indeed, as I tried to hold my cereal bowl in one hand, my tea in the other, and peel a banana with a third hand I don't have, I was so incensed that I came very close to complaining. But you know how it is. I'm British and we don't complain about anything. We save it all up and put it in books.

So, in full view of one of the other guests, I deposited everything in the trash, then left these scenes of ritualized Caligulan trough feeding behind and went in search of my tour guide.

Oh, and there she was! I spotted her straight away: Nicole, sitting in her car, smiling and waving. My God, what a treat. A delightful slip of a thing; smart and good-humored, with short light brown hair, and the largest, most true and trusting, bluest eyes I'd ever seen.[65] In addition, I learned that her boyfriend was plagued by irritable bowel and a long-term hemorrhoid sufferer. But more of that later!

---

64. Oddly, since I found out how Cheerios are made, I'm less inclined to eat them. I've walked through silos of this stuff; why would I want to put it in my body?

65. In the movie, I think we'll ask Carmen Electra to play Nicole. Or, if we can't get her, maybe Gene Hackman. He's not right for the part, I know; I'd just like to meet him. He was so good in *The Birdcage*.

"I'll be taking you around Memphis for the rest of the week," she beamed.

"Oh, you don't have to do that," I said, tossing my bag on the backseat and retuning her radio from soft rock to country. "Are you sure?"

"Of course. That's my job."

Smart, good-humored, *and* willing to save me money on bus fares. What bliss!

SEVERAL TOURS AND EVENTS HAD BEEN organized for the next few days, many of them Elvis-related, because that's what Memphis is in essence: one great big Elvis-related tour. But before we could embark on any of this, I had to have a decent breakfast.

"I want a full-grease, full-cholesterol, artery-clogging blow-out," I said. "And I want your office to pay for it."

"Sure," Nicole replied, agreeing with everything up to the bit about her office paying for it. And, with that, she threw the car into Drive and rushed me to a diner less than a mile away.

Less than a mile, yet it took us an unbelievable fifty minutes to get there. Put this down to Nicole's driving. Or rather to the fact that halfway to the diner she ran a STOP sign and was pulled over by the cops.

The diner, when we finally did arrive, after much tearful phoning to her office and her boyfriend Tony, turned out to be a great place. This used to be one of Elvis Presley's favorite haunts in the '60s and '70s, though less so in the '80s after he died. He even had his own booth—farthest from the door on the left—where he would sit for hours with friends and chew the fat. Sometimes literally. His feeding habits were a disgraceland.

As luck would have it, his table had just been vacated when we walked in, so we ran over and grabbed it.

"I'm going to order the thing that killed him," I hissed to Nicole over my menu.

"I don't think you can," she replied with a giggle. "They don't sell Valium."

Nothing makes a person more attractive, I find, than a ready wit.

As it is, there's plenty of time for joking in a joint like this. Southern service takes forever. Waiters in Memphis get around to your table not when you look like you're ready to order but when they're good and ready to serve you; and if you don't like it . . . well, America's a big place; there must be somewhere else you can go to indulge your freakish need to be attended to speedily and efficiently.

"Elvis eats peanut butter and banana sandwiches," our server said when she arrived after what seemed like ten years. By the way, it's customary around here to pretend The King isn't dead and to speak of him in the present tense. A silly quirk, but you have to indulge them. "We fry them on the grill."

"And that's what killed him? Peanut butter and banana sandwiches?"

"No—it's the Valium that killed him."

Holding her notebook to her face, she lapsed into fits of laughter. Nicole joined in too, and soon we were all helpless again. Though not factually accurate, clearly this is one of those local jokes that never grows tired.

THE BEST TOUR IN MEMPHIS, FOR MY MONEY, and I'd even widen that to one of the best in the whole of America, takes place at Sun Studio, the dingy one-room recording shop started up by visionary producer Sam Phillips in the 1950s.

"Hi, I'm Mick. Welcome to Sun Studio, the birthplace of Rrrrrrack 'n' Roll."

Twenty people, two of them stuffed to bursting with country ham and grits, were jammed into Sun's dingy reception area, watching a tall, lanky guy with Buddy Holly horn-rims who up to this point we'd all assumed was part of the group, step to the front and start recapping events that took place here all those decades ago.

It was January 1954 when an eighteen-year-old delivery boy from the nearby Crown Electric Company popped into the studio during his lunch hour to record an acetate demo. His name was

Elvis Presley (at least, I hope it was, or this story's going to suck big-time!). Doubtless he'd heard that Sun Studio was the birth-place of rock 'n' roll and he decided to help nanny this phenom-enon through its early, difficult years.

Needless to say, when Sun's owner Sam Phillips listened to the demo he was blown away, and some time later invited Elvis to cut his first single, called "That's All Right" (I'd hum it for you, only this is a book). And that's when the Presley career roller-coaster ride began in earnest.

Shuffling through into the main studio, our little group fanned out and stood in awed silence, taking in the smells and the feel of the place, listening for echoes of those bygone days, though realis-tically this is about as useless as looking for undiscovered clues in the Lizzie Borden House. The ghost of Elvis doesn't walk these halls anymore. All the same, it's nice to make-believe sometimes, and the environment conspires in every way to help you in your reverie. Sun has been painstakingly preserved to look exactly like it did back then. Or perhaps it hasn't. Sometimes neglect can be better than preservation. Either way, it's a trip.

For some reason, I'd expected the experience to be tacky and exploitative. Actually, I was counting on it. But to my joy, and yes, I admit, to my disappointment, I was swept along like everybody else and sucked into the Elvis phenomenon.

In case you're unfamiliar with the minutiae of his career, I've compiled a comprehensive time-line for you:

1935: Elvis born, one of twins. Other twin dies at birth without establishing a recording career. 1953: Elvis graduates from high school; 1954: first hit for Sam Phillips; 1955: RCA Victor buys out Presley's contract from Phillips; 1956: success starts in earnest; 1957: more success; 1958: Elvis joins Army; 1960: Elvis leaves Army; 1961: more success; 1962: more suc-cess; 1963: more success; 1964: more success: 1965: more suc-cess; 1966–1976: Elvis takes success to new heights; 1977: Elvis dies on toilet.

Now, I've never had much truck with the past. It always seems too distant to me, too remote. I can't relate. But Elvis's life is different. This guy means something to every one of us. So it's astonishing to think that the very acoustic tiles he stared at as he sang that demo all those years ago are still right there on the wall today, staring at *you*. The same tiles he walked on lie underfoot. The white X's marking the position of his guitarist Scotty Moore, bass player Bill Black, and drummer Johnny Something-or-other (I was standing at the back and couldn't hear properly) are still on the floor. Even the microphone Elvis crooned into when he sang "That's All Right"—one of those funny silver ones that looks like a scented-soap container—stands in the same place it did then, ready for you to finger and admire and stroke, though they do ask you not to lick it, which I think is fair.

The tour, if you can call it that—you move from one room (reception) into another room (the 30-by-18-foot studio), stand for twenty minutes listening to Mick talk and tapes of Elvis singing, and then you come out again—is over only too fast, but it's terrific fun and highly atmospheric.

Many of the older members of the group, having waited years for this, were reluctant to leave. They kept on posing for photos beside the drum kit and the microphone long after it was all over.

"What was it about Elvis that made him so special?" I asked a young woman, who, since she was only sixteen, must surely have missed certain key moments in Elvis' life—such as *all of them*.

"Because he's never forgotten where he came from," she said. (I wish they wouldn't do that: talk about him as if he's still around and he might just leap out on you at any moment, shouting "Surprise!") "He's talented," she went on, "he loves his fans, and he's the greatest entertainer who's ever lived—simple as that."

"You do know he's dead, though, right?"

"No he's not," she blurted out, shocked that I would say such a cruel, albeit pretty widely known thing. "He lives on in our hearts."

I mean, what do you say to someone like that? Other than maybe, "You're delusional. Get help!"

After a moment's thought, I added: "Has anyone told you about John Lennon yet?"

With a slow, uncomprehending shake of the head, she said, "What about him?"

Oh dear. "I'm afraid the news isn't good."

And everyone laughed.

Everyone except her.

ONE OF THE MOST PLEASANT SURPRISES of the week was finding a Starbucks close to my hotel.

STARBUCKS WELCOMES ELVIS FANS, a sign said as I picked up my scone and latte at the checkout.

Pocketing the change, I asked the server what kind of people they were, these fans they welcomed so much, because thousands of them turn up every year during Elvis Week and virtually take over the town with their fashion shows, look-alike contests, special luncheons, and fancy '70s parties.

"They're the Las Vegas show type," he said in a tortured, whining tone that sounded as if his nostrils had been stapled together. "Big hair, bedazzled sweaters, 'What would Anita Bryant do?' pins. Humble, down-home people who just want to be wowed. They relate to Elvis. It feeds something within them to come here. It's almost like a pilgrimage. I've lived in Memphis for a while and sometimes it's hard to take it seriously. But they do. Put the word *Elvis* on anything and someone will be dumb enough to buy it."

Oh yeah?

STARBUCKS WELCOMES ELVIS FANS.

I rest my case.

ALSO ON OUR AGENDA THAT DAY WAS AN ELVIS fashion show being held in a restaurant at the top of Beale Street. I won't bother you with the details, if only because, for the most part, there are so few details to bother you with. All it was was some models prancing around in retro-looking shirts and jackets while a large crowd of people who are receptive to such things stood by clapping and having a grand time.

Me, I was mystified. I guess it's a bit like satellite TV; you either have a dish and are able to tune in or you don't. I thought I had, actually. I thought that, by personally living through the latter half of the 1950s, I would at least have paid my subscription. But it seems not, and it rapidly became clear, when five hundred people went wild over a coy, fair-haired child modeling a quite ordinary-looking T-shirt, that the "these clothes were inspired by Elvis and the '50s and that's why they're great and you should wear them yourself" signal definitely wasn't reaching my box.

For that reason I didn't stay long and indeed probably wouldn't have mentioned the event at all had it not been for the fact that this was where, for the very first time in my life, I met my Nemesis. Oh yes.

Small and red-headed, with a sour, owlish face, like a maiden aunt with a head cold, he loitered on the fringes of the audience in a smart blue sports jacket, looking bored and quite out of it, not much like anyone's nemesis at all really. But that's his gift, you see, and that's what makes the events that took place later, on the night of the Elvis Vigil, so shocking: They came out of left field. I wasn't expecting them.

And even if I had been, I'd *still* have been shocked.

As a matter of fact, our little tiff started long before I arrived in Memphis. Back in L.A. Jim had told me of an ongoing spat he'd been engaged in for days with some guy claiming he knew people and could get me into Graceland for free.

Oooh. Now, as we know, the word *free* is like candy for my ears, so I was all for it. Trouble is, the guy wouldn't play ball. From what I heard, he'd been snippy and obstructive from the get-go, making Jim jump through all kinds of hoops before he'd bend, stoop, *condescend* to help.

Well, guess who Mr. Snippy turned out to be. Yup—the guy at the fashion show. Owl-Face.

You know how there are some people you just don't like? And I mean instantly. You can't explain it in words, but the moment you lay eyes on them you're overcome with a . . . a weird frisson of ennui. Well, that's what happened with Owl-Face. To me, there was something quite unnerving about him. He was friendly, but cold; agreeable, but sinister; helpful, but arrogant; a whole bunch of "this, but that's," giving him an obnoxious, insolent air that reminded me of so many officials, tourist officers, bureaucrats, PR people, agents, managers, and God-knows-who-else I've been forced to deal with over the years, just to get my job done. I don't know what his problem was. Probably he was loved too much as a child by doting parents and spoiled, or maybe he wasn't loved enough by his parents. Maybe they sensed his nemesis-potential straight off the bat, like *Damien—Omen II*, and in those circumstances regarded nurturing him as a waste of time. Either way, he'd grown up to be cold, sinister, arrogant, angry, pompous, and petulant—and not in a good way.

"Hi," he said, sounding friendly, but suspicious.

"Hi," I said back, calling his bluff on that one. Then I pitched right in with: "My producer tells me you won't help me visit Graceland."

The friendly smile vanished faster than toiletries from a hotel bathroom.

"Well, er . . ."

Just as I thought. These people are so audacious on the phone or hiding behind the cool anonymity of e-mails, but corner them, get them face to face, pull a microphone out of your pocket and start recording, and they invariably crumple like tents in a tornado.

"There seems to have been some confusion," he said at last, his eyes roaming the far reaches of the restaurant, looking for exits. "I wasn't sure who you were."

Not altogether true. I found out later that, not only did he know who I was, but either he or one of his cronies had heard a couple of my radio reports and hadn't cared for the tone. They thought I might not take Elvis and his legacy seriously, and that's why he'd been so difficult, but also evasive, with Jim.

"So now that you do know who I am, do I get to see Graceland?"

"I'm sure I can arrange something. Okay?"

"Great!" Injecting a steely edge into my voice. "I'm looking forward to it."

And with that we went our separate ways.

"So?" I'm sure you're thinking. "What's the big deal? The guy's just trying to be helpful. He's taking care of business, like Elvis. You're reading him all wrong."

Ah, but the subtext of menace was ever-present, believe me. I could sense it in his dapper, but tense demeanor. He was clearly very ruffled by my direct approach and didn't enjoy being put on the spot like that, or having to concede defeat so readily, especially to a journalist. These may have been early days in our hero–nemesis relationship, but already I detected tremors of unrest there, tremors which would, as I said, burgeon into something quite horrible and unexpected later on in the week.

THAT EVENING, NICOLE AND ONE OF HER FRIENDS, Anne, drove me into the suburbs to see 1034 Audubon Drive, a small and fairly unremarkable one-story house that you wouldn't look at twice were it not for the fact that Elvis lived there for thirteen months in 1956[66] during the in-between period after he moved out of the two-roomed shack his parents owned in Tupelo, Mississippi, but before he bought Graceland.

To commemorate Elvis Week, the current owners were throwing a small party for friends, neighbors, and fans, many of them the same age Elvis would have been had he not done that dying thing in 1977.

Some plodded inquisitively around the house, taking in the angular fiftiesness of the fixtures and decor and gasping in all the right places, while many more sat out by the pool fighting off mosquitoes. It seemed harmless enough, and yet, even before I got there, as Nicole, Anne, and I came through the gates and up the

---

66. It wasn't until the early 1960s that years were finally reduced to the standard twelve months we enjoy today.

driveway, I had a dark premonition. I knew something bad was going to happen. Remember how I said that Memphis was my very last outing as a radio reporter? Well, the decision wasn't made all at one go, it came in stages, and stage one happened that night at 1034 Audubon Drive.

Once inside, Nicole and Anne began doing the rounds, shaking hands, saying hi's and how're-ya-doings to people they recognized, leaving me to make my own entertainment. So I set off along the tight angular passageways that connected kitchen to den to bedroom, admiring as I went the hard work and love the owners had put into re-creating the place exactly as it was in Elvis's day. What a spectacular job, even if the end result does look a bit like an old sitcom set. My only complaint, if I had one, was that the place was in color.

By the time I got back to the living room, Nicole had drifted onto the patio, looking for a snack table. While she was gone, I took the opportunity to home in on a prim-looking woman who seemed like she might benefit from being asked stupid questions by a reporter.

"What did you think of Elvis?" I asked playfully, whipping out my recorder.

"He was innocent and cunning with a touch of evil about him," came her immediate reply.

Ah.

Given the nature of the event, it was an odd start.

Odd and yet . . . strangely intriguing.

It's true, many of Elvis's neighbors in those days considered him to be a crude and sinful delinquent, though you'd think that, half a century later, these overly sensitive fuddy-duddies would either have forgiven him (especially in light of the dying thing) or at least relaxed their silly puritanical value system just a tad and let the sun shine in. But evidently not.

"Oh yeah? How so?"

"Well . . ." She went on to cite the time when Elvis shot live bullets at a TV set and destroyed it. According to the story, his father Vernon saw the incident and went berserk. But Elvis didn't care. "It's only a TV," he smoldered, probably adding a perfunctory "Uh-huh-huh" to please the fans.

As anecdotes go, even dead-celebrity anecdotes, this rates as a total clunker. But Miss Prim, who I suspect had never fired a gun at a television in her life and so didn't appreciate the fun involved and how much it impresses your friends, took great exception to Presley's cavalier attitude toward an emerging technology.

"I just think he could have behaved more responsibly, that's all."

"Okay. Well, thank you. Good-bye."

Great. Only my first interview and already I had an excellent sound bite—"Extra! Extra! 'Elvis Presley could have behaved more responsibly,' says narrow-minded old woman! Extra! Extra!"—now, who else could I talk to?

Just then, across the room, I spotted my next mishap of the evening, in the shape of a stocky, large-breasted blonde in her mid-to-late fifties.

"What did you think of Elvis?"

"He's like a member of my family," she said. "To people like me, who've lost a loved one, it's good to know Elvis is always there . . ."

"You mean your husband passed away?"

"Yes he did."

"Aw, I'm sorry to hear that. But of course Elvis is dead too."

This never gets a good response—I should have known that by now.

"Elvis lives on in our hearts. He's still very important to us."

"Yes," I said, "but rather than look to him to help you, wouldn't it be better to find yourself another husband? A real live one?"

Suddenly her mood changed. "What are you saying?"

"Er . . . well, just suppose, here I am—I come along. I have nobody in my life and I ask you out on a date, wouldn't you rather be with me, a live person, than Elvis, who's . . . ?"

"*What?*" The jugs heaved defensively. "What do you mean? Where is this going?"

"I *mean*," I persisted—Oh my God! When will I learn? Why can't I recognize when I'm onto a loser and quit?—"wouldn't you rather go with someone like me than . . . ?"

Than with a dead guy!!!

"How *daaaaaaare* you!" That was all it took. WHOOOOSH! She went up like a bottle rocket. Couldn't have been angrier if I'd set upon her with scissors, cut out her intestines, and worn them as a hat. "I don't know who you think I am or what game you're playing, but if this is going where I think it's going . . ."

"It's not going anywhere!"

". . . you're very much mistaken."

And you're insane! You think I'm coming on to you? I'm a reporter! I'm working. I wouldn't come on to you if you were the last uptight, bad-tempered, small-minded, large-breasted old bag on the planet!

"This is *disgusting*!" she wailed. And now people were looking. "*You* are disgusting."

"What are you talking about? I simply . . ."

"You come here, pretending to interview people . . ."

"I'm not pretending, I *am* interviewing people."

It was a dangerous situation, unlike anything I'd experienced before. The only thing I can compare it to is climbing Mount St. Helens, peering into the crater and saying, "Is this thing still dorma . . . ?" then having it erupt in your face.

KA-BOOOOM!

". . . asking personal questions of total strangers, then you start making suggestive comments—you're *sick*! Get away from me!"

Brushing the microphone aside, Mount St. Helens stormed off across Elvis Presley's living room and made a formal complaint to the hostess of the event.

Looking back on it now, I can see that what we had here was a clear example of Self-Evident Life Truth No. 6: Some folk enjoy conflict. They get a real kick out of feeling victimized and blaming others for their own problems. The law courts are full of 'em, all busy suing each other and everyone else they can think of, starting on page one of the phone book. They're not content until they've taken umbrage, become annoyed, and made the rest of the world as unhappy as they are.

And her plan worked, because now I was just as unhappy as she was.

"See that man over there? No, the one with the goatee. Yes, *him*! D'you know what he just said to me?"

Straight away Miss Prim joined in, relating how the same terrible reporter man had tricked her into saying bad things about Elvis, which was *totally* not true. I hadn't tricked her at all.

A disgruntled murmur began circulating around the room.

You know that scene in *Jurassic Park* where the kids are trapped in the kitchen and the raptors are closing in? It felt like that. Presley purists are a notoriously straitlaced, humorless bunch when they climb on their hobbyhorse. "Don't mess with them," Nicole had warned me in the car, "or they'll turn on you." How I wish I'd listened!

The news of what had happened to Mount St. Helens—i.e., nothing; it was all in her head—spread like herpes. People stepped in from the garden.

"He said *what*?"[67]

Not only was it *the* most cripplingly dispiriting moment in a career which, as you know by now, is pretty much littered with them, but this unpleasant episode also served to accelerate what was fast becoming an inevitable decision.

At that moment, though, as I stood lost and shell-shocked and inwardly panicking, with the raptors closing in all around me, a small miracle happened.

"Don't worry," a concerned voice muttered in my ear. Turning, I found myself being stared at by two large true-blue eyes. "We'll take care of it."

---

67. I've listened to my tape of what happened that night on a couple of occasions. Both times I was reminded of the commotion you hear on a black box voice recorder seconds before the plane goes down. It's horrible.

And amazingly, that's exactly what they did.

Over the next five minutes, in one of the most incredible displays of heroics ever witnessed in peacetime, Nicole and her friend Anne muscled their way across the room in systematic bursts, making amends and apologizing profusely to anything with a pulse, including the hostess, Miss Prim, Mount St. Helens, and even a sheepdog lying half asleep behind a chair, for what had just taken place ("He's British, he doesn't understand," they kept saying; which, as panaceas go, seems to work every time), before scooping me up, one at each elbow, and escorting me out of the door.

AT THE END OF ANOTHER SUFFOCATINGLY muggy day— fifteen hours of feeling like I'd been walking around with my head jammed up a sumo wrestler's ass—the elements had taken pity on Memphis, allowing the humidity to loosen its grip and the tiniest hint of a wind to disturb the trees.

Back in the car, I was badly shaken. "What if she sues me?"

"Sues you for what?" Nicole said. "You didn't do anything."

"I know, but who's going to believe me? It's her word against mine."

"Oh, quit whining." Anne stepped hard on the gas, causing the SUV to lurch forward. "This is Memphis. Nobody sues in Memphis. And anyway," she threw in as an afterthought, "if she does, my mother's a lawyer. She'll get you off."

Oh goodie! I'm glad one of us was thinking ahead!

"Look . . ." Rather than end the evening this way, on a low note, Nicole had a suggestion. ". . . Why don't we all go for a drink? To unwind?"

"Nah—I'm not in the mood."

"Oh, here's a place." She jabbed at the window.

Damn!

Newby's, it was called; a bare-boards and shadowy corners kind of bar with a rock venue tucked away out back. Popular with trendy types and also, one would imagine, with people who enjoy lurking in shadows.

"I don't want anything," I grunted, sidling in.

Anne was at the bar. "The drinks are on us!" she called over her shoulder. And, well, you know how I feel about that. If it's free or it's a cow . . .

So, installing myself at a corner table, trying hard to ignore the screaming guitar sounds emanating from a sound-check in the next room—if that band isn't called The Migraines, may I recommend they change their name at once? They'll make a fortune—I began tipping one Budweiser after another down my throat. Alcohol blunts fear, I find, the way rock blunts scissors. And, sure enough, five beers later, every last trace of the catastrophic Audubon Drive party with all of its attendant beastly ghastliness had been temporarily erased from my mind.

Also, my bladder was fit to explode and I had to pee.

I was gone three minutes, maybe four, that's all, but by the time I returned Nicole was in tears.

"What's wrong? What happened?"

Shielding her eyes, she shook her head.

"I think she needs a hug," Anne hinted.

"So—hug her," I said, backing off.

"From *you!*"

"Oh."

Tricky, this. The British don't like to hug, intimacy in our eyes being the emotional equivalent of having your home broken into and all your old Fleetwood Mac LPs stolen. It's considered a total affront. I've known my father forty-six years and my brother forty and not once in all that time has either one of them hugged me, or expressed the least desire to. Cold, aloof, awkward, and unreachable—*that's* the British way.

But the poor girl was sobbing fitfully. Plus, as you know by now I'm weak. So, still somewhat mystified, I made comforting noises and pulled her into my shoulder, where she proceeded to cry copious tears over my nice clean shirt.

Out in the parking lot afterwards, both of us were a little unsteady on our feet. Anne offered to drive me to the hotel and Nicole mumbled something about calling Tony, her live-in boyfriend, to ask if he'd come pick her up.

"Good idea," Anne said. Then, the second Nicole's back was turned, she hissed to me out of the corner of her mouth, "You do know she has a crush on you, right?"

"What??"

KA-BOOM!

14

A Lot of Fuss about Ducks

*The National Bird Dog Museum ◆ Count Noble is ambushed
by quail ◆ the Cash Peters Room ◆ weeet-weeeet, errrk, errrk,
weeeet ◆ we're going to Graceland ◆ the American Dream: what's
that about? ◆ the bit of Graceland you don't get to see ◆ I try to
see it and my personal tour ends badly ◆ the problems of loving a
man with hemorrhoids ◆ stealing scones leads to a
reconciliation ◆ the March of the Peabody Ducks*

THE DAY AFTER AUDUBON DRIVE, TO BREAK THE Elvis monotony—because one can tire of celebrating the achievements of a dead guy one never knew or even cared for very much—we decided to abandon Memphis for a spell and, stopping only briefly so that Nicole could pay her traffic ticket for running the STOP sign, head out to Grand Junction, Tennessee.

Due to the pressing nature of our hangovers, we remained subdued for most of the ninety-minute drive. What little conversation there was tended to be low-key and sporadic, thankfully making no mention either of the previous night's fiasco or of female-people having crushes on male-people, especially female-people who had live-in boyfriends and who therefore shouldn't be thinking such things.

Grand Junction is a rural hideaway located close to the Mississippi border. Its only claim to fame, as far as I'm aware, is that it's the home of a museum dedicated entirely to the historic sport of field trialing. Which, let's face it, isn't much of a claim to fame at all.

"Go down there and have a look-see, you might like it!" Jim had said, in the same tone of voice he'd used when suggesting the Kansas Barbed Wire Museum.

"What on earth for? And what is field trialing anyway?"

But he'd already hung up.

I even thought I heard him snicker as the phone went down.

THE NATIONAL BIRD DOG MUSEUM exists to honor "the partnership of man and dog in the quest for feathered game in the farmlands, prairies, woods and marshes of our beloved land." Which I guess is another way of saying they endorse the idea of a bunch of guys ganging together and terrorizing innocent creatures before they have a chance to get away. If so, then, speaking as a Buddhist, the very concept has me on edge.

The way I understand it, what field trialing boils down to is this: a handler sets out on horseback with two dogs, a pointer and a setter, bounding along beside him. Using a complex code of whoops and whistles that only a dog could ever be bothered to learn—*eeeek, whoooop, uh-uh, neeeeeee*[68]—the handler gives them a mission: go out there, guys, and find quail.

And away they go.

Apparently, quail have a built-in mechanism that tells them not to flee when chased. Intuitively, the birds know that dogs are not really the danger here, it's the guys in charge of the dogs you have to worry about, and that the second they flutter into the skies they'll be shot dead. So, driven by instinct, they don't move. They stay put in their nest while the dogs stand on point close by, waiting for the handler to arrive and flush out their prey. It's very clever. The dogs are then awarded marks on how many finds they make, how they go on point, and also on endurance. The quail, for their part, get nothing, except, if they're really smart, a good lawyer.

According to one of the founders of the museum, field trialing is the nonviolent wing of the hunting movement, and they make

---

68. A language closely allied to Dutch, unless I'm very much mistaken.

sure no birds get hurt during the competition. Good for them! However, when I voiced my objections to the very notion of creatures being hounded for pleasure, he insisted strongly that hunting, when you got down to it, is really an okay thing.

"This country, a long time ago," he said, "lived on hunting, lived on fishing, lived on vegetables, all of which have to be killed before you can eat them, including cabbages and cucumbers . . ."

Er . . . run that by me again. Vegetables get killed?

"Sure they do."

Now, I may not be the brightest bulb on the tree, but even *I* managed to spot the flaw in that one. "But cabbages and cucumbers don't have feelings," I said.

"How do you know they don't?" he responded in a flash.

And I confess I buckled, crushed by a superior mind.

THE MUSEUM IS BILLED AS A PLACE where "history comes alive."

I hate it when it does that.

Surely, one of the great benefits of history is that it's stone-dead and can't harm you, especially where animals are concerned.

I was badly bitten by an Alsatian once, almost severing my right hand.[69] It wasn't the dog's fault—I had a hold of its tongue at the time—but ever since then I've tried to maintain a respectable distance between man's best friend and dog's worst enemy: me. Fortunately, it's only history that comes alive in the Bird Dog Museum; the exhibits don't. They're either painted on canvas, molded in bronze, or stuffed, then stuck in a glass display case. All the same, it brought back bad memories.

The walls of the main room are lined with official portraits of championship setters, each one with a tough-sounding name:

---

69. I was five years old. It happened about a month after I almost drowned in a pond and about a month before I fell up to my neck in quicksand on a building site and was damn near asphyxiated. After that, I pretty much stayed indoors 'til I was twenty-five.

Titan, Rogue, King Valiant—something that would look magnificent on a movie poster, or, failing that, a kennel. Much of the artwork is beautifully crafted and quite captivating, although the most captivating thing of all—and it takes you a while to realize this—is that most of the dogs in the paintings have no feet! I mean, how bizarre is that?

According to Wendy, the manager, there's a good reason for this.

First, a **Question:** What's the chief thing we discovered at the Museum of Bad Art? (And no flicking back the pages to look!)

Answer: That monkey hands are tricky, right?

Well, as it turns out, a setter's feet are even trickier. So rather than risk screwing up on such an important detail, and since they can't just cut a dog's legs off at the ankles and hope you don't spot it, because you will, some artists have taken a leaf out of the Bad Art Book of Tips and Tricks and painted the animals standing in long grass. Or even behind rocks. Which isn't exactly original, but it's effective.

Aside from the portraits, the museum has displays of saddles, trophies, and riding hats. They also have a mannequin outfitted in hunting clothes.

"What's *that* about?" I asked Wendy.

"I don't know," she said, bending to look. "I never read the plaque on it."

But who cares? Once you're done with the mannequin, you are but a couple of steps away from the greatest exhibit of them all: Count Noble. (Left to me, there would be a resounding bugle fanfare here. And I did suggest it, but they tell me it can't be done. Such are the limitations of print.) Anyway, Count Noble is the museum's pride and joy.

This Llewellin setter originated in Pembrokeshire, South Wales. After arriving in New York in 1880 he enjoyed a pioneering and prestigious career as a field champion, dominating the sport for many years, right up until the end. Given what I know now about hunting, it would please me greatly to hear that his death wasn't a happy one and that maybe a bunch of super-intelligent quail ambushed Count Noble from above, pecking the bastard to slivers and shreds before transporting his beak-ravaged carcass (using very tiny pulleys and harnesses) to the nearest dumpster and tossing him in.

But that's not how it happened. More than likely, he just yelped and keeled over.

Which, in most instances, would be the end of it. Popular for a while, but then dead, buried, and instantly forgotten. Like game-show hosts. But you know what? Bird-dog enthusiasts are a feisty, willful lot. They are. And Count Noble wasn't just any old pooch (it's okay, I'm a journalist[70]), he was the very cornerstone of the American Llewellin setter dynasty.

"Basically, he was too important to stay in the ground," Wendy concluded.

"So what did they do?"

"They dug him up."

"They dug the dog up? Then what?"

"They stuffed him."

And to be honest, he still looks furious about it.

These days, Count Noble holds center stage at the museum. He's been mounted on a specially created 3-D hillside setting, somewhere he can stand commandingly on point for all eternity like the true reigning champ that he is. More importantly, he's behind glass. That way Wendy can be absolutely sure the Quaila Nostra won't get to him after lights-out and peck him to slivers and shreds all over again.

ONCE YOU'RE DONE WITH THE MAIN EXHIBIT room, you'll be wanting to leave. Trust me, you will. But there's one other corner

---

70. Self-Evident Life Truth #19—page 123.

of this place you must visit before you make a mad dash for the exit. It's called the Wildlife Heritage Center. I don't think I'm spoiling the surprise by telling you that it's where they keep the rest of their stuffed animals.

In this small but unusual sanctuary stand some amazing creations: a wide variety of woodland animals, including raccoons, hogs, owls, bobcats, a laminated rattlesnake, and a coyote chasing a quail. Each one sports a strange, glazed look on its face, the sort of look I guess you too would wear if you'd just had your insides ripped out and replaced with a wire frame and padding.

According to Wendy, schoolchildren adore this part of the museum, especially those who have yet to learn to read. I know this to be true because, despite the prominent DO NOT TOUCH signs that are everywhere, someone had clearly been touching rather a lot. The coyote, for instance, had a leg missing. And the quail it was chasing had no head.

"Yes, I know about that," Wendy grinned. "The head is on my desk."

Which I imagine must have come as a terrible blow to Mr. Yoshimoto when he was told.

He's the guy who so generously donated the tri-ped coyote when it was still a quadruped and the headless quail before it was decapitated. He's also one of the more prominent field-trialers on the circuit. So much so that he had an entire room of the museum dedicated to him.

"An entire room?" I exclaimed. "Oooh, how exciting. I'd like one of those too."

Imagine! The Cash Peters Room at the National Bird Dog Museum—now that *would* be something. We could have a portrait on the wall of me, with no feet, standing in long grass, and everyone who comes through would be given a free strawberry margarita. Oh, and schoolchildren would be handcuffed to prevent them stealing stuff. It would be so great. I'm convinced it's entirely doable. Pull a few strings, buy them a brand new coyote for their Wildlife Heritage Center, one with four legs, or maybe even five . . . and hey presto.

My mind was buzzing. It was simply too good an opportunity to pass up. So, choosing my moment, I cornered Wendy and put it to her straight: "I want a room in this place dedicated to me. What are the chances?"

Without giving it a thought, she replied, "Slim to none," and walked off.

LOOKING BACK ON IT, IT'S HARD TO SAY WHAT the best part of my trip to the Bird Dog Museum was, although jumping in the car and driving away ranked pretty high.

Heading back into Memphis, Nicole was broody and quiet again, apparently still under a cloud from the previous night. And, to tell you the truth, even though the Wildlife Heritage Center had given me a slight lift—helpless laughter makes great therapy, I find—underneath I wasn't feeling all that wonderful either.

Every season has a watershed moment, a time when what-might-yet-be suddenly becomes what is. For instance, there's a point around early October time each year when summer seems to become exhausted. Sick of listening to our complaints— "When will it rain?", "I can't stand this sticky heat, can you?", "I think I have skin cancer"—she washes her hands of us and heads south for eight months to torment the Australians. And that's when you feel it. I'm sure you're familiar with the kind of day I'm talking about. When the wind blows noticeably chillier, and the atmosphere has an indefinable crackle to it and there's a different look in the eyes of people you meet, because they sense the change too. And although the sky's blue and the sun's doing that shining thing it's so good at, somehow it can't quite expel the enduring nip from the air. Overnight, everything has shifted. The world is new. Autumn has arrived.

Well, in a way this is what happened post-Audubon Drive. One day I awakened to a distinct chill and the beginnings of a new world. Except, we were still in August and it was like the Mojave, only moist, outside, so the cause was nothing seasonal.

Perhaps it was dawning on me that this was it. After many false stops, I'd finally reached the end of my radio/wilderness years. And not the "Barbra Streisand's Retirement" kind of end either, but the very *end*-end, one that doesn't allow for comebacks or for brief cameos at Democratic fund-raisers. The time had come to say farewell to something that had been the mainstay of my life for too long. The Bird Dog Museum would be the very last kooky museum the Begotokomugubu would ever visit, and it would be followed soon enough by the last goofy tour he would ever go on too. Only one remained: Graceland, which had been fixed for two days later, the day of the Elvis Vigil (another disaster just waiting to happen, as you'll see). Then, nothing. Done. Finished. Sayonara.

After that, when my phone rang with the offer of a new assignment it would be met with a firm "No thanks, Jim; I'm not available," followed by a quick hang-up. And when it rang after that: "Jim, I just told you—no. Now please stop calling," I'd hang up a second time and put the machine on. It was over. I was about to create a vacuum, one that Nature could abhor at its leisure. After sixteen years spent perched on life's cliff-top, unsure whether, when I jumped, my wings would open or if they'd simply stick together like two ends of a Band-Aid, leaving me to plummet to the ground, I was preparing to leap into the unknown. Here, at last, was where I moved on to better things; better things that had yet to materialize admittedly, but better things nonetheless. And for once, I was very, very scared.

Weeeeet-weeet, erk, horrrrk, weeeet-weet.

Oh shut up.

ELVIS BOUGHT GRACELAND AT THE AGE OF twenty-two, after Audubon Drive got to be inundated with screaming, doting fans and the neighbors started to complain.

"You see that man over there? No, the good-looking one with the guitar? Yes, *him*. D'you know what he just did with his hips? It's disgusting. *He's* disgusting."

No wonder he couldn't wait to get the hell out of there.

The stone-fronted Colonial-style mansion lies half-concealed at the top of an oak-lined driveway overlooking Elvis Presley Boulevard.[71] Back in Historical Times the estate was huge, extending over 500 leafy acres. It was owned originally by a press baron called S. C. Toof, who bequeathed the house to his daughter Grace (which is where the name Graceland comes from), who later bequeathed it to her niece Ruth, who, before she could screw around with rock 'n' roll history by changing its name to Ruthland, offloaded the property onto Elvis for $100,000. Interestingly, by the time he moved in, the estate's original 500 acres were down to a paltry 14. I'm not sure what happened to the other 486, but something tells me that finding out would take a helluva lot of time and research, so for now I'm perfectly happy attributing it to soil erosion.

Sweeping through the white wrought-iron gates you've seen hundreds of times on TV and into the curling tree-lined driveway, you're immediately gripped by a sense of occasion, one that quite took me by surprise. For twenty years Elvis drove in and out of these gates. Now it's your turn. *Wow!* How wonderful!

It's a moment that even people with Alzheimer's will never forget.

FOR ANYONE VISITING GRACELAND for the first time, there are two ways to get in:

a. You pay: Buy a ticket at the Visitors Center across the street and climb on a bus, which then takes you up to the

---

71. I mean, what are the chances of finding a house on a street with the same name as yours? Talk about uncanny! The only thing *more* uncanny, to my mind, is Crapper inventing the crapper. That still gives me goose bumps.

house for a leisurely two-hour digital audio-tour narrated by Lisa Marie Presley. (She's on tape, by the way, not crouching in a cupboard with a flashlight reading the script into a microphone). Or,

b. You don't pay: This I call "the radio journalist's way." When you're media, you're shown around for free by a member of the marketing department who you get the feeling has something far more productive he could be doing with his time, but who endeavors to be pleasant to you nonetheless.

Nicole had warned me about the marketing guys here and how leery they were of journalists they'd never heard of (a category into which I fitted most comfortably). Many writers and reporters, it seems, don't take Elvis as seriously as those who are making money off him do. They've even been known to come here and start poking fun at Graceland—can you *believe* that? Those scheming, underhand, notebook-carrying fact-pimps!

They giggle at Elvis's over-the-top '60s custom design furniture, mock his questionable-at-best taste in decor: the yellow leather bar, the carpet on the walls, the mirrored sofa cushions.[72] And, horror of all horrors, they've even been known to ask if they can bring in a big fat Elvis impersonator with dyed black hair and pan-scourer sideburns to lounge on the couch strumming a guitar for a photo shoot. Jeez! They make the mistake, in other words, of thinking that the people who run Graceland have a sense of humor about all of this, and as far as I could tell they don't. If anything, they're more intense and more protective of their man, his

---

72. My guess is that these were bought as a gift for Liberace. Then at the last minute Elvis thought, "Let that fat prancing jester buy his own mirrored cushions" and kept them for himself. Liberace—or Lee, my pet name for him (although around the house I'd refer to him by his official title: Mr. Showbusinessness)—wouldn't have cared. He didn't need any more mirrored *anythings*. He already owned a mirrored piano and a mirrored Rolls-Royce, and that was quite enough to be going on with. You can see a collection of his personal clutter, including capes, feathered outfits, candelabra, and the World's Biggest Rhinestone—*ooooooh!*—at the Liberace Museum in Las Vegas.

legend, and his image than the fans are. And frankly who can blame them? After all, Elvis is the cash cow that laid the golden eggs (so to speak) and understandably they want to keep it that way.

That must be why Owl-Face had been so wary about helping us. I even suspect, though she would neither confirm nor deny this, that he'd had a word with Nicole on the quiet beforehand, in that light, but quietly aggressive manner of his, warning her to make sure I stayed on my best behavior: ABSOLUTELY—NO—FUNNY—BUSINESS—okay?

Well, of course! I was more than happy to oblige. I'm never out to make trouble. I even went so far as to pledge to myself and also to Nicole in the car on the way over that I would be respectful at all times; low-key, friendly, and wholly unassuming. The very model of professionalism, in fact. Which is why, given that I honored this pledge *to the letter*, I'm still shocked that things turned out as badly as they did.

TO MAKE SURE I DIDN'T RUN AMOK IN THE PLACE, peeing behind the furniture perhaps, or even leaping over the velvet rope and cooking a hearty meal for six in Elvis's ground-floor kitchen—really, who knows what they were imagining?—my tour was supervised by one of the marketing guys, a dark-haired, friendly, accommodating sort of chap with a laconic drone to his voice that, at times, made it a challenge to stay awake.

Then I discovered: It wasn't the voice that was sending me off to sleep, it was Graceland itself. My goodness, what a boring place this is if you're not at least somewhat intrigued by Elvis.

For fifteen arduous minutes we trekked between exhibits:

• Into Elvis's living room with its white sofas and carpet, and stained-glass partitions. It was here that his body lay in state. Then it was removed (well, you can't just leave it there!), and now he's buried out back where he won't get dusty or be in the way;

• Into Elvis's dark and gloomy poolroom, which has the feel of a turn-of-the-century Moroccan brothel about it, thanks to four hundred yards of pleated cotton fabric that have been nailed to the ceiling in a propeller shape;

- Upstairs;

- Downstairs again;

- Into the kitchen where Elvis would fix himself a snack;

- Down more stairs;

- Into the TV room where Elvis would watch TV;

- Into the dining room where Elvis would eat;

- Outside to the Meditation Gardens where Elvis is buried;

- Inside to the Jungle Room where Elvis liked to relax before he was buried . . . oh my God, enough enough *enough!*

Graceland, since it's a museum, a memorial, and a tour, will be a real treat for some, I have no doubt; it's beautifully preserved and could be quite absorbing. But for me all it did was prove something I'd suspected all along: that my interest in Elvis Presley falls at the "could give a rat's ass" end of the curiosity spectrum.

Of course, I'm not typical, I know that, and 600,000 visitors a year—second only to the White House and, someday, I predict, the Cash Peters Room at the National Bird Dog Museum—would disagree with me. But I swear, if Elvis weren't revered as one of the greatest entertainers of all time and didn't have all his awards and gold records displayed on a wall out back, I don't think you'd spend twenty minutes in this house, much less twenty bucks. And by the time we reached the Jungle Room, a strange play-area full of ugly African furniture and other '70s relics that Elvis chose personally,[73] I was thinking to myself, "Will this never bloody end!" and overtaken by a mad urge to run around, pulling off everyone's audio-tour headsets shouting, "It's just a house! It's just a house!"

---

73. Before IKEA came to America the world of furnishings was in *total* freefall.

But you can't do that: 1) They'd have you arrested; and 2) It's not just a house. Not to them. To those who pay to come through here each year, and sometimes year after year, it's a temple. A living, breathing shrine to the American Dream.

I'm astonished that Elvis Presley is viewed in this way. I mean, yes, he started out with nothing and used his considerable skills, talents, and charisma to make a fortune and amass a heap of expensive stuff. But ultimately he wasn't happy, was he? And right there is the double-handed fallacy of the American Dream: You're led to believe that if you apply yourself diligently and follow your star, then you can have it all; not only that, but once you have it, it will make you happy.

Remember the question I asked several chapters ago, the one I said absolutely fascinated me and always has: "What went wrong?" Well, here, I think, is the answer. I tracked it down in Memphis of all places.

Self-Evident Life Truth #32 states: The meaning of life is: a) to have fun; b) to loosen up; and c) to unlearn 75 percent of the things you learned as a child.

Look closely, and you'll see it makes no mention of owning a passenger jet called *Lisa Marie*, or having a yellow leather bar in your TV room, or a house on a street with the same name as yours. And the reason it doesn't is because none of these things is important; they're merely the icing on the cake, not the cake itself. Yet most Americans have staked their whole life on achieving similar goals: having, owning, possessing, winning, beating the next guy past the post. What they don't realize is: Eat lots of cake and you get full; eat lots of icing and you get sick.

In short—before this cake and icing talk does your brain in— ordinary Americans need to learn one simple lesson: that they don't have to win *all the time*, to be the best that they can be *all the time*, to come out on top and control everything *all the time*. It's okay to kick back once in a while and relax, drift. Be more like me, in fact, only without all the frustrated, resentment-ridden, stuck-in-radio-and-can't-break-free bits. There's nothing shameful about opting out and deciding not to keep up with the Joneses. Or in living a low-impact, ordinary, cake-eating life if coincidentally it also happens to be a happy one.

So if anyone walks up to you, as they might one of these days, and asks you why you think millions of ordinary Americans seem to be so angry and so desperately unhappy with their lot, don't hold back. Don't beat about the bush. Just tell 'em straight. Say, "Because they've eaten too much icing and are making themselves sick."

Then run away before they ask you to explain what the hell you're talking about!

IN THE END, THE ONLY THING I WAS EVEN mildly curious to see at Graceland, and this is what kept me going, was the place where Elvis died.

Is there anything more interesting than that? Hardly! Get a photo of the bathroom next to his bedroom, I thought to myself, and you can go home happy.

"Up those stairs," the marketing guy said, passing quickly by, "is the entry to the master suite."

"Ooooh! At last."

And I was just starting to climb when he rushed back to stop me. "No, no, the bedroom is out of bounds," he said. "The door's locked and no one's allowed up there."

"Aw, come on. I promise I won't sleep on the bed."[74]

"No. The rooms have been closed off since 1982."

"So? This would be the perfect time to open them. Perhaps they need airing."

"I'm sorry, no, that won't happen."

Grrrrrrr.

I hadn't paid a penny to come on this tour, but you know what? I was *very* close to demanding a refund. You can't open a famous person's home to the public and then not open up the

---

74. As I recall, I gave a similar undertaking at the Three Bears' House.

famous person's bedroom too. It's not right. And I desperately wanted to inspect the area where this particular famous person died. I'd heard he was sitting on the can reading about the Turin Shroud when he just toppled over onto his face.

"I'm sorry, Cash. I can't help you."

"Oh go on. Can't I at least take a quick look?"

"I told you, it's locked."

"Well, unlock it."

"I don't know who has the key." He was absolutely adamant.

"Okay, then," I sighed. It was time to bring out the big guns. "Tell me, whom do I have to sleep with in this organization to get to see Elvis's bedroom?"

His mouth fell open. "Oh *my!*"

Behind him, Nicole had her hands over her eyes.

"What? What did I say?" I gasped, nonplussed.

Hard to believe, but I was the first journalist ever to offer an "Access all areas" pass around his own body in return for the same around Graceland.

"I can work my way through them all by teatime," I threw in, thinking a rapid turnover might clinch it.

"That's very fast."

"Well, that's me—fast. And loose."

He actually laughed at this, still unsure if I was kidding around or not. And it was while he laughed that I made *the* biggest mistake of the day.

Actually, there was nothing at the time to suggest I'd done anything wrong, but since asking nicely, arguing logically, talking straight, glibly prostituting myself, and even putting on my Sad Clown Face (Bela Lugosi, mostly *Chandu of the Magic Isle*, but with a little *Return of Chandu* thrown in for good measure) had all come to nothing, I thought I'd try one last ruse, one I like to call "saying something stupid." When all else fails, this invariably produces results. Alas, on this occasion, not only did it get me into even more trouble than I was in already, but also, ultimately, it finished off my career as a travel reporter.

Leaning in closer, I whispered, "Is it because you're embarrassed? Are there stains on the sheets?"

Someone sucked in their breath sharply. Must have been
Nicole, because the laconic marketing guy just stood and stared.
Then after thinking the matter through for what must have been
three-tenths of a nanosecond, he blurted out a curt "*No!!!*" and,
shazam, as if by magic, Nicole and I found ourselves being led
down the driveway to the car, which—call me psychic—I took to
be a very definite signal that I'd come to the end of my personalized tour of Graceland.

Though sadly, this was not the last I'd be hearing of those
stained sheets.

AFTER ALL OF THAT, WE WERE BOTH FEELING drained and
needed a couple of hours to recuperate, so we decided to grab a
late lunch at the Peabody Hotel on Union Street.

Nicole had nagged me almost nonstop from Day One about
something called the Peabody Ducks. "You have to see the Peabody
Ducks," she kept saying. "You *have* to see the Peabody Ducks."
And despite telling her on 273 separate occasions (and those are
just the ones I counted) that I had only a passing interest in creatures of any kind—did she learn nothing from our trip to the
Wildlife Heritage Center?—her cheerful pestering became so
insistent that I finally caved in. "Okay, okay, okay—I'll see
them!"

"Good. The next show's at five. We've still got time to go eat."

The Peabody's quite a place. If you've never been, you should.
Once "the social hub of the Southern Aristocracy"—I'm reading
from a leaflet—"this 14-story hotel with its Italian Renaissance
architecture . . . blah blah blah . . . dates back to 1869." Ooh—
Historical Times again! My favorite era. "In these dark-beamed
halls, plantation owners and traders would come together to drink
and celebrate the rise of King Cotton, and . . ." Okay, I get the
idea: it's old.

In the elegant grand lobby, as moody as a crypt and as sumptuously grand as the dining room on board the *Titanic* shortly before seawater burst through the windows and flooded it, drowning everybody, the air crackles with a constant tumultuous chatter and clatter. Porters rush about doing stuff, though you're not sure what; children cry, wheelchair tires squeak, the usual batch of men in dull homogenized gray suits with plastic name tags around their neck sit staring glumly at their cell phones, and everywhere you look, pretty waitresses balancing trays of cups glide between tables arranged around an impressive travertine fountain (the kind that tinkles constantly and makes you want to pee). Behind the fountain is a man in a tuxedo sitting at a grand piano. He tinkles constantly also, though usually it's old ABBA hits.

Lunch was a series of rambling silences punctuated by chewing. There had been a worrying deterioration in Nicole's mood, I noticed. The bubbles had gone from her champagne personality, leaving her flat and almost undrinkable. Twice in two days she'd burst into tears for no apparent reason, and in the car on the way down here, when I'd launched into a spontaneous chorus of "I'm Gonna Wash That Man Right Outta My Hair," she'd all but told me to shut up!

Finally, I broke down. "Nicole, is there something wrong?"

"It's Tony," she said.

"What about him?"

"I . . . I just don't know if I love him any more."

"I'm sorry to hear that." Already I'd heard enough. Time to lighten the mood. "I see Martha Stewart's got a new line of bed linen out . . ."

But it's never that simple. You make one brief inquiry, just to be nice, and they give you their whole life story from conception onwards.

"We've been going through a rough time recently."

"Oh?"

Their two-year relationship had hit a wall—that's the peas and beans of it. Her boyfriend was spending all of his free time racing motorcycles, drinking with pals, and generally pretending he was still single, while poor Nicole was left at home waiting for him. On top of which, and frankly this alone would have killed it for me, the guy had a chronic hemorrhoid problem—*yeeeeeeeuw!*— though astonishingly the piles part of his character appeared to trouble her less than the bike-racing and the drinking and the not coming home at nights parts.

"It's all going wrong," she groaned, dragging her knife and fork together over the remains of her salad. "I'm so bored with this job. I like Memphis, but I want to see the world, not be stuck here for the rest of my life . . ."

She started to cry again.

"But what would you want to do instead?"

"I want a life like yours."

"What on earth for?"

How come everyone thinks it's so great being me? Admittedly, there are a thousand worse things to be than a travel reporter. A zeppelin attendant for one! Or the driver of the Oscar Mayer Wienermobile, having to pretend that you're happy and not embarrassed as you wave at passers-by from a car shaped like a sausage. Or I could have one of those awful outdoorsy jobs, pro-tecting nature. Aaagh! Could it get any more ghastly than that?

"What you do, it's so varied," she went on. "You get to learn so much stuff."

"Yes, but it's stuff about barbed wire and Parisian sewage and feet. It's no use to anyone."

"I want to travel the way you do. Meet new people. Fly first class . . ."

"Oh God!"

"Hey! Here's an idea!" she perked up. "Maybe I could come with you . . ." Leave my boyfriend. Run off with an older man. ". . . be your assistant!"

What???

I wasn't ready for this. I had a partner back home, for God's sake. No way!

"Er . . ." I mumbled, "no. No thank you. That's okay. I don't
. . . you know . . . no."

"Oh."

And so, leaving her aspirations of a) cheating on her man, and
b) trailing wearily behind her new beau through one crappy
museum after another, to wither on the vine, I performed the last
rites on my entree—a savory dish that involved chicken, cream,
and corn, though in what order and to what overall effect I don't
now recall—and we left.

TO FILL YOU IN ON THE MARCH OF the Peabody Ducks:
Sometime in the 1930s the then general manager, Frank Schutt,
returned from a hunting trip[75] and, just for a laugh, placed some
of his duck decoys in the hotel fountain (proving once again that
they had absolutely no sense of humor in those days). Right there,
in that instant, another fine American tradition was born, one that
has lasted to the present day, although now those early wooden
ducks have been replaced with something a little less fake: i.e.,
real ones.

The March takes place twice a day in the Peabody's grand
lobby: once at 11 A.M. when they—and by they I mean the
ducks—are escorted down from their sanctuary on the hotel roof
to swim in the fountain, and at 5 P.M. when they're taken back up
again. On the face of it this sounds about as entertaining as a root
canal, but I guess one must remain open-minded.

---

75. It's amazing how many lunatic traditions started after a hunting trip. In Texas, a
plumber called Barney Smith used to go hunting with his dad. One day they shot a
deer—for which I hope they suffer karmically over many, many lifetimes. Bringing
it home, they found they had nothing to mount it on. So Barney, being a bright kind
of chap, rushed into the shed and came back carrying a toilet seat. He then proceeded to glue the deer's antlers to it. Ta-daaa! Well, after that, there was no stopping him. He developed a passion for gluing things onto other things—silly things
a lot of the time: money, photos, plumbing equipment, even the leftover parts from
his eye operation . . . and in the end wound up with 600+ decorated toilet seats in
his garage—enough to open Barney Smith's Toilet Seat Museum. I've been there
and seen them and, quite honestly, they're cute but for the most part very ama-
teurish. At least half of the exhibits would qualify for pride of place in the Museum
of Bad Art under the mixed-media section.

Originally, we'd been planning to shoot for the five o'clock performance, then head off to Graceland for the Elvis Vigil. But the vigil wasn't 'til 8 P.M. and it was still only 3:35.

"Let's skip it," I said.

"No, you *have* to see the Peabody Ducks."

"Hm. Well, okay. But it had better be good."

To kill some time, Nicole decided to head off back to her office to see what was cooking there. Meanwhile, I installed myself on one of the big overstuffed couches in the bar with a margarita, happy to hang loose and watch the world go by.

It's a popular place, the Peabody lobby, and very busy. Every seat was occupied and every table too, mostly with couples taking afternoon tea, working their way through giant stacks of sandwiches and cakes too numerous in some cases to be eaten at one sitting.

What happens to the leftovers, I wondered? Wouldn't it be a crime if they got slung in the trash rather than into, say, my stomach?

Unwilling to contemplate such a cruel, senseless tragedy, and since lunch had been just the one course, leaving plenty of room for dessert, I set about devising a plan. Every time a group of people got up and left, I would scoot across the room, grab whatever they'd left behind that didn't have visible teeth-marks in it, and sneak back to my couch with the item tucked under my shirt flap. (It's a scavenger mentality you develop after years of working on a tight budget. And it was hugely successful. I don't think even a battalion of camouflaged Marines could have done better.) Altogether, I managed to filch a total of five scones and eight sandwiches from neighboring tables in under twenty minutes. Isn't that wild? And by the way, I heartily recommend the Peabody scones. They're yummy and filling, especially if you eat five of them one after the other, something I also heartily recommend.[76]

---

76. I say this playfully. Do it, choke, and die, and it's your problem. I take no responsibility.

By four o'clock, more tourists than ever were flooding through the doors until, in the end, I'd estimate three or four hundred people had congregated around the octagonal marble fountain, sitting, kneeling, crouching, and elbowing each other for the best position.

Meanwhile, several feet away, trying to distance themselves from this circus, sat the usual smattering of lone middle-aged businessmen in dull homogenized gray suits, looking suicidal. Some yakked on cell phones, others sipped at cappuccinos, slowly turning the pages of a novel without taking anything in.

Sip and turn, sip and turn.

I watched them for a while, same way I watch any animal in captivity: fascinated and yet filled with sadness. And as I did so, for the very first time I realized something important: Oh my God. This must be what my dad did for thirty years of his life back home in England.

He was a sales rep for a company that made printing ink. Looked at from an orbiting satellite, his territory was roughly the right-hand side of the UK (including the nobbly bit halfway down that looks like a washerwoman's backside) which meant he was forever on the road, spending long weeks away from home, encased in a dull gray suit like these guys and sitting each evening in a hotel bar with only a drink and a book for company. Though the hotels were not, I suspect, as fancy as the Peabody. Like me, he was on a budget, so more likely they were those murderous two-star penitentiaries I get rerouted to all the time.

While on his travels Dad would practice magic tricks. This was his hobby. He was an expert at sleight of hand. He could take a red sponge ball and make it disappear, then pull it out of somebody's ear, which you have to admit is a real gift. In fact, up to the age of nine, I genuinely believed my head was filled with red sponge balls and this was why I could never think straight like the other kids.

Could he have turned conjuring into a career? Perhaps. Truthfully, though, he was never in a position to find out. Not with a family to support and a mortgage to pay. And anyway, I

imagine that pulling sponge balls out of people's ears is only good
for one TV special; after that, the audience wants new thrills. So,
like many tens of millions of others in his situation, he did the
right thing, or if not the right thing then the responsible thing: He
took his place on the Hamster Wheel and kept running.

"Hey—you!"

"Aw, hell's bells! What are *you* doing here?"

"How's it going?"

"Please *go away*. I'm not speaking to you!"

"I know, Dad, and I will. Just tell me something first . . ."

"No!"

". . . if you had the chance to live it all over again, would you
do what I did? Quit your conventional life and follow your d . . . ?"

"What, and become a drifter? Stealing scones off other
people's plates? Living job to job the whole time? No money in
his pocket? Unhappy?"

"I'm not unhappy. I'm discontented, and discontentment's a
good thing. It keeps you interested. As a matter of fact, I'm writing
a book about my final six months as a travel reporter."

"Six months?"

"Well, two years. This scene may even be in it, I haven't
decided. I'm done with radio, though, that's for certain. The Elvis
Vigil is my last assignment. After that, I'm going to do something
I should have done a long time ago: either shoot myself, or go into
television. I haven't decided that either. Hey, you know what? We
should hug."

"Not on your bloody life!"

"Yes, we should. Come on! We never hug."

"That's because we're British, we . . . hey . . . stop that! Let go."

"Is this still about the gay thing?"

"No, it's *not* about the gay thing?"

"Then hug me."

"No. There are people watching."

"They're watching the ducks. They don't care about us. Put
your arms around here . . ."

"*Let go of me!*"

"Tighter. Hug me like you mean it . . . there—now, doesn't that feel good?"

"This is so embarrassing."

"See what you've been missing all these years? Feel how life-affirming that is? Look at us, we have a whole father-son thing going on suddenly . . ."

"And you plan to release me—when?"

"Oh. Okay. Well, it was worth a try."

As I say, sometimes I fantasize.

"WELCOME TO THE HISTORIC PEABODY HOTEL," a deep male voice boomed from nearby speakers, causing two old dears next to me to jump out of their cardigans.

There was no sign of Nicole. She'd gone back to the office and not returned. Then again, she must have seen this a hundred times already.

Close to 450 people were scrunched in around the fountain. The heightened anticipation of earlier when absolutely nothing was happening had given way now to a chainsaw-buzz of excitement as *the* moment approached. Children jumped to their feet, parents reached for cameras.

"LADIES AND GENTLEMEN, THE MARCH OF THE PEABODY DUCKS."

"Hurray!"

With a sparkling fanfare, a brass band struck up, followed by a burst of spirited ceremonial music that I think used to be the title theme to *Monty Python's Flying Circus.* Or maybe it was *Dragnet.* (Honestly, I'd be hopeless in a quiz.) At that point, a man in a uniform appeared, walked to the fountain, and began corralling the five brown ducks into action with a stick. Offering no resistance, they hopped out of the water, shook themselves off, and waddled, amid a shock-blaze of camera flashes and much cheering, toward the elevator. Ten seconds more, the doors opened and closed, and they—and by they I mean the ducks

again—were whisked up to the roof, where they'd stay until their
11 A.M. performance tomorrow.

And that's it. That's the March of the Peabody Ducks that
everyone talks about, and which all these tourists had sat around
for almost two hours waiting to see.

The second it was over, a breath of plentiful release descended
over the multitude. Cameras were put away, seniors came out of
hiding, kids lost interest and started talking about the next thrill—
"Mom, can I have an Xbox?"—and everyone quickly dispersed,
their faces aglow with duck-induced satisfaction.

At 5:10, Nicole reappeared, clattering red-faced across the
lobby. As she drew closer, I'd saw she'd been crying *again*.

"Where were you? You missed it."

"I know. Sorry. What did you think of the ducks?"

"Er . . . they were good. Very good." Just being polite. On the
inside, I was thinking *Aaaaaaaaaaaaaaaaaaghghghgh!!!!* "Is something wrong?"

She took a deep sniff. "It's Tony . . ."

No! You don't say.

"He sent a big bouquet of red roses to the office. They were on
my desk."

Still blubbering, she handed me the card he'd sent her.

"Nicole. I'm sorry," it read. "I love you very, very much. Tony."

A fresh spurt of tears hit her cheeks. "Isn't that the *sweetest*
thing?"

Oh boy.

Either men are intensely clever or women are total suckers, I
can't decide which.

15

Candlelight, Music, and Owl-Face

An unfortunate incident at the Elvis Vigil ◆ Owl-Face attacks ◆ I
get angry at Owl-Face ◆ Owl-Face on the run ◆ bearing down on
Owl-Face ◆ at last, something for Dame Judi to get her teeth into ◆
Owl-Face gets what's coming to him, and ◆ I'll stop there, before
I give too much away ◆ good-bye to Memphis

AND SO, AT LONG LAST, TO THE WHOLE POINT OF my trip: the Elvis Vigil.

"The Vigil is a religious experience," the head of the Convention and Visitors Bureau warned me beforehand (which, if I read it correctly, was her way of saying, "For God's sake, don't giggle when you're there or you may never get out alive"). "I mean, you wouldn't go to someone's funeral and laugh, would you?" she said, adding after a moment for reflection: "Well, *you* might, but usually one doesn't."

What a fine judge of character she is!

As I write, Elvis Presley has been dead for twenty-five years, though, annoyingly, the figure keeps going up and will probably have risen yet again by the time you read this.

He croaked on August 16, 1977, and each year since then, up to ten thousand hardcore fans from all over the world have marked the anniversary by migrating to Memphis for a candlelit procession past his graveside.

It's really something to behold. Quite splendid. A pilgrimage every bit as solemn and moving as Lourdes. Orchestrated mass mourning executed on such a formidable scale and with such love that it surely compels even the hardest of cynics to reach inside themselves and feel something. Regrettably, due to certain problems beyond Graceland's control, it's a love that flows only one way right now, Elvis being out of commission and unable to reciprocate. But that's hardly the point.

"He lives on in our hearts," the fans will tell you.

And tell you. And tell you.

Many of them, for reasons only they understand, go to the trouble of making themselves up to look like Elvis. Some even drag their kids along too — "Hey, Duane, git yer lazy ass over here 'n' say howdy to the reporter man." And out from behind a car, but very begrudgingly, will step an infant in a white jumpsuit.

Now *that* I find scary.

Where I come from, a five-year-old with a snarling top lip, glued-on sideburns, and a pompadour is one step away from robbing 7-Elevens for a living.

Aside from the mainstream impersonators who are mainly there to pose and get attention — it worked too, I was all over them like a rash! — there's the usual bevy of oddballs paying affectionate tribute to a man they adored but whom they bear no resemblance to whatsoever. Walking around idly, I spotted what I assumed to be a Japanese Elvis, as well as a bald Elvis, a black Elvis, and, later on, a couple of thuggish female Elvises sharing a cigarette. The rest I had no problem with, but these two terrified me. There's something unsettling, I find, about a woman with sideburns — I can't quite put my finger on what it is. But I'm paid to do interviews not to be a pussy, so, undaunted — well, okay, slightly daunted — I approached them, thinking to myself, "Hey, what harm can it do?"

It was no use, though. I couldn't go through with it. Five feet away, afraid I might burst out laughing and get beaten up for it, I had second thoughts and fled.

Not everyone's a dud, however. I came across guys who looked and acted uncannily like The King. Then, when they'd open their mouths to sing, they'd sound like a cocktail waitress from Hackensack. Conversely, some had the voice down to a science — "Are you lone-summmm . . . tonight . . . ?" they warbled into microphones that weren't connected to anything, getting the tone, diction, and pitch absolutely spot-on — but, on the downside, looked nothing like Elvis. Misshapen and small, they simply couldn't carry it off, not even in a white jumpsuit. (By the way, don't go telling them that, okay? After years spent perfecting their moves in the bedroom mirror, they really won't thank you for complimenting them on their Danny DeVito impression. In their heads, they're Elvis, the King of Rock 'n' Roll. Just accept it.)

But these were the kooks. Everyone else on the boulevard that night seemed to me to be good, ordinary, rational people caught up in the thrall of a superstar and united by a common infatuation. A few, to their credit, had not bothered dressing up at all. In fact, I think they deliberately dressed down to be inconspicuous. And that's fine too. Who cares if you look like you stowed away in the wheel housing of the aircraft? You're here! You're welcome. You're among friends. So what are we waiting for? Let the Vigil begin!

"LADIES AND GENTLEMEN, THIS is a solemn occasion . . ."

On the dot of 8 P.M. the voice of the MC soared over our heads, reverberating off the souvenir shops opposite.

It was growing dark already. Ahead of me were the Graceland gates, and beyond them the coiling driveway disappearing through oak trees toward the mansion, its stone frontage and white columns brightly illuminated, like a shuttle launch. Over to my right and back a bit, a large electronic billboard flashed up a rapid-fire sequence of archive shots, showing a young, still-attractive Elvis Presley[77] at his peak, gyrating to a soundtrack of guitars and visceral screaming. And over to my left, a woman

---

77. I spoke to a lot of fans, and it's astonishing how readily they overlook Elvis's older, drug-dependent, colon-twisted, fat-pudding years. "A regrettable decline, but why dwell on it?" seems to be their take on things. "He's a good, kind person at heart. The fact that he has destroyed himself is sad but we forgive him." I only hope future visitors to the Cash Peters Room are half this accommodating. When I die, I want to be stuffed like Count Noble and flown, preferably by zeppelin, to Grand Junction, where I shall be positioned in a specially made diorama at the Bird Dog Museum with a glazed look on my face—the look of someone who's just had his insides ripped out and replaced with foam padding.

with a large homemade letter E stuck to her forehead crunched her way through a family-size bag of Reese's Pieces without offering me a single one, despite the fact that I smiled at her and even eyed the bag very obviously when she glanced my way one time. With her big E jiggling up and down, she continued wedging whole handfuls of candy into her tight little piggy mouth while she listened distractedly to a brief rundown of the evening's events.

I don't remember the exact list—I was busy concentrating on the bag—but it went something like this: welcome speech; Elvis fans form orderly line; torch comes down driveway, Elvis fans light candles from torch, Elvis fans file up driveway to grave of mystery dead rock 'n' roll star,[78] Elvis fans sob (optional); Elvis fans come back down again and go home.

Neither Nicole nor I had brought candles. Frankly, we were disinclined to stand in line for two hours just to go somewhere we'd already been to once today. Besides, you know how mopey everyone gets at gravesides, all somber and crying and stuff: mourning's *such* a downer. For that reason, we decided to keep it simple: Stick around for the welcome speech and the pre-event hullabaloo, then skip the rest and go celebrate the anniversary of Elvis's death in our own way, by getting drunk and forgetting he ever existed.

"Nicole!" I whispered and shouted simultaneously.

She'd muscled her way to the front of the crowd to watch the ceremonial torch arrive and the first candles being lit.

"Hey—Nicole!" I tried waving, but she missed that too.

Unfortunately—and here's where the world around me turned from Kansas to Oz in seconds—my frantic waving was spotted by someone it wasn't intended for, a strange little red-haired man wearing a dark blue sports jacket, who was already barreling this way.

---

78. I suggested awarding prizes for guessing who the mystery dead rock 'n' roll star is, but apparently it's too easy.

Owl-Face!

He seemed upset. His eyes narrowed as he approached and his face bore the pained expression of someone who's lived under power lines for too long.

Once he was standing directly in front of me, his back stiffened and he blurted out, "Was it you?"—speaking in a direct, but condescending way, as if this was a restaurant and I was an inept waiter in need of a dressing down.

"Me what?"

"That asked about the stains on the sheets?" He took a step closer. "Was it?"

Man, he was sooooo pissed.

"Yes," I confessed outright. "Yes, it was me."

"Oh."

Maybe he'd been expecting a staunch denial, or at the very least to have to beat an admission of guilt out of me. Not for a single second did he imagine that I would give in without a fight. Obviously, he doesn't know many British people.

"Oh—right!" he said.

Not "okay," note, the way Americans do, but "right," the way I do, which I thought odd. Maybe he does know some British people!

After this he seemed to flounder a little. Still giving me the evil eye, he began searching around for something new to add: a threat perhaps—"If you broadcast those asinine remarks, I'll . . ."—or some suitably withering comment, a trenchant rapier-slash of a quip that would not only pull me down a peg or two but at the same time top his less-than-inspired "oh—right" as a comeback, and *really* put me in my place.

Sadly, the best he could come up with under pressure was another "Right," but extended this time, like this: *"Riiiiight!"*

Now, had this been *Hello, Dolly!* and had he been wearing a multilayered chiffon ball gown, I'm sure he'd have scooped it up in both hands and flounced off to a rousing *thump-ya, thump-ya* brass band chorus. But, damn these sports jackets, they're notoriously bad for flouncing. Ask anyone. They make no impact at all. So instead, Owl-Face, doing the best he could with what little he had, spun around on one heel and huffed his way into the crowd, steering a zigzag line to safety.

For a few seconds I did nothing. Just watched him go, relieved that I was still in one piece. But then, as it dawned on me what had just gone on here, a different set of emotions took over. Relief turned to something stronger and far darker.

"Oh yeah??" I thought. "Oh *yeah??*"

I could feel my blood starting to boil.

Who was *he* to push *me* around? What was he *thinking*, marching up to a journalist he didn't know, however dumb and pathetic that journalist might seem, and questioning the integrity of his work, however nonexistent that integrity might be? By *whose* say-so did this annoying creep have the right to hit and run? How *dare* he pick on me?

And the more I chewed it over, the more incensed I became.

So incensed, in fact, that for the very first time in my career—hell, what am I saying? In my entire *life*—I freaked out.

I mean, you know me—*I don't do anger.* I don't even write with lots of italics as a rule. Buddhists never use italics. We're calm and cursive and infinitely forgiving. We're not prone to over-reaction or to impulsive outbursts, and we *certainly* don't throw high-decibel pyrotechnic tantrums in the middle of candlelit vigils. That's not our style at all. But this little upstart was so arrogant, so annoying, that even Buddha himself would have given up on the peace-and-love and respect-for-all-living-things crap, if only for five minutes, just for the chance to beat him up.

And so, on a hot, clammy August night in Memphis, Tennessee, a night I swear I shall never forget as long as I live, my waters of British self-restraint finally broke. Without stopping to calculate the consequences—which is just as well, because they could have been horrible and filled with all manner of beastly ghastliness, possibly putting me in the hospital—and fueled by a quiet rage that had built up over four decades of being trodden on by little bullies like Owl-Face, from my schooldays onwards, I sprinted through the crowd after him.

"Come back here! Don't you walk away from me!"

Behind us, a contemplative hush had fallen across the scene. The procession was under way. On a signal, the first few Elvis fans shuffled in silence through the gates into Graceland. Tiny flickering flames, protected by cupped hands, marked their advance, drifting one at a time up the driveway with an almost churchlike reverence that was both eerie and magical. And while all this was going on, I was standing in the middle of Elvis Presley Boulevard yelling at a man in a sports jacket.[79]

After plowing through waves of Elvis impersonators and young women with production stills from *Blue Hawaii* stapled to their coats, I hounded this dog as far as the curb, then circled him until the little bastard was cornered and couldn't get away.

"What d'you mean—'right'?" I spat. "Hm? What d'you mean *right*?" The back of my neck was hot and tingling—the first signs of a stroke, unless I'm very much mistaken. "Who the hell are you anyway?"

Instantly, he backed down. "It's okay. Don't worry about it."

Don't worry about it?

"Listen to me!" I raised my voice. "The stains-on-the-sheets question was a perfectly good question. I'm a journalist. I have a right to ask anything I want to. If you don't answer it, good, that's your business. But you're *not* telling me what to ask. I will not be ordered around—alright?"

"Okay, fine," he bleated. "I don't want to editorialize your report."

"Yes you do. Yes you bloody do! If you don't want me to play the question on-air, I won't play it, but at least have the guts to ask.

---

79. This is the part Dame Judi Dench will enjoy playing the most, I feel. It'll really test her range. If she can just get through the scenes early on in which I tour all the crap museums, then by the time she gets to this bit, set against a soundtrack of Elvis singing and a line of candles snaking its way silently up to Graceland, she'll blow the audience away. Go, Judi!

How *dare* you threaten me! What're you going to do?"

"*Nothing*. I told you, it's fine."

Grrrrrrrrrrrrrrr.

With the blood rushing to my head and my brain swimming, most of what came next was a blur. I remember snarling, jabbing a finger at him, telling him how sick to my stomach I was of being pushed around by ignorant nobody assholes like him, and how I wasn't going to take it anymore. And I also remember the poor guy standing there, repeating over and over, "It's fine. It's fine. Do what you like."

"Oh, I will, pal. Believe me, I will."

But that's all I remember.

I hope it went further than mere empty threats and bravado. I'd like to think I ripped off my jacket, removed my glasses (and perhaps, if there was time, checked my hair) and, before ten thousand cheering spectators, with one well-aimed punch, leveled the irritating little prick, smashing his jaw like a beer glass.

Alas, I doubt it went that far.

In fact, I know it didn't, or I'd be in jail now.

More likely, at the last moment the Buddhist in me, the voice of reason and love and a respect for all living things—except PR people, big dogs, and snakes—took over. Being a Brit, I may even have gone as far as apologizing to him for losing my cool in such an embarrassing manner, while offering a guarantee that the comment about the stained sheets would be expunged from my radio report. "You have my word on it." Whereupon he, I have no doubt, smiling weakly, accepted my apology, then, after shaking hands, scurried—dazed, but relieved—into the crowd and out of my life forever.

"What was *that* about?" Hearing a commotion, Nicole came running over. She'd witnessed everything.

I swung around. Owl-Face was a dot in the distance, and still going. "No idea."

We stood for a short while, at a loss, watching the slick of candle-bearers trickle slowly graveward, neither of us sure what to do next, or what to say.

"You will be playing the stains-on-the-sheets thing on the radio, right?" Nicole cut in after a while, which is as good a thing to say as any.

"Of course," I replied, and flashed her a triumphant smile. "Why wouldn't I?"

"Good."[80]

ON MY FINAL MORNING IN MEMPHIS, Nicole took an hour off work to drive me to the airport, which I thought was very kind of her. Then again, that's how the majority of Memphians are: kind, hospitable, generous to a fault.

Before climbing out of the car at the terminal I gave her a hug. Not a feeble British "Ugh, you're touching me, you're touching me!" hug either, but a full-bodied, heartfelt thank-you hug, long and warm and close. Then I grabbed my bags and left.

"Write when you can," she shouted through the open window.

"I will."

"Don't forget."

"I won't."

"'Bye."

This time the crack in her voice made me turn around. "Hey, are you okay?"

"Yeah," she nodded

But those big blue dinner-plate eyes couldn't lie about anything.

For once, here was someone who was genuinely sad to see me go. I can't tell you how rare that is! Most times when I leave a place it's to muted cheers as the tension that accompanied my visit gives way to profound relief. But this was different. For a few days one August, this woman had done something she'd never done before: jumped off the Hamster Wheel. Only for the

---

80. But I didn't. I should have, but I couldn't bring myself to break my word. I'm just too bloody honorable, that's my problem.

shortest time, mind, but long enough to get a taste of the spon-
taneity and unpredictability, as well as the many wanton pleas-
ures that a life without direction or rules can bring. It was like a
Showtime Preview Weekend. Her appetite had been whetted,
her curiosity aroused, but now it was over and the Drifter was
moving on again, and as appealing as cable niche programming
is at times, she wouldn't be subscribing to it. Instead, she would
pick up where she left off, going back to her cute, conventional
boyfriend with his chronic hemorrhoid problem, ready to work
with him at ironing out the wrinkles of their relationship, and
rejoining the rest of Southern society in that ritual dance of
small-town delusion they call life.

"'Bye, then."

"'Bye. Write when you can."

"You said that already." Throwing her one last wave I headed
into the terminal building. But—and don't ask me what prompted
this—halfway to the check-in desk something made me turn and
look.

Back at the curb, the car hadn't moved. It was still sitting
where I'd left it, engine ticking over, with Nicole, motionless, her
little white knuckles wrapped around the wheel, staring directly
ahead, a translucent scree of tears, tinged red by the taillights of a
departing shuttle bus, drizzling down her cheeks.

I could have gone back and comforted her. Should have, perhaps. But in the end I thought better of it.

It's a principle of Buddhism: Don't make other people's problems your problems. Whatever she was going through it was for a
reason, and she must face her challenges alone in her own time,
the way the rest of us have to. It wasn't my job to interfere. I was
only passing through. After all, what am I? Only a journalist. And
we all know what that means: I don't actually do anything. I just
comment on what everyone else is doing.

16

Good-bye to All That

In which we end the book

I CALLED MANDY LAST WEEK IN LONDON, JUST TO touch base, because it had been a while. I also wanted to update her on my progress.

"You've finished the book? Congratulations. That's terrific."

"Yup!" I said, holding the phone away from my ear. When she's excited, she has an edge to her voice so sharp you could dice carrots with it. "Not that it achieves very much. It just confirms for a general audience what a select few of us knew already."

"All the same, I'm proud of you. Well done. And what about the museums and tours? Still doing those?"

"Nope." After the Memphis debacle, I hadn't been near a museum. Couldn't face it. Instead, I'd diverted my attention elsewhere. Appeared on a couple of TV shows, though nothing worth bragging about; done some general radio work for the BBC, which went down well. I even got to go on CNN finally, on a day the Pope did us all a favor and refrained from walking down a flight of steps, releasing hours of airtime for other topics. Unbelievably, they had me on to talk about the "Elvis Presley phenomenon," a subject on which, despite my quite breathtaking ignorance, I am now considered an expert. None of it amounted to very much, but at least I wasn't reporting from a kooky museum. On that basis alone, things were definitely looking up.

"You'll go back to it, though," Mandy chuckled. *"I know what you're like. You say you hate it, but you're hooked. You won't be able to resist."*

Hm.

She was right, of course. I'm weak. It didn't take much for the Begotokomugubu to fall off the wagon. Determination wasn't enough. Merely quitting wasn't the answer either, because I knew what would happen. It would only take some neophyte editor to pick up the phone and start squealing: "Oh my God, you won't believe it! There's this awesome attraction in Salzburg, Austria — a tour of *the Sound of Music* locations! You *have* to go!" That's all it would take. "No! You're kidding me!" I'd gasp as usual. "It can't be true. Really?" and ten days later, there I'd be once again, on a tour bus roaring through the Salzkammergut, singing "The Lonely Goatherd" at the top of my voice.

No, if I was to put a stop to this nonsense once and for all, I needed a plan. Something final. And I don't mean a *Freddy's Dead: The Final Nightmare* kind of final either, where, just because I made a ton of money on my fourth sequel, I'd say to hell with logic and return for a fifth. No, what I'm talking about is a totally radical, end-of-the-line, no-going-back, once-and-forever final. Only less hyphenated.

Given these parameters, I thought it might be hard to come up with a satisfying idea. Yet, to my surprise, three days later I hit on exactly that.

On Saturday morning early, I took a bus to Santa Monica, a coastal suburb of Los Angeles that, on an initial encounter, looks like it was the brainchild of a marketing genius with a hugely ambitious idea: "Hey, why don't we build a massive sprawling metropolis of condos and hotels and souvenir shops and restaurants and bistros and movie theaters and clothes stores that will be bigger than Tokyo but without so many Japanese people in it? And let's make it stretch right to the horizon and beyond. What d'you say?" — only to find that, due to a sizeable oversight at the planning stage, during which everyone in all their excitement forgot to factor in the Pacific Ocean, this sprawling metropolis had to be scaled down to the size of a fairground and stop at the beach.

But Santa Monica has a pier, and today the pier was the only thing I was interested in.

Threading my way down the slope onto the boardwalk, past the food stands, the tiny roller-coaster, the amusement arcades, and through hundreds of milling tourists—including a group of Japanese students who'd heard all about this place they call Tokyo But Smaller and had come to see it for themselves—I kept on walking 'til I couldn't walk any further.

With a little more forethought, I'd have brought some words to say. Something poignant about creating crossroads and fresh starts, the way I had five years ago in Yorkshire. But this—this wasn't like that. It was all very impromptu. There wasn't room for anything so elaborate. And anyway, this time I wasn't alone. There were a dozen Hispanic fishermen close by, watching me as they fiddled with their rods.[81]

"Poor bastard," I bet they thought as I approached the guardrail, looking as if I might throw myself over. "Probably another one of them public radio guys."

Once in place, I dipped into the pocket of my jacket and pulled out my mini-disc recorder. It's nothing much to look at, just a flat, silvery metallic box no bigger than a coaster, but it's been my friend and constant companion through just about everything these past few years. Wherever I went, it went. Each tour I'd been on, each museum I'd visited, and every cheesy, mid-range hotel I'd stayed in, my mini-disc recorder had been on, visited, and stayed in too. On this machine was recorded every interview, every sound effect, every last argument and incidental comment that went into my radio reports. This box had been a key part of my life. But now I'd outgrown it. And like all friends and companions who have outlived their usefulness, the time had come for it to be tossed into the ocean.

So that's what I did. Without fuss I leaned into the rail and, hard as I could, flung it out to sea, watching as the steel casing glinted briefly in the morning sunlight, tumbling over and over itself in a sharp parabola to strike the waves at an angle.

---

81. In a nice way! Shame on you for thinking that!

Plop!

I waited a few moments, wondering if, without telling us, those geniuses at Sony had raced ahead of the competition yet again by devising a mini-disc recorder that floats—or, better still, grows wings and flies.

But nobody's that clever.

The machine had gone, slipping beneath the waves, dragging my old life down with it. Neither of them was ever coming back, I was sure about that. A vacuum had been created and as from today I was walking into it.

One of the Hispanic fishermen, who'd watched the mini-disc recorder meet its death, stared at me quizzically.

"I'm television now," I assured him with all the confidence of someone who knows he's lying.

"Ah," he said, not understanding a word.

Then I turned and walked away, free at last.

Those Who Have Served

I NEVER KNOW WHAT TO SAY. YOU GET TO THE END OF a book and suddenly you feel duty-bound to show appreciation to the various people who helped you along the way. You don't *have* to, I guess, but it's a good idea, if only because you might do another book soon and need their help again. At the same time you don't want it to get all heavy and turn into an Emmy acceptance speech.

For that reason I intend to keep this light and frothy.

First, let me say that I'm shocked. I really wasn't expecting to win and had nothing prepared. So let me quickly thank the following:

Kristen Auclair, my agent, for her professionalism, and for putting up with my endless questions and changes of heart and hysterical outbursts, and for talking me down off the ledge when everything was getting on top of me. They hand out medals for less. She is THE BEST!

Len Richmond, for being uncompromisingly honest. His insights and criticisms were invaluable. It can't be much fun having friends call up while you're in bed and read entire pages of text to you, saying, "Is this too weird, d'you think?" But he never complained. He hung up sometimes, but he never complained.

For Stanley Penner. No need to go into details. He knows why.

For my editor Laura Strom, who already feels like she's known me a lifetime. Sadly, I have that effect on people. But I admire her for sticking to the principles she so firmly believed in until, eventually, I came around to believe in them too. Without her this book would not be . . . well, what it is.

And for everyone else who stood by, watched it happen, yet were seemingly powerless to intervene: Gary Robertson, Jeff Greenberg, Adreana Robbins, Gary and Lulu Leva, Andrea

Horvath, Michelle Kholos, Sylvana Robinson, Jim Gates, J. J. Yore, Larry Hudspeth, Cheryl Glaser, Ellender Sahr, Imee Curiel, Marc Abrahams, Jeff Van Bueren, and of course the lovely Nicole in Memphis (who apparently has been to counseling with Tony to fix the bits of their relationship that were broken and says things are working out just fine) . . . oh God, and now the music's started . . . er . . . I'd also like to thank everyone ·at the BBC end, everyone at the MPR end, my family—no, not my family—but everyone else, particularly those who scanned this page for their name and found they weren't mentioned: a *very special* thanks goes out to you for what you did, whatever the hell it was.

Goodnight, and I love you all.

Details, Details

CHAPTER 6

The American Museum of Sanitary Plumbing

32 Piedmont Street
Worcester, MA 01610
(508) 754–9453

The Museum of Dirt

*Personal visits are actively discouraged.
Do not go. Instead, visit their Web site:*
www.planet.com/dirtweb/flash/html

CHAPTER 7

Salem, Massachusetts

*Currently trying to overhaul their whole
"we only do witches" image thing. To check
on progress, go to* www.salemweb.com.

CHAPTER 8

The Annals of Improbable History

To subscribe:
Marc Abrahams
P.O. Box 380853
Cambridge, MA 02238
(617) 491–4437
www.improbable.com
*The Ig Nobel Prize Ceremony is held at
Sanders Theater, Harvard University,
Cambridge. For tickets: (617) 496–2222.*

CHAPTER 9

The Gibbs Farm Museum

2097 West Larpenteur Avenue
St. Paul, MN 55113
(651) 646–8629

www.rchs.com/gbbsfm2.htm
*Tuesday–Friday: 10 A.M.–4 P.M. Sunday:
noon–4 P.M. Closed mid-November to
mid-April.*

The Museum of Questionable Medical Devices

*Bob McCoy has retired. The museum
has shifted to the Science Museum of
Minnesota at 120 West Kellogg (ironi-
cally) Boulevard, St. Paul, MN 55102.
(651) 221–9444.*
www.smm.org
www.mtn.org/quack
www.quackwatch.com

The Orange Show

2402 Munger Street
Houston, TX 77023
(713) 926–1506
www.orangeshow.org

The Mall of America

60 East Broadway
Bloomington—not Minneapolis—
MN 55425
(952) 883–8800
www.mallofamerica.com

CHAPTER 10

The Glore Psychiatric Museum

3406 Frederick Avenue
St. Joseph, MO 64506
(816) 387–2310
www.ci.st-joseph.mo.us/glore_
museum.htm
*Monday–Saturday: 9 A.M.–5 P.M.
Sunday: 1–5 P.M.
Admission is free, but donations are accepted (and they mean money, not
relatives, so leave Grandma at home to
watch wrestling).*

William P. Didusch Museum at the American Urological Association

1120 North Charles Street
Baltimore, MD 21201
(410) 727–1100
www.auanet.org
Open office hours.

The Mutter Museum

The College of Physicians of
Philadelphia
19 South 22nd Street
Philadelphia, PA 19103
(215) 563–3737
www.collphyphil.org
Tuesday– Saturday: 10 A.M.–4 P.M.
Sunday: noon–4 P.M.

The Kansas Barbed Wire Museum

120 West First Street
LaCrosse, KS 67548
(785) 222–9900
www.rushcounty.org/barbedwiremuseum

CHAPTER 11

The Precious Moments Chapel

4321 Carthage Road
Carthage, MO 64836
(417) 358–7599
www.preciousmoments.com

Ripley's Believe It Or Not

3326 West Highway 76
Branson, MO 65616
(417) 337–5300
www.ripleysbranson.com

Branson, Missouri

www.bransonmissouri.com

CHAPTER 12

The American International Rattlesnake Museum

202 San Filipe Street NW, Suite A
Albuquerque, NM 84104
(505) 242–6569
www.rattlesnakes.com
Year-round 10 A.M.–6 P.M. Closed major
holidays.

CHAPTER 13

Sun Studio

706 Union Avenue
Memphis, TN 38103
(901) 521–0664
www.sunstudio.com

CHAPTER 14

The National Bird Dog Museum

Grand Junction, Tennessee
As a small protest, I refuse to give out
the museum's address. But their phone
number is (901) 764–2058. If you're
really that interested, you can pick it
up from there.

Graceland

3734 Elvis Presley Boulevard
Memphis, TN 38186
www.elvis.com/graceland

The Liberace Museum
1775 East Tropicana Avenue
Las Vegas, NV 89119-6529
(702) 798–5595
www.liberace.org/liberace/museum.cfm
  Monday–Saturday: 10 A.M.–5 P.M.
  Sunday: 1–5 P.M.

Barney Smith's Toilet Seat Museum
239 Abiso
San Antonio, TX 78209
(210) 824–7791

The March of the Peabody Ducks
The Peabody Hotel
149 Union Avenue
Memphis, TN 38103
(901) 529–4000
www.peabodymemphis.com